Intelligence

A BEDFORD SPOTLIGHT READER

Intelligence

A BEDFORD SPOTLIGHT READER

Barclay Barrios
Florida Atlantic University

bedford/st.martin's
Macmillan Learning
Boston | New York

Vice President: Leasa Burton
Program Director: Stacey Purviance
Senior Program Manager: John E. Sullivan III
Director, Content Development: Jane Knetzger
Executive Development Manager: Susan McLaughlin
Senior Development Editor: Jesse Hassenger
Editorial Assistant: Samantha Storms
Executive Media Editor: Adam Whitehurst
Advanced Media Project Manager: Rand Thomas
Executive Marketing Manager: Joy Fisher Williams
Director, Content Management Enhancement: Tracey Kuehn
Senior Managing Editor: Michael Granger
Senior Manager of Publishing Services: Andrea Cava
Senior Content Project Manager: Louis C. Bruno Jr.
Senior Workflow Project Manager: Jennifer Wetzel
Production Coordinator: Brianna Lester
Director of Design, Content Management: Diana Blume
Interior Design: Castle Design; Janis Owens, Books By Design, Inc.;
    Claire Seng-Niemoeller
Cover Design: William Boardman
Director, Rights and Permissions: Hilary Newman
Text Permissions Researcher: Elaine Kosta, Lumina Datamatics, Inc.
Photo Permissions Editor: Angie Boehler
Photo Researcher: Krystyna Borgen, Lumina Datamatics, Inc.
Senior Director, Digital Production: Keri deManigold
Project Management: Lumina Datamatics, Inc.
Project Manager: Vanavan Jayaraman, Lumina Datamatics, Inc.
Editorial Services: Lumina Datamatics, Inc.
Copyeditor: Kathleen Lafferty, Roaring Mountain Editorial Services
Composition: Lumina Datamatics, Inc.
Cover Image: RichVintage/E+/Getty Images
Printing and Binding: LSC Communications

Library of Congress Control Number: 2020936456
ISBN 978-1-319-20720-5

Printed in the United States of America.
1 2 3 4 5 6   25 24 23 22 21 20

Acknowledgments
*Text acknowledgments and copyrights appear at the back of the book on
pages 273–74, which constitute an extension of the copyright page. Art
acknowledgments and copyrights appear on the same page as the art
selections they cover.*

For information, write: Bedford/St. Martin's, 75 Arlington Street, Boston,
MA 02116

The Bedford Spotlight Reader Series is a growing line of single-theme readers, each featuring Bedford's trademark care and quality. The readers in the series collect thoughtfully chosen readings sufficient for an entire writing course—about thirty-five selections—to allow instructors to provide carefully developed, high-quality instruction at an affordable price. Bedford Spotlight Readers are designed to help students make inquiries from multiple perspectives, opening up to critical analysis such varied topics as American subcultures, food, happiness, language diversity and academic writing, monsters, music, science and technology, and sustainability. An editorial board of more than a dozen compositionists whose programs focus on specific themes have assisted in the development of the series.

Bedford Spotlight Readers offer ample material for a composition course while keeping the price low. Each volume in the series offers multiple perspectives on the topic and its effects on individuals and society. Chapters are built around central questions such as "How is sustainability a political issue?" and "What makes people happy?" and so offer numerous entry points for inquiry and discussion. High-interest readings, chosen for their suitability in the classroom, represent a mix of genres and disciplines as well as a choice of accessible and challenging selections to allow instructors to tailor their approach. Each chapter thus brings to light related—even surprising—questions and ideas.

A rich editorial apparatus provides a sound pedagogical foundation. A general introduction, chapter introductions, and headnotes provide context. Following each selection, writing prompts provide avenues of inquiry tuned to different levels of engagement, from reading comprehension (Understanding the Text), to critical analysis (Response and Reflection), to the kind of integrative analysis appropriate to the research paper (Making Connections). A tab labeled "resources" on the book's catalog page at **macmillanlearning.com** offers sample syllabi and suggests additional readings.

Preface for Instructors

Thematic readers can make writing classes more interesting for students and instructors by offering a single focus and sustained inquiry across the length of a course. As an instructor myself, I find that this approach works particularly well with a topic that cuts *across* different domains of knowledge, skipping across various disciplines, subthemes, approaches, and ideas. That is what brought me to *Intelligence*. The readings in this book focus on the concept of intelligence while encompassing classic questions of race, class, and gender and expanding the conversation with emerging questions about animality, technology, ethics, and success. With this book, you can talk about intelligence and what it means to be human, or talk about intelligence and racism, classism, and misogyny, or talk about intelligence and our technological world. Even better, you can talk about how all these ideas intersect.

Intelligence is also a central concern for students in higher education. If you think about it, the very concepts of "student" and "intelligence" are intrinsically yoked, both implicitly and explicitly. By the time students reach your classroom, they've already taken a gamut of standardized tests designed to evaluate both their academic success and their future potential, often also acting as a mechanism of ranking and sorting that affects opportunities for their future. This track continues as they are graded each semester, supposedly to reflect the development and deployment of their "intelligence" (and not their effort, as we do not generally subscribe to an "A for effort" mentality). The question of intelligence is thus embedded in their academic careers, making it vitally relevant to students—and a topic they're uniquely positioned to investigate.

That investigation begins in Chapter 1 by asking, "How smart are animals?" Buried within that question is a much larger one: what does it mean to be human? The readings include classic thinkers in this area, including Frans de Waal and Jane Goodall, whose discovery of tool usage in chimpanzees troubled the existing line between human and animal, as well as essays on curious phenomena like cat psychics and counting horses. Students explore what it means to be intelligent and what that implies for the way we treat animals.

Chapter 2 provides a little critical distance by thinking about intelligence in an area that is outside ourselves: artificial intelligence, or AI. Hanging over this discussion is the central question, "Are the risks of artificial intelligence worth the rewards?" Ray Kurzweil and Tim Adams delineate those positions while other readings look at the troubling way

AI has reproduced existing cultural bias and the inscrutable way machine learning works.

Chapter 3 moves to intelligence in humans, but it does so by exploding the boundaries of that term and thinking about multiple intelligences, asking, "Is there more than one kind of intelligence?" Readings in this chapter explore answers to this question by looking at theories of multiple intelligences, emotional intelligence, and working memory. Implicit in these readings is a critique of prevailing notions of intelligence, based solely on IQ.

But that's not the only critique of intelligence we can make. The popular notion of what it means to be intelligent has too often reflected entrenched lines of race, class, and gender. These discussions are at the center of the readings in Chapter 4, which asks, "Does identity determine intelligence?" The authors featured here, including Malcolm Gladwell and Jennifer Lee, offer tools to decouple intelligence from identity by looking at the debate around race, genetics, and intelligence as well as the unique intelligence of the working class.

Finally, one way to examine the workings of any concept is to push it to its extreme. In asking "What is extreme intelligence?" in Chapter 5, we explore what it means to be a genius or prodigy. That exploration reveals problems with the term "genius," including its gendered application and the ethical problem of giving geniuses leeway for their behavior.

Each reading is accompanied by a set of questions to help students think and write. Understanding the Text questions point students to key concepts or issues in the reading. Reflection and Response readings then invite them to write in relation to the reading. Finally, Making Connections questions encourage deeper critical thinking by asking students to connect the current reading to another. Through these readings and questions, students will come to understand that intelligence is a lot more complex than we generally think and that if we think it has everything to do with IQ, we do so because of existing structures of power. Perhaps students will also find the tools to challenge those structures.

Acknowledgments

I am grateful to all the reviewers who offered their time, insights, and feedback during the development process: Laura Bowles, University of Central Arkansas; Lynée Gaillet, Georgia State University; Karen Gardiner, University of Alabama; Wendy Hinshaw, Florida Atlantic University; David Leight, Reading Area Community College; Daniel Libertz, University of Pittsburgh; Heather McGrane, Daytona State College; Pam Stone, North Arkansas College; and Jack Tabor, Mercer County Community College.

At Bedford/St. Martin's, I'd like to thank John Sullivan, program manager at Bedford, for making this project happen; my editor, Jesse Hassenger, who kept me on track; Lexi DeConti, who worked with me on the early stages of this manuscript; Louis Bruno, who shepherded this book through the production process; Lumina Datamatics, Inc., for publication management and composition services; and William Boardman, for his work on the cover design. Thanks also go to Leasa Burton, vice president at Macmillan Learning.

Finally, I'd like to thank Eric Auciello for his amazing support.

Barclay Barrios

From day one, our goal has been simple: to provide inspiring resources that are grounded in best practices for teaching reading and writing. For more than thirty-five years, Bedford/St. Martin's has partnered with the field, listening to teachers, scholars, and students about the support writers need. We are committed to helping every writing instructor make the most of our resources.

How Can We Help *You*?

- Our editors can align our resources to your outcomes through correlation and transition guides for your syllabus. Just ask us.
- Our sales representatives specialize in helping you find the right materials to support your course goals.
- Our learning solutions and product specialists help you make the most of the digital resources you choose for your course.
- Our *Bits* blog on the Bedford/St. Martin's English Community (**community.macmillan.com**) publishes fresh teaching ideas weekly. You'll also find easily downloadable professional resources and links to author webinars on our community site.

Contact your Bedford/St. Martin's sales representative or visit **macmillanlearning.com** to learn more.

Print and Digital Options for *Intelligence*

Choose the format that works best for your course and ask about our packaging options that offer savings for students.

Print

- *Paperback*. To order the paperback edition of *Intelligence*, use ISBN 978-1-319-20720-5.

Digital

- *Achieve for Readers & Writers*. Achieve puts student writing at the center of your course and keeps revision at the core, with a dedicated composition space that guides students through drafting, peer review, source check, reflection, and revision. Developed to support best practices in commenting on student drafts, Achieve is a flexible, integrated suite of tools for designing and facilitating writing assignments, paired with actionable insights that make students' progress towards outcomes clear and measurable. Achieve offers instructors a quick and flexible solution for targeting instruction based on students' unique needs. For details, visit **macmillanlearning.com /college/us/englishdigital**.

- *Popular e-book formats.* For details about our e-book partners, visit **macmillanlearning.com/ebooks**.

- *Inclusive Access.* Enable every student to receive their course materials through your LMS on the first day of class. Macmillan Learning's Inclusive Access program is the easiest, most affordable way to ensure that all students have access to quality educational resources. Find out more at **macmillanlearning.com/inclusiveaccess**.

Your Course, Your Way

No two writing programs or classrooms are exactly alike. Our Curriculum Solutions team works with you to design custom options that provide the resources your students need. (Options below require enrollment minimums.)

- *ForeWords for English.* Customize any print resource to fit the focus of your course or program by choosing from a range of prepared topics, such as Sentence Guides for Academic Writers.

- *Macmillan Author Program (MAP).* Add excerpts or package acclaimed works from Macmillan's trade imprints to connect students with prominent authors and public conversations. A list of popular examples or academic themes is available upon request.

- *Mix and Match.* With our simplest solution, you can add up to fifty pages of curated content to your Bedford/St. Martin's text. Contact your sales representative for additional details.

- *Bedford Select.* Build your own print anthology from a database of more than eight hundred selections or build a handbook and add your own materials to create your ideal text. Package with any Bedford/ St. Martin's text for additional savings. Visit **macmillanlearning.com /bedfordselect**.

Instructor Resources

You have a lot to do in your course. We want to make it easy for you to find the support you need—and get it quickly. The additional instructor's resources for *Intelligence* are available as downloadable files from the Bedford/St. Martin's online catalog at **macmillanlearning.com /spotlight**. In addition to sample syllabi, the instructor's resources include a list of additional readings and films to assign with the book.

Contents

Chapter 2 Are the Risks of Artificial Intelligence Worth the Rewards? 59

complex decision-making, but those calculations are a quagmire of mathematical functions and variables,"

Chapter 3   Is There More Than One Kind of Intelligence?   121

Chapter 4   Does Identity Determine Intelligence?   169

Contents by Discipline

Education

History

Philosophy and Ethics

Psychology

Sociology

Contents by Theme

The Future

Gender and Sexuality

Measuring Intelligence

Race

Intelligence

A BEDFORD SPOTLIGHT READER

Introduction for Students

Right now, right at this very moment, someone is judging your intelligence.

This statement is based on the assumptions that you're reading this book for a college writing class, that your school assigns grades (not all do), and that you're likely taking more than this one class. Across all your classes, your instructors are evaluating your intelligence with every class meeting, assignment, discussion, quiz, project, and test. At the end of the term, they will offer a final assessment in the form of a single letter grade, perhaps modified with a plus or minus sign, which will then become part of your official record. Although it is in many ways an oversimplification of the function and supposed importance of grades, it's fair to say that they are, on some level, taken to be measures of intelligence.

As a teacher of writing myself, I am deeply uncomfortable with that fact because I want to believe that as teachers our main goal is *not* to issue a judgment of how smart you are; instead, it is to help you become the best writer and thinker you can be. But even though effort or overall improvement might factor into your final grade, that grade won't be based on that factor alone. The unavoidable reality is that your grade will be based on your demonstrated abilities as a thinker and writer, and no matter how deeply we as teachers wish for it to mean something else, it's easy to read grades as a quantifiable measurement of intelligence.

If that sounds disturbing, it should. Regardless of how intelligent you are or how well you do in school, you are always more than your smarts. Our systems don't always reflect that, however, and you may not have thought much about intelligence and how we measure and interpret it. The best path to understanding how these constructions affect your life is knowing how they work (and work against you). Intelligence has been shaping your future, but that doesn't mean it has to determine it.

That's why this book is designed to help you think about intelligence and, through that process, grow your skills in ways that expand your intelligence as well. That's what college writing is about anyway. Generally, we're not here to make you a perfect writer. Sure, we want you to write clearly and correctly, but we're generally more interested in what you have to say than how you say it. This book is about thinking critically, and that means tackling thorny questions without clear answers. It means spending time thinking your way through these murky questions. It means explaining in writing what you think, taking a position in relation to the questions at hand, and offering evidence so that readers can understand why you think that way. You may not become a perfect writer, but I hope you'll become a great thinker. This book will help you grow toward that goal.

Why Intelligence?

As I've already discussed, intelligence — what it is, how it's measured, and what we think of it — is a topic close to you whether you realize it or not. In fact, you might say that the very concepts of "student" and "intelligence" are inseparably linked: to be a student is to learn, which is to say that to be a student is to use and develop your intelligence. By the time you've reached this class, you've already run through a gauntlet of standardized testing designed to evaluate both your success and future potential in school. Such tests can also act as a mechanism of ranking and sorting, putting some students on top and others on the bottom, which impacts opportunities for your future. Clearly, the question of intelligence is central to your educational career. Reading, thinking, and writing about intelligence offer you the means to understand your educational experiences in new ways. For example, you'll be able to critique what intelligence means and how it operates both inside and outside classrooms and educational settings.

At the same time, not much is really known about intelligence, which is surprising given that it is something so close to you and with such power to shape your life's paths. That's another reason this topic deserves our attention. We often think of intelligence in relation to success in school — the ability to memorize information or take tests well, for example — but as the readings in this book illustrate, intelligence is a lot more than that. Even if we accept that central definition of intelligence as academic success, we still don't know a lot about how to measure it accurately or what factors impact it. One central theme throughout these readings is that we don't know what we think we know. In other words, it turns out that we are not very smart about being smart. And because the answers aren't clear, there's a lot of room for critical thinking on this topic. Critical thinking requires complex issues that you need to think through, and intelligence itself is deeply complicated.

The topic of intelligence also crosses a lot of territory, offering the opportunity to approach the concept from many directions and generate new insights. It's like turning an object over in your hands while looking at it closely: seeing it from many angles gives you a better understanding of its overall shape. For example, going beyond humans to explore animal intelligence or artificial intelligence provides entirely new contexts for working out just what intelligence is. Within the realm of human intelligence, we can look at different forms of it to get a larger picture and find its limits. These various approaches will give you many different opportunities to think and write about this issue.

Finally, intelligence is worth studying because it's a subject that appears across many disciplines, a fact reflected in the selections gathered here. Regardless of your major, you'll get a sense of how different academic areas look at a topic. The readings in this book come from a variety of academic fields, including primatology, anthropology, history, journalism, philosophy, mathematics, computational science, education, and psychology. This diversity gives you a chance to see how different disciplines approach the study of a topic, what counts as evidence in research, and how the debate about intelligence continues in just about every area of academic study.

The Organization of This Book

To get you started on your study of intelligence, this book collects a range of essays that speak to this topic. Many of them are from contemporary conversations, but some represent key historical turning points in the study of intelligence. Many of them have been chosen at least in part for their approachability and readability to better emphasize their ideas. Reading these pieces shouldn't take a lot of work, but thinking about them should.

To offer you a structure for your investigations, each chapter is framed with a question that provides both an organizing principle for the selections in that chapter and a starting point for critical thinking around that theme. Each chapter also includes an introduction that offers a sense of what the selections are about, what's at stake in the question being asked by the chapter, and how all that relates to your larger inquiry around intelligence as a concept.

Other tools to encourage critical thinking also accompany each selection. For context, a headnote gives some background about the author and the piece. Three sets of questions follow each reading. The first set addresses important concepts from the essay to aid in your understanding of it, the second asks for critical thinking and a written response, and the third set invites you to connect that reading to other readings in the chapter, which is a more developed form of critical thinking. Some of these questions are multimodal, which means that you'll be asked to work in modes beyond just writing, including opportunities to incorporate visual, video, and audio elements.

The first chapter asks the question, "How smart are animals?" Starting with the question of animal cognition offers two advantages. First, because the question of human intelligence is so close to home, turning to animal intelligence provides a little bit of critical distance, which allows for more objective analysis of the issue. Second, the science behind animal cognition is quite complex and, as discussed above, complexity promotes critical thinking. Part of what makes this issue so complicated is that it's not only a question of whether or not animals can think but also a question of what it means to be human. To acknowledge animal cognition is to trouble the line we've drawn between humans and animals, which raises ethical questions in addition to the scientific ones. The science here is also complex because of the number of historical hoaxes involving thinking animals. Therefore, working through these issues means not only working toward an answer for the question this chapter asks but also working toward a basic understanding of what makes something — anything — intelligent.

That conversation continues in Chapter 2, which asks, "Are the risks of artificial intelligence (AI) worth the rewards?" Proponents of AI imagine it as the next stage of human evolution, but equally strident voices on the other side of the conversation warn that AI can mean the end of humans. That opposition makes this question seem binary, but like all the questions around intelligence, the answer is anything but simple. Other readings look at how aspects of AI are already embedded in our world; how they carry over social biases around race and gender; and how simple, stupid bots are as dangerous as AI. Again, these questions are as much about human intelligence as artificial intelligence because the only way to determine the validity of AI is to work from a definition of what makes human intelligence.

After having explored the question of intelligence away from the human context in the early chapters, Chapter 3 brings your investigation directly to the question of what intelligence is — or, more properly, what *intelligences* are — by asking, "Is there more than one kind of intelligence?" This chapter turns to multiple understandings of intelligence developed by psychologists, educators, and others who study intelligence. The kind of "book smarts" represented by intelligence in school and on IQ tests is only one kind. Chapter 3 examines some of the others, including multiple intelligences, emotional intelligence, and successful intelligence. In expanding the range of intelligences, we also expand the category of people who are intelligent, thus challenging the kind of ranking and sorting at the center of schools and grades.

Chapter 4 then turns to a different sort of challenge: uncoupling the troubling stereotypes that link certain identities to a certain level of intelligence. By asking the question, "Does identity determine intelligence?" this chapter is also asking whether or not who we are determines how smart we can be. For once, the answers are a little less ambiguous, as these readings debunk the model minority stereotype of Asian American academic success, the idea of which gender is smarter, and the myth that blue-collar workers aren't very smart. In so doing, these readings also offer you the chance to define your own intelligence independent of your identity markers. Intelligence, in this sense, remains complex and worthy of critical thought, as it cannot be reduced to any one aspect of who a person is.

Geniuses and prodigies, on the other hand, are often reduced entirely to their extreme intelligence and talent. Chapter 5 asks, "What is extreme intelligence?" The pursuit of that answer involves looking not only at the intellectual factors that create genius or foster a prodigy but also at the social and cultural factors that circulate around these terms. That's where things get complex as we consider the gendered nature of the term "genius" or the moral valuation of genius as good, even though some people considered geniuses do things that are very bad.

Throughout all these chapters, my hope is that you will push and pull against the concept of intelligence, learning new concepts, exploding old myths, and finding your own ground in relation to the questions asked by each chapter and in relation to intelligence itself. That's the real work of this book — and the core of both critical thinking and critical writing. You may also find that it's the true mark of intelligence. In many ways, intelligence is less a thing someone or something has — like an amount of information stored in your brain — and more a way of moving through the world — like certain habits of mind that include questioning, investigating, evaluating, and concluding. This book will give you a lot of practice with those habits of mind. In the process, you'll expand your skills with them, which is another way of saying you'll expand your intelligence.

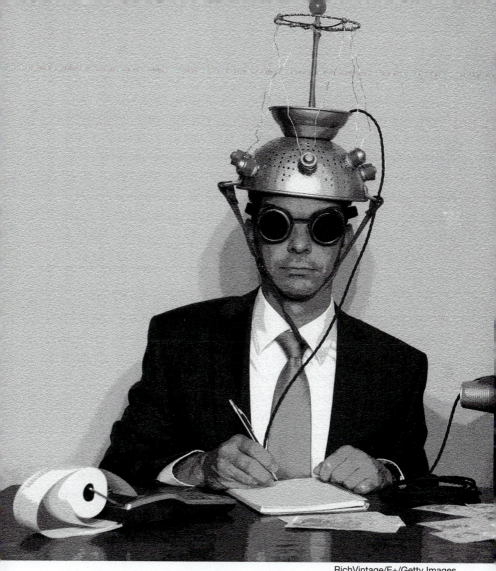

1

How Smart Are Animals?

I f you've ever owned a pet, you probably already have a good idea of just how smart animals can be. Pets can behave in ways that suggest complex minds at work — surprising us, delighting us, frustrating us, and at times even outsmarting us. But animal intelligence can also allow us to look more closely at ourselves, and that is the aim of this chapter. One potential problem with studying intelligence is that in some ways it's just intelligence thinking about itself; that is, we are a little too close to our own intelligence to think about it clearly. Turning to animal intelligence first gives us some objective distance, allowing us to begin to think critically about the concept of intelligence as a whole.

Animal intelligence also raises the question of what it means to be human. Ever since the time of the ancient Greeks, when Aristotle articulated the *scala naturae*, the "ladder of being," humans have believed themselves to be better than animals. Humans are special: we use language, we make and use tools, we recognize ourselves in a mirror. What happens, then, when we discover animals that use language, make and use tools, and recognize themselves in a mirror? Our intelligence was supposed to make us unique. If animals are smart too — if they think too — what separates humans and animals?

That's one of the questions you will explore in this chapter. But these readings cover more than just the central question of whether or not animals think, or even the larger question of what it means to be human. They also explore the conditions required for good science, the history of animal thinking hoaxes (like an early form of "fake news"), the special relationships we form with some animals, and the moral and ethical questions of how we should treat other living beings. Across all these issues, the question of animal intelligence often rebounds to the question of intelligence more generally, how to define it, who has it, and how to measure it.

Frans de Waal opens this exploration by offering an overview of what we've learned about animal intelligence and the challenges of creating solid scientific studies to expand our knowledge in this field. Jane Goodall, the famous conservationist, enacts some of de Waal's requirements for solid animal cognition science in her firsthand account of her study of chimpanzees and, in particular, her revolutionary discovery that they made and used tools. Goodall's work was one of the first to trouble the definitional links between humans and animals, but it was certainly not the last. Dinitia Smith continues in Goodall's direction with a profile of Irene Pepperberg, whose work focuses on a parrot's language use. Philip Sopher broadens this discussion again by looking at several examples of animal intelligence, while also noting the specific challenges to pursuing this scientific field.

Rachel Monroe shifts the conversation to more familiar territory by sharing her experiences with her cat Musa and the use of a pet psychic. Pet psychics may or may not be legitimate, but Alicia Puglionesi looks at thinking animals that were definitely hoaxes — although not always to the detriment of continuing research in this field. Rather than trying to answer the question of whether or not animals think, John Horgan asks a different and perhaps more troubling question: do fish suffer? If they do, as he suggests, how can we justify our treatment of them? Horgan reminds us that the question of animal intelligence is not just a matter of scientific curiosity. It's also a matter of human behavior, in its ethical and moral dimensions.

As you read through this chapter, you will find a lot of terms and examples repeated across the readings. These readings are in conversation with one another, which is a central part of the process of academic conversation, a process you will learn and practice in this class. The readings also, both explicitly and implicitly, question the nature of intelligence itself, offering a start to your own exploration of this complex concept.

Magic Wells

Frans De Waal

Primatologist Frans de Waal is the C. H. Candler Professor of Psychology at Emory University and the director of the Living Links Center, which focuses on the study of human behavioral evolution through the investigation of primates. He is a prolific author with more than a dozen books published, including *Our Inner Ape* (2005), *The Age of Empathy: Nature's Lessons for a Kinder Society* (2009), and *The Bonobo and the Atheist* (2013). This selection is from his 2016 book, *Are We Smart Enough to Know How Smart Animals Are?*, which focuses on animal cognition.

On Becoming a Bug

Opening his eyes, Gregor Samsa woke up inside the body of an unspecified animal. Equipped with a hard exoskeleton, the "horrible vermin" hid under the sofa, crawled up and down walls and ceilings, and loved rotten food. Poor Gregor's transformation inconvenienced and disgusted his family to the point that his death came as a relief.

Franz Kafka's *Metamorphosis*, published in 1915, was an odd opening salvo for a less anthropocentric° century. Having selected a repulsive creature for metaphorical effect, the author forced us from the very first page to imagine what it is like to be a bug. At around the same time, Jakob von Uexküll, a German biologist, drew attention to the animal point of view, calling it its *Umwelt*. To illustrate this new concept (German for the "surrounding world"), Uexküll took us on a stroll through various worlds. Each organism senses the environment in its own way, he said. The eyeless tick climbs onto a grass stem to await the smell of butyric acid emanating from mammalian skin. Since experiments have shown that this arachnid can go for eighteen years without food, the tick has ample time to meet a mammal, drop onto her victim, and gorge herself on warm blood. Afterward she is ready to lay her eggs and die. Can we understand the tick's *Umwelt?* It seems incredibly impoverished compared to ours, but Uexküll saw its simplicity as a strength: her goal is well defined, and she encounters few distractions.

Uexküll reviewed other examples, showing that a single environment offers hundreds of realities peculiar to each species. *Umwelt* is quite different from the notion of *ecological niche,* which concerns the habitat that an organism needs for survival. Instead, *Umwelt* stresses an organism's self-centered, subjective world, which represents only a small tranche° of all available worlds. According to Uexküll, the various tranches are "not comprehended

anthropocentric: regarding humankind as the central or most important element of existence, especially as opposed to animals.
tranche: a portion of something, often money.

and never discernible" to all the species that construct them. Some animals perceive ultraviolet light, for example, while others live in a world of smells or, like the star-nosed mole, feel their way around underground. Some sit on the branches of an oak, and others live underneath its bark, while a fox family digs a lair among its roots. Each perceives the same tree differently.

Humans can try to imagine the *Umwelt* of other organisms. Being a highly visual species ourselves, we buy smartphone apps that turn colorful images into those seen by people without color vision. We can walk around blindfolded to simulate the *Umwelt* of the vision-impaired in order to augment our empathy. My most memorable experience with an alien world, however, came from raising jackdaws, small members of the crow family. Two of them flew in and out of my window on the fourth floor of a student dorm, so I could watch their exploits from above. When they were young and inexperienced, I observed them, like any good parent, with great apprehension. We think of flight as something birds do naturally, but it is actually a skill that they have to learn. Landing is the hardest part, and I was always afraid they would crash into a moving car. I began to think like a bird, mapping the environment as if looking for the perfect landing spot, judging a distant object (a branch, a balcony) with this goal in mind. Upon achieving a safe landing, my birds would give happy "caw-caw" calls, after which I would call them to come back, and the whole process would start anew. Once they became expert flyers, I enjoyed their playful tumbling in the wind as if I were flying among them. I entered my birds' *Umwelt*, even though imperfectly.

Whereas Uexküll wanted science to explore and map the *Umwelten* of various species, an idea that deeply inspired students of animal behavior known as ethologists, philosophers of the last century were rather pessimistic. When Thomas Nagel, in 1974, asked, "What is it like to be a bat?" he concluded that we would never know. We have no way of entering the subjective life of another species, he said. Nagel did not seek to know how a human would feel as a bat: he wanted to understand how a bat feels like a bat. This is indeed beyond our comprehension. The same wall between them and us was noted by the Austrian philosopher Ludwig Wittgenstein, when he famously declared, "If a lion could talk, we could not understand him." Some scholars were offended, complaining that Wittgenstein had no idea of the subtleties of animal communication, but the crux of his aphorism was that since our own experiences are so unlike a lion's, we would fail to understand the king of fauna even if he spoke our tongue. In fact, Wittgenstein's reflections extended to people in strange cultures with whom we, even if we know their language, fail to "find our feet." His point was our limited ability to enter the inner lives of others, whether they are foreign humans or different organisms.

Rather than tackle this intractable problem, I will focus on the world that animals live in, and how they navigate its complexity. Even though we can't feel what they feel, we can still try to step outside our own narrow *Umwelt* and apply our imagination to theirs. In fact, Nagel could never have written his incisive reflections had he not heard of the echolocation of bats, which had been discovered only because scientists did try to imagine what it is like to be a bat and did in fact succeed. It is one of the triumphs of our species' thinking outside its perceptual box.

As a student, I listened in amazement as Sven Dijkgraaf, the head of my department at the University of Utrecht, told the story of how, at about my age, he was one of only a handful of people in the world who was able to hear the faint clicks that accompany a bat's ultrasonic vocalizations. The professor had extraordinary hearing. It had been known for more than a century that a blinded bat can still find its way around and safely land on walls and ceilings, whereas a deafened one cannot. A bat without hearing is like a human without sight. No one fully understood how this worked, and bats' abilities were unhelpfully attributed to a "sixth sense." Scientists don't believe in extrasensory perception, however, and Dijkgraaf had to come up with an alternative explanation. Since he could detect a bat's calls, and had noticed that the rate increased when bats encountered obstacles, he suggested that the calls help them traverse their environment. But there was always a tone of regret in his voice about the lack of recognition he had received as the discoverer of echolocation.

This honor had gone to Donald Griffin, and rightly so. Assisted by equipment that could detect sound waves above the 20 kHz range of human hearing, this American ethologist had conducted the ultimate experiments, which furthermore demonstrated that echolocation is more than just a collision warning system. Ultrasound serves to find and pursue prey, from large moths to little flies. Bats possess an astonishingly versatile hunting tool.

No wonder Griffin became an early champion of animal cognition—a term considered an oxymoron° until well into the 1980s—because what else is cognition but information processing? *Cognition* is the mental transformation of sensory input into knowledge about the environment and the flexible application of this knowledge. While the term *cognition* refers to the process of doing this, *intelligence* refers more to the ability to do it successfully. The bat works with plenty of sensory input, even if it remains alien to us. Its auditory cortex evaluates sounds bouncing off objects, then uses this information to calculate its distance to the target

---

oxymoron: a figure of speech in which seemingly contradictory terms appear together.

as well as the target's movement and speed. As if this weren't complex enough, the bat also corrects for its own flight path and distinguishes the echoes of its own vocalizations from those of nearby bats: a form of self-recognition. When insects evolved hearing in order to evade bat detection, some bats responded with "stealth" vocalizations below the hearing level of their prey.

What we have here is a most sophisticated information-processing system backed by a specialized brain that turns echoes into precise perception. Griffin had followed in the footsteps of the pioneering experimentalist Karl von Frisch, who had discovered that honeybees use a waggle dance to communicate distant food locations. Von Frisch once said, "The life of the bee is like a magic well, the more you draw from it, the more there is to draw." Griffin felt the same about echolocation, seeing this capacity as yet another inexhaustible source of mystery and wonder. He called it, too, a magic well.

Since I work with chimpanzees, bonobos, and other primates, people usually don't give me a hard time when I speak of cognition. After all, people are primates, too, and we process our surroundings in similar ways. With our stereoscopic vision, grasping hands, ability to climb and jump, and emotional communication via facial muscles, we inhabit the same *Umwelt* as other primates. Our children play on "monkey bars," and we call imitation "aping," precisely because we recognize these similarities. At the same time, we feel threatened by primates. We laugh hysterically at apes in movies and sitcoms, not because they are inherently funny — there are much funnier-looking animals, such as giraffes and ostriches — but because we like to keep our fellow primates at arm's length. It is similar to how people in neighboring countries, who resemble each other most, joke about each other. The Dutch find nothing to laugh at in the Chinese or the Brazilians, but they relish a good joke about the Belgians.

But why stop at the primates when we are considering cognition? Every species deals flexibly with the environment and develops solutions to the problems it poses. Each one does it differently. We had better use the plural to refer to their capacities, therefore, and speak of intelligences and cognitions. This will help us avoid comparing cognition on a single scale modeled after Aristotle's *scala naturae*, which runs from God, the angels, and humans at the top, downward to other mammals, birds, fish, insects, and mollusks at the bottom. Comparisons up and down this vast ladder have been a popular pastime of cognitive science, but I cannot think of a single profound insight it has yielded. All it has done is make us measure animals by human standards, thus

> "Why stop at primates when considering cognition?"

10

ignoring the immense variation in organisms' *Umwelten*. It seems highly unfair to ask if a squirrel can count to ten if counting is not really what a squirrel's life is about. The squirrel is very good at retrieving hidden nuts, though, and some birds are absolute experts. The Clark's nutcracker, in the fall, stores more than twenty thousand pine nuts, in hundreds of different locations distributed over many square miles; then in winter and spring it manages to recover the majority of them.

That we can't compete with squirrels and nutcrackers on this task—I even forget where I parked my car—is irrelevant, since our species does not need this kind of memory for survival the way forest animals braving a freezing winter do. We don't need echolocation to orient ourselves in the dark; nor do we need to correct for the refraction of light between air and water as archerfish do while shooting droplets at insects above the surface. There are lots of wonderful cognitive adaptations out there that we don't have or need. This is why ranking cognition on a single dimension is a pointless exercise. Cognitive evolution is marked by many peaks of specialization. The ecology of each species is key.

The last century has seen ever more attempts to enter the *Umwelt* of other species, reflected in book titles such as *The Herring Gull's World*, *The Soul of the Ape*, *How Monkeys See the World*, *Inside a Dog*, and *Anthill*, in which E. O. Wilson, in his inimitable fashion, offers an ant's-eye view of the social life and epic battles of ants. Following in the footsteps of Kafka and Uexküll, we are trying to get under the skin of other species, trying to understand them on their terms. And the more we succeed, the more we discover a natural landscape dotted with magic wells.

Six Blind Men and the Elephant

Cognition research is more about the possible than the impossible. Nevertheless, the *scala naturae* view has tempted many to conclude that animals lack certain cognitive capacities. We hear abundant claims along the lines of "only humans can do this or that," referring to anything from looking into the future (only humans think ahead) and being concerned for others (only humans care about the well-being of others) to taking a vacation (only humans know leisure time). The last claim once had me, to my own amazement, debating a philosopher in a Dutch newspaper about the difference between a tourist tanning on the beach and a napping elephant seal. The philosopher considered the two to be radically different.

In fact, I find the best and most enduring claims about human exceptionalism to be the funny ones, such as Mark Twain's "Man is the only animal that blushes—or needs to." But, of course, most of these claims are deadly serious and self-congratulatory. The list goes on and on and changes every decade, yet must be treated with suspicion given how hard it is to prove a negative. The credo of experimental science remains that an absence of evidence is not evidence of absence. If we fail to find a capacity in a given species, our first thought ought to be "Did we overlook something?" And the second should be "Did our test fit the species?"

A telling illustration involves gibbons, which were once considered backward primates. Gibbons were presented with problems that required them to choose between various cups, strings, and sticks. In test after test, these primates fared poorly compared to other species. Tool use, for example, was tested by dropping a banana outside their cage and placing a stick nearby. All they had to do to get the banana was pick up the stick to move it closer. Chimpanzees will do so without hesitation, as will many manipulative monkeys. But not gibbons. This was bizarre given that gibbons (also known as "lesser apes") belong to the same large-brained family as humans and apes.

In the 1960s an American primatologist, Benjamin Beck, took a fresh approach. Gibbons are exclusively arboreal. Known as *brachiators,* they propel themselves through trees by hanging by their arms and hands. Their hands, which have tiny thumbs and elongated fingers, are specialized for this kind of locomotion: gibbon hands act more like hooks than like the versatile grasping and feeling organs of most other primates. Beck, realizing that the gibbon's *Umwelt* barely includes the ground level and that its hands make it impossible to pick up objects from a flat surface, redesigned a traditional string-pulling task. Instead of presenting strings lying on a surface, as had been done before, he elevated them to the animal's shoulder level, making them easier to grasp. Without going into detail—the task required the animal to look carefully at how a string was attached to food—the gibbons solved all the problems quickly and efficiently, demonstrating the same intelligence as other apes. Their earlier poor performance had had more to do with the way they were tested than with their mental powers.

Elephants are another good example. For years, scientists believed them incapable of using tools. The pachyderms failed the same out-of-reach banana test, leaving the stick alone. Their failure could not be attributed to an inability to lift objects from a flat surface, because elephants are ground dwellers and pick up items all the time, sometimes tiny ones. Researchers concluded that they just didn't get the problem. It occurred to no one that perhaps we, the investigators, didn't get the elephant. Like the six blind men, we keep turning around and poking the big beast, but we need to remember that, as Werner Heisenberg put it, "what we observe is not nature in itself, but nature exposed to our method of questioning." Heisenberg, a German physicist, made this observation regarding quantum mechanics, but it holds equally true for explorations of the animal mind:

In contrast to the primate's hand, the elephant's grasping organ is 20 also its nose. Elephants use their trunks not only to reach food but also to sniff and touch it. With their unparalleled sense of smell, these animals know exactly what they are going for. But picking up a stick blocks their nasal passages. Even when they bring the stick close to the food, it impedes their feeling and smelling it. It is like sending a blindfolded child out on an Easter egg hunt.

What sort of experiment, then, would do justice to the animal's special anatomy and abilities?

On a visit to the National Zoo in Washington, D.C., I met Preston Foerder and Diana Reiss, who showed me what Kandula, a young elephant bull, can do when the problem is presented differently. The scientists hung fruit high up above Kandula's enclosure, just out of his reach. They gave the elephant several sticks and a sturdy square box. Kandula ignored the sticks but, after a while, began kicking the box with his foot. He kicked it many times in a straight line until it was right underneath the fruit. He then stood on the box with his front legs, which enabled him to reach the food with his trunk. An elephant, it turns out, can use tools—if they are the right ones.

As Kandula munched his reward, the investigators explained to me how they had varied the setup, making life more difficult for the elephant. They had put the box in a different section of the yard, out of view, so that when Kandula looked up at the tempting food, he would need to recall the solution while distancing himself from his goal to fetch the tool. Apart from a few large-brained species, such as humans, apes, and dolphins, not many animals will do this, but Kandula did it without hesitation, fetching the box from great distances.

Clearly, the scientists had found a species-appropriate test. In search of such methods, even something as simple as size can matter. The largest land animal cannot always be tested with human-sized tools. In one experiment researchers conducted a mirror test—to evaluate whether an animal recognizes its own reflection. They placed a mirror on the floor outside an elephant cage. Measuring only 41 by 95 inches, it was angled up so that the elephant probably mostly saw its legs moving behind two layers of bars (since the mirror doubled them). When the elephant received a body mark that was visible only with assistance of the mirror, it failed to touch it. The verdict was that the species lacked self-awareness.

But Joshua Plotnik, then a student of mine, modified the test. He gave 25 elephants at the Bronx Zoo access to an eight-foot-square mirror placed directly inside their enclosure. They could feel it, smell it, and look behind it. Close-up exploration is a critical step, for apes and humans as well; that had been impossible in the earlier study. In fact, the elephants' curiosity worried us, as the mirror was mounted on a wooden wall that was not designed to support climbing pachyderms. Elephants normally don't stand up against structures, so having a four-ton animal lean on a flimsy wall in order to see and smell what was behind the mounted mirror scared us to death. Clearly, the animals were motivated to find out what the mirror was all about, but if the wall had collapsed, we might have ended up chasing elephants in New York traffic! Fortunately, the wall held, and the animals got used to the mirror.

One Asian elephant, named Happy, recognized her reflection. Marked with a white cross on her forehead above her left eye, she repeatedly rubbed the mark while standing in front of the mirror. She connected her reflection with her own body. By now, years later, Josh has tested many more animals at Think Elephants International, in Thailand, and our conclusion holds: some Asian elephants recognize themselves in the mirror. Whether the same can be said of African elephants is hard to tell, because up to now our experiments have resulted in a lot of destroyed mirrors due to this species' tendency to examine new items with vigorous tusk action. This makes it hard to decide between poor performance and poor equipment. Obviously, the destruction of mirrors is no reason to conclude that African elephants lack mirror self-recognition. We are just dealing with species-typical treatment of novel items.

The challenge is to find tests that fit an animal's temperament, interests, anatomy, and sensory capacities. Faced with negative outcomes, we need to pay close attention to differences in motivation and attention. One cannot expect a great performance on a task that fails to arouse interest. We ran into this problem while studying face recognition in chimpanzees. At the time, science had declared humans unique, since we were so much better at identifying faces than any other primate. No one seemed bothered by the fact that other primates had been tested mostly on human faces rather than those of their own kind. When I asked one of the pioneers in this field why the methodology had never moved beyond the human face, he answered that since humans differ so strikingly from one another, a primate that fails to tell members of our species apart will surely also fail at its own kind.

But when Lisa Parr, one of my coworkers at the Yerkes National Primate Research Center in Atlanta, tested chimpanzees on photographs of their own species, she found that they excelled at it. Selecting images on a computer screen, they would see one chimpanzee portrait immediately followed by a pair of others. One portrait of the pair would be a different picture of the same individual as presented before, while the other would show a different individual. Having been trained to detect similarity (a procedure known as matching to sample), the chimpanzees had no trouble recognizing which portrait most resembled the first. The apes even detected family ties. After having seen a female portrait, they were given a choice between two juvenile faces, one of which was the offspring of the female shown before. They picked the latter based purely on physical similarity, since they did not know any of the depicted apes in real life. In much the same way, we can leaf through someone else's family album and quickly notice who are blood relatives and who are in-laws. As it turns out, chimpanzee face recognition is as keen as ours. It is now widely accepted as a shared capacity, especially since it engages the same brain areas in humans and other primates.

In other words, what is salient° to us — such as our own facial features — may not be salient to other species. Animals often know only what they *need* to know. The maestro of observation, Konrad Lorenz, believed that one could not investigate animals effectively without an intuitive understanding grounded in love and respect. He saw such intuitive insight as quite separate from the methodology of the natural sciences. To marry it productively with systematic research is both the challenge and the joy of studying animals. Promoting what he called the *Ganzheitsbetrachtung* (holistic contemplation), Lorenz urged us to grasp the whole animal before zooming in on its various parts.

> *One cannot master set research tasks if one makes a single part the focus of interest. One must, rather, continuously dart from one part to another — in a way that appears extremely flighty and unscientific to some thinkers who place value on strictly logical sequences — and one's knowledge of each of the parts must advance at the same pace.*

The danger of ignoring this advice was amusingly illustrated when a   30 famous study was replicated. In the study, domestic cats were placed in a small cage; they would wander about impatiently meowing — and in the process rub against the cage interior. In so doing, they accidentally moved a latch that opened a door, which allowed them to get out of the cage and eat a scrap of fish nearby. The more trials a cat performed, the quicker she'd escape. The investigators were impressed that all the tested cats showed the same stereotyped rubbing pattern, which they thought they had taught them with food rewards. First developed by Edward Thorndike in 1898, this experiment was considered proof that

salient: important.

even seemingly intelligent behavior (such as escaping from a cage) can be fully explained by trial-and-error learning. It was a triumph of the "law of effect," according to which behavior with pleasant consequences is likely to be repeated.

When the American psychologists Bruce Moore and Susan Stuttard replicated this study decades later, however, they found that the cats' behavior was nothing special. The cats performed the usual *köpfchengeben* (German for "head giving") that all felines—from house cats to tigers—use in greeting and courting. They rub their head or flank against the object of affection or, if the object of affection is inaccessible, redirect the rubbing to inanimate objects, such as the legs of a kitchen table. The investigators showed that the food reward was not needed: the only meaningful factor was the presence of friendly people. Without training, every caged cat that saw a human observer rubbed its head, flank, and tail against the latch and got out of the cage. Left alone, however, the cats were unable to escape, since they never performed any rubbing. Instead of a learning experiment, the classical study had been a greeting experiment! The replication was published under the telling subtitle "Tripping over the Cat."

The lesson is that before scientists test any animal, they need to know its typical behavior. The power of conditioning is not in doubt, but the early investigators had totally overlooked a crucial piece of information. They had not, as recommended by Lorenz, considered the whole organism. Animals show many unconditioned responses, or behavior that develops naturally in all members of their species. Reward and punishment may affect such behavior but cannot take credit creating it. The reason all cats responded in the same way derived from natural feline communication rather than operant conditioning.

The field of evolutionary cognition requires us to consider every species in full. Whether we are studying hand anatomy, trunk multifunctionality, face perception, or greeting rituals, we need to familiarize ourselves with all facets of the animal and its natural history before trying to figure out its mental level. And instead of testing animals on abilities that *we* are particularly good at—our own species' magic wells, such as language—why not test them on *their* specialized skills? In doing so, we will not just flatten Aristotle's scale of nature: we will transform it into a bush with many branches. This change in perspective is now feeding the long-overdue recognition that intelligent life is not something we must seek at great expense only in the outer reaches of space. It is abundant here on earth, right underneath our nonprehensile° noses.

---

nonprehensile: not involved in grasping or seizing.

Anthropodenial

The ancient Greeks believed that the center of the universe was right where they lived. What better place, therefore, than Greece for modern scholars to ponder humanity's place in the cosmos? On a sunny day in 1996, an international group of academics visited the *omphalos* (navel) of the world—a large stone shaped like a beehive—amid the temple ruins on Mount Parnassus. I couldn't resist patting it like a long-lost friend. Right next to me stood "batman" Don Griffin, the discoverer of echolocation and author of *The Question of Animal Awareness*, in which he lamented the misperception that everything in the world turns around us and that we are the only conscious beings.

Ironically, a major theme of our workshop was the anthropic principle, according to which the universe is a purposeful creation uniquely suited for intelligent life, meaning us. At times the discourse of the anthropic philosophers sounded as if they thought the world was made for us rather than the other way around. Planet Earth is at exactly the right distance from the sun to create the right temperature for human life, and its atmosphere has the ideal oxygen level. How convenient! Instead of seeing purpose in this situation, however, any biologist will turn the causal connection around and note that our species is finely adapted to the planet's circumstances, which explains why they are perfect for us. Deep ocean vents are an optimal environment for bacteria thriving on their superhot sulfuric output, but no one assumes that these vents were created to serve thermophile bacteria; rather, we understand that natural selection has shaped bacteria able to live near them.

The backward logic of these philosophers reminded me of a creationist I once saw peel a banana on television while explaining that this fruit is curved in such a way that it conveniently angles toward the human mouth when we hold it in our hand. It also fits perfectly in our mouth. Obviously, he felt that God had given the banana its human-friendly shape, while forgetting that he was holding a domesticated fruit, cultivated for human consumption.

During some of these discussions, Don Griffin and I watched barn swallows flying back and forth outside the conference room window carrying mouthfuls of mud for their nests. Griffin was at least three decades my senior and had impressive knowledge, offering the Latin name of the birds and describing details of their incubation period. At the workshop, he presented his view on consciousness: that it has to be part and parcel of all cognitive processes, including those of animals. My own position is slightly different in that I prefer not to make any firm statements about something as poorly defined as consciousness. No one seems to know what it is. But for the same reason, I hasten to add, I'd never deny it to any species. For all I know, a frog may be conscious. Griffin took a more positive stance, saying that since intentional, intelligent actions are observable in many animals, and since in our own species they go together with awareness, it is reasonable to assume similar mental states in other species.

That such a highly respected and accomplished scientist made this claim had a hugely liberating effect. Even though Griffin was slammed for making statements that he could not back up with data, many critics missed the point, which was that the assumption that animals are "dumb," in the sense that they lack conscious minds, is only that: an assumption. It is far more logical to assume continuity in every domain, Griffin said, echoing Charles Darwin's well-known observation that the mental difference between humans and other animals is one of degree rather than kind.

It was an honor to get to know this kindred spirit and to make my own case regarding anthropomorphism, another theme at the conference. Greek for "human form," the word *anthropomorphism* came about when Xenophanes, in 570 BC, objected to Homer's poetry because it described the gods as if they looked like people. Xenophanes ridiculed the arrogance behind this assumption—why couldn't they look like horses? But gods are gods, far removed from the present-day liberal use of the word *anthropomorphism* as an epithet to vilify any and all human-animal comparisons, even the most cautious ones.

In my opinion, anthropomorphism is problematic only when the human-animal comparison is a stretch, such as with regards to species distant from us. The fish known as kissing gouramis, for example, don't really kiss in the same way and for the same reasons that humans do. Adult fish sometimes lock their protruding mouths together to settle disputes. Clearly, to label this habit "kissing" is misleading. Apes, on the other hand, do greet each other after a separation by placing their lips gently on each other's mouth or shoulder and hence kiss in a way and under circumstances that greatly resemble human kissing. Bonobos go even further: when a zookeeper familiar with chimpanzees once naïvely accepted a bonobo kiss, not knowing this species, he was taken aback by the amount of tongue that went into it!

Another example: when young apes are being tickled, they make breathy sounds with a rhythm of inhalation and exhalation that resembles human laughter. One cannot simply dismiss the term *laughter* for this behavior as too anthropomorphic (as some have done), because not only do the apes sound like human children being tickled, they show the same ambivalence about it as children do. I have often noticed it myself.

They try to push my tickling fingers away, but then come back begging for more, holding their breath while awaiting the next poke in their belly. In this case, I am all for shifting the burden of proof and ask those who wish to avoid humanlike terminology to first prove that a tickled ape, who almost chokes on its hoarse giggles, is in fact in a different state of mind from a tickled human child. Absent such evidence, *laughter* strikes me as the best label for both.

Needing a new term to make my point, I invented *anthropodenial*, which is the a priori° rejection of humanlike traits in other animals or animallike traits in us. Anthropomorphism and anthropodenial have an inverse relationship: the closer another species is to us, the more anthropomorphism will assist our understanding of this species and the greater will be the danger of anthropodenial. Conversely, the more distant a species is from us, the greater the risk that anthropomorphism will propose questionable similarities that have come about independently. Saying that ants have "queens," "soldiers," and "slaves" is mere anthropomorphic shorthand. We should attach no more significance to it than we do when we name a hurricane after a person or curse our computer as if it had free will.

The key point is that anthropomorphism is not always as problematic as people think. To rail against it for the sake of scientific objectivity often hides a pre-Darwinian mindset, one uncomfortable with the notion of humans as animals. When we are considering species like the apes, which are aptly known as "anthropoids" (humanlike), however, anthropomorphism is in fact a logical choice. Dubbing an ape's kiss "mouth-to-mouth contact" so as to avoid anthropomorphism deliberately obfuscates the meaning of the behavior. It would be like assigning Earth's gravity a different name than the moon's, just because we think Earth is special. Unjustified linguistic barriers fragment the unity with which nature presents us. Apes and humans did not have enough time to independently evolve strikingly similar behavior, such as lip contact in greeting or noisy breathing in response to tickling. Our terminology should honor the obvious evolutionary connections.

On the other hand, anthropomorphism would be a rather empty exercise if all it did was paste human labels onto animal behavior. The American biologist and herpetologist Gordon Burghardt has called for a *critical anthropomorphism*, in which we use human intuition and knowledge of an animal's natural history to formulate research questions. Thus, saying that animals "plan" for the future or "reconcile" after

---

a priori: relating to knowledge gained from theoretical deduction, rather than from observation or experience.

fights is more than anthropomorphic language: these terms propose testable ideas. If primates are capable of planning, for example, they should hold on to a tool that they can use only in the future. And if primates reconcile after fights, we should see a reduction of tensions as well as improved social relationships after opponents have made up by means of friendly contact. These obvious predictions have by now been borne out by actual experiments and observations. Serving as a means rather than an end, critical anthropomorphism is a valuable source of hypotheses.

Griffin's proposal to take animal cognition seriously led to a new label for this field: *cognitive ethology.* It is a great label, but then I am an ethologist and know exactly what he meant. Unfortunately, the term *ethology* has not universally caught on, and spell-checkers still regularly change it to *ethnology, etiology,* or even *theology.* No wonder many ethologists nowadays call themselves behavioral biologists. Other existing labels for cognitive ethology are *animal cognition* and *comparative cognition.* But those two terms have drawbacks, too. *Animal cognition* fails to include humans, so it unintentionally perpetuates the idea of a gap between humans and other animals. The *comparative* label, on the other hand, remains agnostic about how and why we make comparisons. It hints at no framework whatsoever to interpret similarities and differences, least of all an evolutionary one. Even within this discipline, there have been complaints about its lack of theory as well as its habit of dividing animals into "higher" and "lower" forms. The label derives from *comparative psychology,* the name of a field that traditionally has viewed animals as mere stand-ins for humans: a monkey is a simplified human, a rat a simplified monkey, and so on. Since associative learning was thought to explain behavior across all species, one of the field's founders, B. F. Skinner, felt that it hardly mattered what kind of animal one worked on. To prove his point, he entitled a book entirely devoted to albino rats and pigeons *The Behavior of Organisms.*

For these reasons, Lorenz once joked that there was nothing comparative about comparative psychology. He knew what he was talking about, having just published a seminal study on the courtship patterns of twenty different duck species. His sensitivity to the minutest differences between species was quite the opposite of the way comparative psychologists lump animals together as "nonhuman models of human behavior." Think for a second about this terminology, which remains so entrenched in psychology that no one takes notice anymore. Its first implication, of course, is that the only reason to study animals is to learn about ourselves. Second, it ignores that every species is uniquely adapted to its own ecology, because otherwise how could one serve as a model for another? Even the term *nonhuman* grates on me, since it lumps millions of species together by an absence, as if they were missing something. Poor things, they are nonhuman! When students embrace this jargon in their writing, I cannot resist sarcastic corrections in the margin saying that for completeness's sake, they should add that the animals they are talking about are also nonpenguin, nonhyena, and a whole lot more.

Even though comparative psychology is changing for the better, I'd rather avoid its leaden baggage and propose to call the new field *evolutionary cognition*, which is the study of all cognition (human and animal) from an evolutionary standpoint. Which species we study obviously matters a great deal, and humans are not necessarily central to every comparison. The field includes phylogeny, when we trace traits across the evolutionary tree to determine whether similarities are due to common descent, the way Lorenz had done so beautifully for waterfowl. We also ask how cognition has been shaped to serve survival. The agenda of this field is precisely what Griffin and Uexküll had in mind, in that it seeks to place the study of cognition on a less anthropocentric footing. Uexküll urged us to look at the world from the animal's standpoint, saying that this is the only way to fully appreciate animal intelligence.

A century later we are ready to listen.

Understanding the Text

1. De Waal argues that testing animal intelligence requires some crucial factors. What are they? Reread the text to locate quotations where de Waal delineates the elements necessary to test animal intelligence accurately.

2. De Waal coins the term "anthropodenial." Define this term using his text and then think of an example of what he means.

Reflection and Response

3. How does bias influence the conversation around animal intelligence, and how can we correct for that bias? Consider not only de Waal's argument and use of terms such as "anthropodenial" but also de Waal's own bias. Is it possible to eliminate this bias? If not, what are the best steps we can take to minimize it when considering animal intelligence?

4. De Waal titles this selection "Magic Wells," drawing from a quotation from Karl von Frisch. In what ways do animals function as "magic wells"? Using your smartphone or another recording device, make a video essay response to this question. Be sure to consider all the visual factors that go into a video, including elements such as the background and what you wear, and how you can use them to further support your position.

Making Connections

5. De Waal offers a number of examples of studies suggesting that animals have intelligence. Alicia Puglionesi ("How Counting Horses and Reading Dogs Convinced Us Animals Could Think," p. 51), in examining the history of "thinking" animals that were actually just well trained, seems to challenge some of the underlying premises of de Waal's examples and his argument as a whole. Evaluate de Waal's essay using Puglionesi's ideas. How credible is the evidence of cognition in animals?

6. How would accepting the idea of animal intelligence change human behavior? Consider the changes to how we eat, our home and recreational life, and how some people make a living. How might the magnitude of these changes shape the conversation around animal intelligence? Use one other essay from this chapter to support your response.

At Long Last I Belong

Jane Goodall

Primatologist and anthropologist Jane Goodall is widely recognized as the world's foremost expert on chimpanzees, having studied them since 1960, and is the founder of the Jane Goodall Institute, a global conservation organization. She has written more than two dozen books, including *The Chimpanzees of Gombe: Patterns of Behavior* (1986), *The Ten Trusts: What We Must Do to Care for the Animals We Love* (with Marc Bekoff, 2002), and the children's book *The Eagle and the Wren* (2000), and she has been the subject of more than forty films. This selection is from her landmark 1967 book, *My Friends the Wild Chimpanzees* (1967), in which she documented chimpanzees' creation and use of tools, the first such documented observation of tool creation in the animal kingdom.

At the start of the rainy season in 1960, after four long, difficult months in the field, I made my first really exciting observation—I saw a chimp fashion and use crude tools!

That morning I felt rather despondent, for I had trudged the mountains for hours and had seen no chimpanzees at all. Then, as I headed for the Peak, I spotted a black shape beside the red-earth mound of a termite nest.

Quickly I sat down (even today the chimps seem more at ease if we observe them from their own level) and peered through my binoculars. I saw David Greybeard, and as I watched him I could hardly believe my eyes. He was carefully trimming the edges from a wide blade of sword grass!

I gazed, scarcely daring to breathe, as he pushed the modified stem into the nest. He left it for a moment, then pulled it out and picked off something with his lips. The chimp continued probing with the stem until it bent double. He then discarded it and reached out to pick a length of vine. With a sweeping movement of one hand, he stripped the leaves from the vine, bit a piece from one end, and set to work again with his newly prepared tool.

For an hour I watched. From time to time David changed position, 5
opening up new holes in the termite mound by scratching at the soil with his index finger. Finally, after again trying each of the holes in turn, he dropped the piece of vine and wandered away.

I hurried to the place and found a horde of worker termites busily sealing the holes David had opened. Each moistened bits of clay with saliva and pressed the minute pellets into place. Poking a blade of grass down one hole, I felt the insects bite it. When I pulled the stem out, four workers and a couple of the larger soldiers clung to it. I tasted one, for I make it a point to try almost everything the chimps eat, but it seemed rather flavorless to me. At that time my mother had not yet left the reserve, and I was so excited I could hardly wait for sunset to hurry down and tell her what I had seen.

"You see," I told her, "some wild animals can *use* objects as tools. There's the sea otter for one. It gets a flat stone from the floor of the sea, floats on its back with the stone lying on its chest, and bangs shellfish against it to open them. And wild chimps have been seen *using* tools. In West Africa an observer saw one poke a stick into honey in an underground bees' nest. A chimpanzee in Liberia hammered with a rock at a dried palm nut. But David didn't simply *use* tools—he actually *made* them!"

"Can you really say that he was truly making tools?" my mother asked.

I described how David had stripped leaves from the section of vine and trimmed the edges off the blade of grass.

"Man isn't the only toolmaker after all!"

"He didn't just make use of any old bit of material lying around," I   10 explained. "He actually modified stems and grasses and made them suitable for his purpose."

"Then that means man isn't the only toolmaker after all!" my mother exclaimed.

Anthropologists, other social scientists, and theologians have defined man in a variety of ways. Until recently one widely accepted element of the anthropologists' definition was that "man starts at that stage of primate evolution when the creature begins to make tools to a regular and set pattern." The grasses and twigs used by the chimps for termite fishing do not, perhaps, comply entirely with this specification. Nonetheless, Dr. Leakey, on learning of my findings and referring to the description above, wrote, "I feel that scientists holding to this definition are faced with three choices: They must accept chimpanzees as man, by definition; they must redefine man; or they must redefine tools."

It is of great satisfaction to me to know that my work at the Gombe Stream Game Reserve is being taken into consideration by many scientists in their continuing efforts to redefine man in a manner far more complex and detailed than ever before attempted.

As the weeks passed, I discovered that when the rains begin the worker termites extend the passages of the nest to the surface and seal them with a thin layer of soil until it is time for the fertile, winged forms to fly out. Then the termites open the passages and the princes and princesses, as they are called, emerge and eventually join swarms from other nests. Pair by pair they burrow into the ground to form new colonies. With one batch gone, the termites again seal the passages until the next group takes wing.

Other inhabitants of the reserve also feed on termites. Baboons, mon-   15 keys, and birds gather around a nest when the emigrations take place, capturing the insects as they fly out. But the chimpanzee, using primitive tools, gets a head start while the nests are still sealed.

Jane Goodall carrying a young chimp in Zambia.
Stephen Robinson/Photoshot Images/Newscom

Many times since that first thrilling day I have watched chimpanzees fishing for termites. Usually they work about an hour. But if the insects refuse to bite, the chimps try one fishing tool after another in quick succession (as though they feel the tools are to blame), then wander away, often to try their luck at another nest.

Some authorities suggest that only when an implement is kept for future use is the toolmaker showing forethought; for this reason people often ask whether the chimps ever save the tools for reuse. This would have little point, since most of the objects would shrivel and become useless if kept. And, anyway, grass stems and twigs abound near the termite nests.

The chimpanzees do, however, select stems beforehand and carry them to termite nests quite out of sight, as far away as 100 yards. Such behavior seems to indicate a certain forethought. A mature male once picked a grass tool that he carried for half a mile while he carefully inspected eight nests. When none of them proved right for working, he gave up and dropped the stem.

The year following the discovery of chimpanzee toolmaking, I found that the apes also eat several species of ant. One, the safari ant, has a particularly vicious and painful sting. Hugo and I once saw Mr. McGregor raiding an underground nest of these insects.

Standing upright, he carefully pushed a yard-long stick into the burrow, then stepped back from the hundreds of ants that emerged. After picking off those that had bitten onto him, he returned to the nest and pulled out the stick with a magnificent gesture. Still upright, he ate the globular mass of ants clinging to the end, seemingly unmindful of the stings. Then he pushed the stick back for more. 20

"I'm sure early man must have used sticks and twigs as tools long before he thought of chipping flakes of stone—don't you think so?" Hugo asked.

I nodded. "In fact, Mr. McGregor looks rather like a prehistoric man himself," I said.

Indeed, the old male chimp with his bald crown, neck, and shoulders, and the little fluff of hair around his head that resembles a monk's tonsure°, did look like some strange hairy man of the forest standing there, stick in hand, among the hanging lianas and gnarled trunks.

Chimps also eat weaver ants in large quantities, and we feel the apes have made quite a discovery here: The ants have a most exotic flavor, rather like curried lemon. One might even be able to market them as tropical delicacies. In addition, we have seen the chimps spend hours eating caterpillars and apparently relishing them.

---

tonsure: part of a monk's or priest's head left bare on top by shaving off the hair.

I vividly recall the day deep in the forest when Hugo and I saw young 25
Evered reach out, strip the leaves from a small branch, and stuff them
into his mouth.

"Whatever is he doing?" asked Hugo as Evered took the leaves out of his
mouth after chewing them slightly. Soon we had the answer. Holding them
between his index and middle fingers, he dipped them into a little hollow
in the trunk of a fallen tree. He lifted out the slightly mashed greenery, and
we saw the gleam of water. Evered sucked the liquid from his homemade
"sponge," and continued to dip and drink until he emptied the bowl.

We have seen many other chimps drink in the same way when they
could not reach the water with their lips—and always, like Evered, they
first chew the leaves briefly. It is the initial crumpling that makes this tool
so sophisticated, for it increases the absorbency of the leaves. Here again,
the Gombe Stream chimps, by modifying natural objects and using them
for a specific purpose, demonstrate their ability to make tools.

Chimpanzees on some occasions use leaves for wiping themselves
clean of sticky or unpleasant substances such as mud, blood, or food
smears. Figan once rubbed his chest with several handfuls of leaves after
carrying a load of overripe bananas. Mothers usually scrub themselves
with bunches of leaves if they are dirtied by their babies. And we watched
Melissa, after a fight, blotting the blood on her nose with a leaf.

"She looks like a fastidious lady dabbing at her nosebleed with a lace
hanky," Edna said. At that moment we all began to laugh, for Melissa, quite
unlike a fastidious lady, licked the blood from her forest handkerchief.

There has long been discussion among some scientists as to whether 30
man first used objects as tools or as weapons. Of course, one cannot draw
firm conclusions from the Gombe Stream chimpanzee community, but
these chimps do employ objects in both food-gathering and fighting.
Weapon use, however, is neither as frequent nor as effective as tool use.

For instance, some adult males throw missiles with definite aim during
aggressive encounters with other chimpanzees, with baboons, and with
humans. Although the missiles usually travel in the right direction, they
often fall short of the target and frequently are too small or ineffective
to inflict damage anyway. Once Mr. Worzle threw three times in quick
succession with a beautiful overarm style, scoring two hits on a big male
baboon only three feet away. As weapons he used a handful of leaves, a
banana skin, and a small pebble.

Only twice have we seen an adult female throw objects. But young Fifi
during her sixth year gradually became a frequent, if unsuccessful, flinger of
missiles, and she developed a technique all her own. Looking in any direction but that of the baboon or chimpanzee that has aroused her hostility,
she unobtrusively gathers as many pebbles as she can hold. Then, with what

we refer to as "Fifi's evil face," she charges toward her target and throws the whole handful. Luckily for her victims, Fifi's aim is far from good—the stones descend on her own head as often as they reach their goal.

It seems somewhat surprising that the chimpanzees do not make more use of rocks and branches as weapons, since all the mature males we know, and most of the adolescent males, throw things at random to enhance what we call their charging displays. These occur when the chimps become socially excited or frustrated. They rush about wildly, hurling rocks or sticks, dragging branches, slapping the ground or stamping, and leaping into the trees to sway branches violently from side to side.

Faben, during his magnificent displays, often runs upright, holding a stick above his shoulder and then hurling it somewhat as one would a javelin. David Greybeard, whose displays are slow, deliberate, and spectacular, frequently throws large rocks.

Once, when Hugo was in bed with malaria, David arrived behind the 35 tent, stamping and slapping the ground and hooting. In his excitement, he hurled a large stone that by chance went straight toward Hugo, missing his head by a bare two inches. Had it not been for those two inches, Hugo undoubtedly would have had his skull smashed in.

Just as the older apes use rocks, sticks, and other items in displays, so the youngsters use many objects in their games. Besides playing together—wrestling, tickling, or chasing through the trees—young chimps love to play with toys.

Their forest home provides any number of delightful and ingenious playthings which even human children would enjoy. *Strychnos* trees produce round, hard-shelled fruit about the size of tennis balls. The youngsters kick them from foot to hand, or roll them over their bodies.

With the fruit, Figan devised a game of his own: Lying on his back, he spins a *Strychnos* ball round and round, balancing it on his hands and kicking gently with his feet, like a circus bear.

Sometimes the young chimpanzees drag objects along the ground, walking slowly and looking back over their shoulders like children with pull-toys. Fifi once pulled a dead rat by its tail, and Gilka dragged a long stem with a cluster of berries on one end. Fifi found another strange plaything. Once while Hugo was absorbed in taking notes, he heard a high-pitched noise, glanced casually at Fifi, and returned to his work, thinking she had a whistle.

"Suddenly," he told me afterward, "I realized that Fifi couldn't possi- 40 bly have a whistle!"

Looking again, he saw that the noise came from a cicada. Fifi held one of its wings in her mouth, and the insect emitted a loud churring sound as it tried to escape.

"Fifi played with it for about half an hour," Hugo told me. "She either held it in her lips, or she put it in the 'groin pocket' between her thigh and abdomen. I could still hear the churring sound in a muffled sort of way. When she apparently had tired of the insect, she looked at it intently, bit off its head, looked at it again, and let it fall to the ground. 'No good any more,' she seemed to say to herself."

Understanding the Text

1. What is Goodall's great discovery in this essay? What makes it so significant? Read back through the selection to identify quotations that underscore not only the discovery but also its greater importance.

2. For a scientist, Goodall uses a fairly informal tone in her writing. First, locate an example of a sentence that offers a good example of this tone. Why do you think she chose to write this way? What audience do you think she is speaking to?

Reflection and Response

3. At the time of Goodall's work, one of the key factors that separated humans from animals was the creation and use of tools. Dr. Louis Leakey, whose work first suggested that humans evolved in Africa and who was Goodall's primary mentor, responded to her discovery of chimpanzee tool usage by saying that scientists must "accept chimpanzees as man, by definition; they must redefine man; or they must redefine tools" (p. 27). Have we changed our definition of humans in the years since Goodall's work? What separates humans from animals now? Why might our definitions be slow to change, and what makes such a definition important anyway?

4. Goodall notes that scientists long wondered if humans first used objects as tools or as weapons. Given her observations of chimpanzees, what conclusions might we draw? How does your answer relate to your answer to question 3 about the difference between humans and animals?

Making Connections

5. Frans de Waal ("Magic Wells," p. 10) explores some of the challenges involved in testing animal cognition. Evaluate Goodall's work in light of de Waal's discussion. Do her observational experiments meet the standards that de Waal suggests are necessary? Present your answer through a slide presentation created in PowerPoint or other presentation software. Consider how using this format affects how you present your argument, including elements such as fonts, transitions, and images.

6. Rachel Monroe ("The Cat Psychic," p. 44) looks at the influence that the special relationship between pets and their owners has on how we think about animal intelligence. Connect Monroe's experiences relating to her cat to Goodall's experience relating to chimpanzees. How does our proximity to, and closeness with, an animal shape the way we think about them and how they think?

A Thinking Bird or Just Another Birdbrain?

Dinitia Smith

Author and filmmaker Dinitia Smith has published four novels and has taught at both Columbia University and New York University. She was a cultural correspondent for the *New York Times*, from which this selection is drawn. In it, she profiles Irene Pepperberg, a research associate at Harvard University's Harvard Animal Studies Project, noted for her work on animal cognition in parrots and, in particular, her work with Alex, an African grey parrot she argued was able to use language in sophisticated ways.

"Calm down," Alex, an African Gray parrot, told Dr. Irene Pepperberg, the scientist at the University of Arizona who owns him. "Don't tell me to calm down," Dr. Pepperberg snapped. Sometimes Dr. Pepperberg and Alex squabble like an old married couple. He even says, "I love you."

For the last 22 years, Dr. Pepperberg has been teaching Alex, who is twenty-three, to do complex tasks of the sort that only a few nonhuman species—chimpanzees, for instance—have been able to perform. But unlike those other creatures, Alex can talk, or at least, he can vocalize. And, Dr. Pepperberg says, Alex doesn't just imitate human speech, as other parrots do—Alex can think. His actions are not just an instinctive response, she says, but rather a result of reasoning and choice.

Assertions like Dr. Pepperberg's are at the center of a highly emotional debate about whether thought is solely the domain of humans, or whether it can exist in other animals. Although many people are intrigued by the idea that animals may be capable of some form of abstract reasoning and communication, scientists often ascribe what looks like clever behavior to mimicry or rote learning or even, in some cases, unconscious cues by a trainer.

So, just how smart is Alex?

The question of animal intelligence goes back at least to Descartes and 5 his famous aphorism, "I think, therefore I am." Animals cannot think, said Descartes, and therefore are inferior to humans. And for many theologians and philosophers, the ability to think gives man a unique closeness to God.

Parrots, of course, are famous mimics, and some parrots have bigger vocabularies than Alex. But no parrot, says Dr. Pepperberg, has been able to perform tasks as complex as Alex can. And she believes that when Alex vocalizes, he is expressing the results of his thoughts, not mere mimicry. For instance, when she asks Alex what color corn is, he answers yellow, even though there is no corn around. This means, she says, he has an abstract concept of what the words "color," "corn," and "yellow" mean. He has not simply memorized them, but can apply them to different objects.

Chimpanzees and dolphins have been able to perform equally complex tasks, though the tasks differ from those given to Alex because of the differences between species. But chimps and dolphins, obviously, cannot vocalize in the way Alex does.

Few scientists would dispute that Alex is doing something unusual in the history of animal studies. At least, his behavior is more advanced than that of most other parrots who have been the subject of scientific experiments. But scientists differ on the implications of Alex's behavior.

Until now, Dr. Pepperberg has published her work in scientific journals, but in January Harvard University Press will publish *The Alex Studies*, a book summarizing her experiments with Alex.

Dr. Pepperberg bought Alex at a garden-variety pet store in Chicago 10 when he was about a year old with the idea of studying him. As far as she knew, he had no particular pedigree, and she is not even sure whether he is particularly smart in relation to other parrots. Now she is trying to replicate his training with another Gray Parrot, Griffin.

Dr. Pepperberg, listing Alex's accomplishments, said he could identify 50 different objects and recognize quantities up to 6; that he could distinguish 7 colors and 5 shapes, and understand "bigger," "smaller," "same," and "different," and that he was learning the concepts of "over" and "under." Hold a tray of different shapes and colored objects in front of him, as Dr. Pepperberg was doing the other day as a reporter watched, and he can distinguish an object by its color, shape, and the material it is made of. (Dr. Pepperberg said she frequently changed objects to make sure Alex wasn't just memorizing things and that she structured experiments to avoid involuntary cues from his examiner.)

But on this day Alex was being recalcitrant. Dr. Pepperberg had been away for three weeks at MIT, where she is a visiting professor this year. When she leaves him, she says, Alex chews at his tail and wing feathers, giving him a rather threadbare appearance, and when she returns he is very demanding, turning his back and saying, "Come here!"

"What matter is orange and three-cornered?" she asked Alex, holding the tray of objects in front of him. First, Alex had to identify which object was orange and three-cornered, and then tell Dr. Pepperberg what it was made of. She allowed Alex to pick up the objects on the tray with his beak and to "examine" each one.

But after he finished, instead of giving an answer, Alex demanded a nut. "Want a nut," he said clearly, sounding almost human. (He also responds to other people's commands, Dr. Pepperberg's graduate students for instance.)

"I know, I'll give you a nut," Dr. Pepperberg said, sounding annoyed. 15

"Wanna go back," said Alex, meaning go back into his cage.

Dr. Pepperberg continued trying to get Alex to perform, but he resisted and she began to lose patience.

"C'mon, Alex," she said.

"I'm sorry," he said. Usually, said Dr. Pepperberg, that means he is about to give in.

"What matter is orange and three-cornered, Alex?" she insisted. 20

"Wool!" said Alex, getting it right.

Dr. Pepperberg refuses to call Alex's vocalizations "language." "I avoid the language issue," she said. "I'm not making claims. His behavior gets more and more advanced, but I don't believe years from now you could interview him." She continued: "What little syntax he has is very simplistic. Language is what you and I are doing, an incredibly complex form of communication."

Still, many scientists and others remain unconvinced. What about unconscious cues from the trainer? Perhaps the most famous instance of that involves Clever Hans, a horse at the turn of the twentieth century who could supposedly count, tell time and make change by tapping his hoof on the ground. It was learned that Hans's trainer was tipping him off to the right answer by tensing his body and moving his head as Hans "counted."

More recently, Dr. Herbert Terrace, a Columbia University psychology professor, famously repudiated his own studies in the 1970s with a chimpanzee he called Nim Chimpsky, after the MIT linguist Noam Chomsky. Dr. Terrace taught Nim to use signs that looked as if they were combined grammatically into sentences. But it turned out they were clever imitations of his teacher.

Asked about Alex, Dr. Terrace said he thought that what Alex was doing 25 was "a rote response." He calls it "a complex discriminative performance."

But is Alex thinking? "I would say minimally," Dr. Terrace responded. "In every situation, there is an external stimulus that guides his response." Thought, he said, involves the ability to process information that is not right in front of you.

"It shows Alex is a smart bird," he said. But if you take away Alex's ability to vocalize in a way that seems human, he went on, it would not seem as impressive: "The words are responses, are not language."

On the other side of the animal-intelligence debate is Dr. Donald R. Griffin, author of *Animal Thinking*, who coined the phrase "cognitive ethology," the study of animal cognition. He believes that animals are capable of complex thought and behavior that is not just instinctive. The discovery that "a bird can express his conscious thoughts and feelings," said Dr. Griffin, "is a great advance. We used to think that was impossible." To Dr. Griffin, Alex's achievements are just one more proof of his contention.

Dr. Griffin's views of animal intelligence have been hotly contested. "The intensity of the aversion is incredible," he said. "It's a very touchy subject. Scientists don't like to be told that a valid reason for what an animal does is the possibility that it does it with any consciousness."

> "Scientists don't like to be told that a valid reason for what an animal does is the possibility that it does it with any consciousness."

Dr. Steven Pinker, an MIT scientist and author of "How the Mind 30 Works," said that at the heart of the debate is the question of human primacy. "In earlier times the issue was of whether we are mere animals, and to separate and exalt human worth. Ironically, there has been the same kind of moralistic return from animal fans who say we shouldn't mistreat them because they think and feel the way we do."

Dr. Pinker believes that human beings alone are genetically programmed to learn language spontaneously and easily. "I think it is rather an ironic definition of animals to tend to enoble them by training them to mimic humans."

Until recently, birds had been thought of as on the low end of the intelligence scale—hence the term "birdbrain." The point, Dr. Pepperberg said, is that Alex "is a nonmammal, nonprimate, with a brain the size of a walnut." And Alex's accomplishments, she added, show that "animal intelligence is more widespread than we thought."

Dr. Pepperberg attributes what she calls Alex's ability to reason and process complex information to her training methods. Most training of birds has followed the conditioning theories of B. F. Skinner, the behaviorist. A bird is taught to say or do a specific thing by a human instructor and is rewarded with food. Dr. Pepperberg initially uses the object itself as a reward so that the bird associates the word with the object. She uses two human trainers instead of one to demonstrate the interaction she is trying to teach Alex.

For instance, Dr. Pepperberg stands in front of Alex with a graduate student and orders the student to select a three-sided orange object and to say what the object is made of—wool, perhaps. She believes that by watching the interaction, Alex connects the graduate student's response to the command. "Orange," she believes, comes to mean to Alex the color of an object rather than the immediate reward of a grape.

Dr. Pepperberg says her experiments have implications beyond 35 determining whether—or how well—animals can think. She says her methods have been successfully used to train autistic children and children with learning disabilities. Alex's achievements, she said, also underscore the need for stricter conservation of parrots, which are an endangered species.

Dr. Pepperberg, who is fifty, was born in New York City, an only child who kept parakeets as pets and taught them to speak. She was studying for her Ph.D. in chemistry at Harvard, she said, when she saw a *Nova* series on PBS about chimps' using sign language, dolphin research and why birds sing. She wanted to change fields, but her advisers discouraged her, she said, so she continued her chemistry studies, continuing nonetheless to read all she could on animal behavior.

When she applied for her first grant to study bird behavior from the National Institutes of Health, she said, "there were reviews asking me what I was smoking."

"People are not at all surprised a chimpanzee can do this," she went on. "You can't imagine—people said birds were stupid."

Dr. Pepperberg expects Alex to live at least twenty more years. Meanwhile, she has added two new birds to the lab. Besides Griffin, now four years old, there is Kyaaro, who Dr. Pepperberg believes exhibits symptoms of attention deficit disorder.

"Alex doesn't like either of them," she said. "Kyaaro is weird. Griffin is 40 a threat." Right now she is trying to train Griffin to do some of the things Alex can do.

Griffin, who learned the word "wool" only recently, has been clinging to it the way a child clings to a new-found possession. One day recently Dr. Pepperberg held up a purple plastic letter S and asked, "What sound is purple?" Griffin stared at the letter. But from the other side of the laboratory Alex made the sound for him, "Sss."

"Buttinsky," Dr. Pepperberg said to Alex, and she turned back to Griffin.

"What sound?" she asked Griffin again, holding up the S. "What sound?"

"Wool," said Griffin.

Griffin has a long way to go.   45

Understanding the Text

1. Smith positions Pepperberg's research in the larger context of animal cognition, but Pepperberg herself represents her work and what Alex can do quite differently. Find passages where Pepperberg talks about her research and its significance. Why might she frame the work in this way?

2. What is "cognitive ethology"? Locate the section of the text where this term is defined, give an example from Smith's essay, and then offer an example of your own.

3. Although Irene Pepperberg is in many ways the main subject of this essay, she is not the author. How does the fact that Smith is writing change the presentation of Pepperberg and Alex? Locate parts of the text where Smith's presence as a writer is clear. How might the essay change in tone or content if Pepperberg were to write it?

Reflection and Response

4. What is the relationship between memory and intelligence? One of the critiques about Alex that circulates in Smith's text is that his use of language doesn't reflect thinking but instead reflects a series of learned responses. Write a response in which you articulate your sense of the role of memory in intelligence and in language use. Is all human language itself a series of memorized responses? What makes human language use special or unique?

5. Does Alex actually use language? Smith presents several different views on this question. Present your own position, supporting it with passages from the text. You might want to incorporate some of your observations about memory and language from question 3. Present your answer through a poster presentation. (A poster presentation is an academic genre used in many disciplines in which researchers summarize their findings on a poster board, using key data and images.) As you craft your poster, be aware of the impact of spacing and visual arrangement.

Making Connections

6. Irene Pepperberg's research, like Jane Goodall's ("At Long Last I Belong," p. 26), evokes passionate responses because it seems to trouble the traditional lines between humans and animals. But why are we so invested in drawing this line? What's enabled by guarding the line between humans and animals? What might be possible instead if we were to redraw — or even erase — that line?

7. As the title of Smith's essay suggests, we generally think that birds aren't very smart. John Horgan ("Do Fish Suffer?," p. 55) makes some similar observations about the ways we think about fish and other marine life. Synthesize the conclusions of both essays. How might we treat birds, fish, and other animals differently if we were to assign them intelligence? What sort of research would be needed before we accepted the intelligence of fish?

What Animals Teach Us about Measuring Intelligence

Philip Sopher

Philip Sopher is a writer turned entrepreneur who works on both novels and smartphone apps. Previously, he spent a year as an editorial fellow at *The Atlantic*, a national magazine known for its commentary on contemporary culture, politics, and foreign affairs. This piece is from his tenure there; in it, he provides an overview of the debate around animal intelligence, examining the many challenges involved in studying if and how animals think. That discussion leads him to questions about measuring human intelligence as well.

My dog Maebe gets very excited whenever my roommate comes home. Due to her heightened sense of smell, she starts her happy dance thirty seconds before the door actually opens, giving me time to sneak the bag of chips that he bought back into the cupboard. Does such olfactory aptitude mean she's a genius, on par with master sommeliers?°

In the midst of her happy dance, she sometimes chases her tail. When she's feeling especially nifty, she'll catch and proceed to chew on it like it's a squeak-toy. Does her lack of awareness with respect to self-mutilation mean she's stupid?

Intelligence is notoriously difficult to measure. For humans, common measures are childhood IQ and SAT scores, metrics that are under constant attack. But this debacle becomes even more apparent when other species are involved. The study of animal intelligence, or cognition, is such a nascent field that most of what has been hypothesized has yet to be replicated in a lab. The biggest challenges to the field's development are that it relies too heavily on anecdotes, that controlled experiments with large-enough sample sizes are difficult to design, that many consider it irrelevant, and that "intelligence" as a concept has been overly anthropomorphized.

The most famous anecdote is that of Rico the dog. In 2004, German researchers discovered a border collie who could learn the name of an object in one try, had a vocabulary of two-hundred words, and remembered them all a month later. Rico was extraordinary, renewing public interest in an animal's language-processing abilities for the first time since the early 1900s, when the public thought Clever Hans the horse could count, make change, and tell time. (He was really just responding to his owner's body language.)

Similarly fascinating individuals exist across species. In 2011, Kandula the elephant couldn't reach a fruit branch, so he rolled a wooden box

---

sommeliers: wine stewards.

over with his trunk and used it as a stool. Beforehand, scientists did not think elephants knew how to use tools. In another instance, Ayumu the chimp repeatedly recalled random sequences of nine digits, even though the numbers had only been displayed for a fraction of a second. The next year, he was pitted against British memory champion Ben Pridmore and emerged victorious.

When studying animal intelligence, scientists typically analyze a subject's self-control, self-awareness, and memory. These abilities are integral to processing information and making rational choices—intelligence in its most generalized form.

The most popular intelligence-assessment tools among such researchers today are the "pointing test" and the "mirror test." In the "pointing test," an animal is trained to expect food in a certain place. The location of the food will then be switched, and a human will point to the new location. If the animal goes directly to the new location, it passes the test, and if it ignores the pointing motion and looks for food where it has been trained to look, it fails. The study assesses self-control and the ability to respond to new information. Human babies start passing the test around their first birthdays—but most animals, even chimps, fail. The ones that pass are typically domesticated mammals. Dogs are especially good at it.

The "mirror test" checks for self-awareness. A disfiguring mark, such as a red dot, is usually applied to the subject's forehead, and if the subject shows an indication—by touching its face, for example—of recognizing that it's looking at its own reflection, the animal passes. Recognizing oneself in a mirror is considered to be a sign of cognition, as doing so requires at least a rudimentary concept of identity.

Unfortunately, when measuring these capacities in animals, it is often difficult to achieve the sample sizes and conditions required for scientific accuracy. A 2013 study found that elephants pass the pointing test about two-thirds of the time. However, the experiment's sample size was eleven, a number that leaves way too much room for error, as each elephant carries a 9 percent weight on the study. After another 2013 study showed that dolphins can remember one another after more than twenty years of separation, *National Geographic's* headline was "Dolphins Have Longest Memories in Animal Kingdom." In this case, the sample size was forty-three, much too small to be cast as definitive in any other behavioral science.

Along with underwhelming sample sizes, tests for animal intelligence often fail to replicate the animal's natural ecological context. An extreme example of such a design flaw is that Kandula, the elephant who used a stool, was initially given a stick for the purpose of batting down the food. However, elephants locate food with their sense of smell. Kandula didn't use the stick because he would've had to pick it up with his trunk,

10

meaning he wouldn't have been able to smell the food. This is analogous to humans with eyes on their hands being told to use silverware.

The pointer and mirror tests might also be ecologically inconsistent. Irene Pepperberg, an animal psychologist at Harvard who works with parrots, explains, "Mirror tests check whether a subject has self-recognition, but the test can be tricky. We gave the mark-test to one of my parrots. He saw the mark in the mirror, scratched at it for a couple of seconds, the mark didn't go away, and he walked off. Parrots get gunk on their faces all the time when they feed, so what did the bird's actions mean? Ditto for the point test: If an animal doesn't have arms, hands, and fingers, what would pointing really mean?"

Therein lies a paradox: Scientists have difficulty accrediting experiments that are not properly controlled, but, with animals, properly controlled studies often cannot account for ecological context because animals would never encounter laboratory conditions in the course of their natural lives. This is why the field still relies mostly on anecdotes.

It follows that, with the current infrastructure, analyzing animal intelligence is nearly impossible. Perhaps with more funding, more complex studies could be done at a greater scale. Earlier this year, the Duke Canine Cognition Center was able to organize a study of 567 animals across 36 species for an assessment similar to the pointer test. The center has also built a network of over a thousand dogs on which they can conduct experiments. Brian Hare, a founder of the center, says his goal is to build a database large-enough to shed light on longstanding questions about behavior, breeding, and genetics.

Labs as resource-abundant as Duke's Canine Cognition Center are rare. Adam Pack, who studies dolphins at the University of Hawaii, explained in an email that researchers rely primarily on funding from the National Science Foundation and that many will set up nonprofit arms to enable donations from family foundations and philanthropic individuals. Universities, too, sometimes sponsor small, species-specific labs for just a few scientists. But, in general, it's difficult to get funding for robust animal-intelligence experiments because the field is competing for grants with areas of research, like those on cancer and AIDS, that have more possibility to improve human life. Animal intelligence is more like space exploration, a field in which the societal gains from additional knowledge appear to be purely academic.

And even when there's progress, it's often discredited. Frans de Waal, a primatologist, explains in a *Wall Street Journal* essay, "The one historical constant in my field is that each time a claim of human uniqueness bites the dust, other claims quickly take its place." Members of the animal-intelligence community think non-humans are unfairly

15

written-off as less smart because marks for mental fitness have been overly anthropomorphized.

With animals, there is an emphasis on disentangling intelligence from mechanization. Intelligence is the ability to process information and make inferences, whereas mechanization is an automatic response to a certain stimulus. An octopus, for example, can change colors to blend into surroundings, something a sniper does by design. Scientists are trying to find out whether octopuses choose to change colors or do so mechanically. But does it matter? Ascribing such importance to design, visualization, and inference is incredibly arbitrary. Within this context, "intelligence" is really an indicator of how similar an animal is to humans.

Another argument from the animal-intelligence community is that the idea of "convergent intelligence" is often overlooked. It is common to believe that the more recently an animal shared an ancestor with humans, the smarter it is. This hypothesis, however, does not always hold. Pigs are very distantly related to humans, as it was over 100 million years ago that the ancestors of hogs and humans diverged. But much of pig and human DNA is identical. Proponents of convergence theory believe that pig and human DNA took different routes to the same solution. True to form, pigs have proven to be astute in very human ways. They can even employ deception, a very advanced cognitive tactic. Pig A will almost instantly follow Pig B if Pig B shows signs of knowing where food is stored, and Pig B will try to throw Pig A off its trail.

Simply put, researchers studying animal cognition believe the concept of intelligence has become caricatured.

For those outside of the community, an important side effect of studying this field is that it offers another way of exploring the quagmire of defining and measuring general intelligence. The challenges that come with this research arise because intelligence in its broadest sense is not something that's comparative. This is true not just across species, but also within them. For humans, tests such as the SAT will always be under attack because it's impossible to shrink intelligence to two dimensions. All that can be gleaned from these tests is that, due to whatever mix of circumstance and inherent ability, a person is currently better than a portion of population and worse than another at a particular type of reasoning.

"Smart" and "dumb" are irrelevant in cross-species comparisons."

Equally important, a person who exhibits or does not exhibit aptitude in one area can only be compared within the relevant frame. It's impossible, for example, to compare Mozart's musical talent to Einstein's facility with physics. As with animal intelligence, measuring human intelligence runs into problems when extrapolation extends beyond its boundaries.

20

That is to say, the SAT might be a good measure of preparedness for college coursework, but no test can put a number on a person's innate intellectual ability across all domains.

So is Maebe a genius with her nose?

All that can be deduced is that, compared to humans, her ability to smell is spectacular. But "smart" and "dumb" are irrelevant in cross-species comparisons. Maebe occupies a different niche, and, for her, as with all animals, the main reason for testing "intelligence" is to reveal the skills necessary for survival in her niche, not to examine how she would fair if she occupied the human one.

Understanding the Text

1. Sopher discusses many different factors that make up intelligence. Using his text, develop a definition of intelligence that applies to both animals and humans.

2. According to Sopher, what are some of the challenges in measuring and testing animal intelligence? Support your response with specific passages from his essay.

3. What is "convergent intelligence"? Define this term using Sopher's text and then explain how it makes studying animal intelligence more difficult.

Reflection and Response

4. How might we reliably investigate animal intelligence, given all the problems Sopher presents with studying this topic? Drawing from your work in question 2, suggest strategies we might use to pursue this issue more reliably.

5. Sopher suggests that one of the problems in looking at animal cognition is that intelligence itself has been anthropomorphized. Using examples from this text, explain what he means and then consider the implications of this approach to intelligence. Why have we approached intelligence this way? What does it say about us, and what does it say about our approach to animals?

Making Connections

6. Sopher uses Irene Pepperberg to point out the limitations of the "mirror test." Pepperberg is the focus of Dinitia Smith's essay ("A Thinking Bird or Just Another Birdbrain?," p. 33), which presents Pepperberg's work with the parrot Alex. Apply Sopher's examination of the problems in studying animal intelligence to Smith's explanation of Pepperberg's work. Does Pepperberg avoid some of these challenges? Is her work subject to Sopher's critique?

7. Sopher ends his essay with a larger argument about intelligence. Extend his claims using one of the other essays in this chapter. What does the study of animal intelligence tell us about human intelligence and its limitations?

The Cat Psychic

Rachel Monroe

Rachel Monroe is a writer whose work has appeared in the *New Yorker*, the *New York Times Magazine*, and *The Atlantic*. Her first book, *Savage Appetites*, about women, obsession, and crime, was published in 2019. This piece is taken from *Hazlitt*, an online magazine featuring fiction and nonfiction. In this essay, Monroe explores the relationship between pets and their owners through the metaphysical interventions of a cat psychic, which prompts her to consider the larger issue of the relationship between humans and animals and what communication is possible between the two.

Last October, I came back from a month away and my cat wouldn't speak to me. He refused to come in the house; if he saw me, he ran away. He'd always been a partly outdoor cat with an independent streak, so at first I wasn't worried. Maybe he hadn't liked the woman who sublet my house in my absence. Or he was punishing me for going away. Maybe he was just savoring the last weeks of a lingering Texas summer—the slow descent of twilight, the fat mice moving in the grass. But a few days passed, and then a week, and he continued to avoid me. Two weeks after I returned home, I spent an afternoon sitting very still, watching him sunning himself in my neighbor's backyard. He looked healthy and self-satisfied, in fine feline form. But then he must've felt my eyes on him; he stood up and hopped easily over the fence, disappearing back into whatever secret space he was spending his time in.

I enlisted my friends to prowl the neighborhood with me, calling his name—as if he had ever been the kind of animal who came when called. I ventured as far as I dared into the thick brush beside the railroad tracks, trying to lure him with catnip. I bought insanely expensive wet food, organic and grain-free, the kind of cat food that comes garnished with herbs, and set it outside the front door. When that didn't tempt him, I bought the cheap Dollar General stuff, ambiguous gray globs suspended in jelly. The message I was trying to send was: Whatever you want, buddy, as long as you come home. But he didn't come home.

My neighbor saw him more than I did—he liked to show up at sunrise to watch her feed her chickens. They had reached a kind of truce, but as soon as I showed up, he'd dash off to one of his hiding places. One morning at the beginning of November the buzzards were gone—supposedly the sign of that the year's first freeze is coming. That night, the weather turned. The wind sounded like an enemy trying to get into the house, and there was frost on the grass in the morning. My neighbor reassured me that Musa had come by to watch the chickens get fed and didn't seem any worse for wear. The inaccessibility of his secret life drove me crazy. Where was he sleeping? What was he eating? Did he know he was breaking my heart?

In December, my friend Brandon came over one day to drop off a book; when he asked me how I was, I started crying and I couldn't stop. I felt foolish, and also so, so sad. "Are you *sure* this is about the cat?" he asked. I could see his point, but I was pretty sure it was. I called my mom for a pep talk. "Maybe you just have to accept that he wants a different kind of life," she said. I hung up on her, and didn't even call back to apologize.

Two weeks before Christmas, I was explaining to a friend in town that   5 if I seemed more distressed than usual, it was just because I was trying to accustom myself to the fact that my cat didn't want to be my cat anymore. "No way," she said. "Here's what you do: You just call Dawn." And then she gave me the cat psychic's phone number.

On the surface, it's ridiculous to say my cat stopped speaking to me, because, of course, he has *never* spoken to me—I'm not a shaman and I don't live in a Disney cartoon. But people who have pets will know what I mean; when you live with animals, you're engaged in constant, low-level communication with them.

> "Our lack of a common, spoken language means there's always a gulf of understanding between us."

The incredible amount of intimacy we share with our non-human companions means we become familiar with their expressions and body language, learn how to decode their yips and mews. And yet our lack of a common, spoken language means there's always a gulf of understanding between us. Perhaps that's why talking to animals is such a persistent fantasy: Ancient Greeks told stories about Orpheus's ability to mystically, musically commune with beasts; two thousand years later, children read about Dr. Doolittle's genteel chats with a crocodile. People actually buy books such as *How to Speak Cat*, which promises to parse the sixteen different kinds of meows your cat is making. In YouTube videos, you can watch otherwise perfectly normal-looking human beings showing off their dogs making garbled noises that are supposed to sound like "I love you."

Our desire to talk to our pets is so strong that we're willing to forgive a lot of nonsense. The guy who wrote *How to Speak Cat* has pretty much admitted that the sixteen meows theory is made up. Most of us who live with animals have been guilty at one time or another of that particular flavor of solipsism° that involves projecting our own human thoughts

---

solipsism: self-centeredness; the view that the self is all that can be known to exist.

and feelings onto the animals we live with. (I once dated a guy who told me the key to understanding his mom was to take every sentence where she talked about what the dog was thinking/feeling and replace his name with her own: *Daisy is so excited to meet you! Daisy is tired. Daisy gets over-excited when there are too many people in the house.*)

Hence the moral objection to anthropomorphism: "To imagine that animals think like humans or to cast animals in human roles is a form of self-centered narcissism: one looks outward to the world and sees only one's own reflection mirrored therein," write Lorraine Daston and Gregg Mitman in *Thinking with Animals: New Perspectives on Anthropomorphism.* Anthropomorphism can also reflect a lack of imagination: "To assimilate the behavior of a herd of elephants to, say, that of a large, middle-class, American family or to dress up a pet terrier in a tutu strikes these critics as a kind of species provincialism, an almost pathological failure to register the wondrous variety of the natural world—a provincialism comparable to that of those blinkered tourists who assume that the natives of the foreign countries they visit will have the same customs and speak the same language as at home."

When I looked her up online, Dawn proved to be much more than just   10 a cat psychic. Her website included photographs of all kind of animals, from horses to small rodents. There were also links to her children's books about a giant rabbit; according to her bio, she enjoyed fabric art, rollerblading, and spending time with animals.

On her website, Dawn was careful to denote where her abilities began and ended. She could communicate directly with animals via telepathy, helping her clients to "learn how [their animals] are feeling, what they need, and who they really are." Initial phone consultations lasted forty minutes—"perfect for getting to know everything you have wondered about one animal friend"—and cost $65. I am not by nature a person who believes in psychics, although I've often wished I were. Compared to my friends who text with their shamans and go on desert vision quests, I've always felt boringly earth-bound, unreceptive to miracles. I had consulted a psychic once before, when I was twenty. She said I was an old soul, but it didn't mean much to me; I had the feeling she told everyone that. But I was desperate, and therefore receptive. I reserved the next available slot.

Dawn called me at 11 a.m. on a Tuesday morning. I explained the situation to her, tripping over my words, worried she was such a good psychic she'd be able to tell I didn't believe in psychics, much less psychics who talk to cats, and much*much* less psychics who talk to cats over the phone from two thousand miles away. I told her the whole story: the month away, the subletter, Musa's persistent cold shoulder. "Hmm," she said, as if I had presented her with a particularly tricky puzzle. "Well, that is a tough one, isn't it?" Dawn's voice was patient but firm; it was easy to imagine her saying soothing words to a panicked animal. She asked if I knew what and where Musa was eating, and if there had been any other significant changes around the house. "My mom says that maybe he just doesn't want to be my cat anymore," I said. "No, of course not," she said. "These things just take time, is all." She sounded confident, optimistic. I realized that the animal she was calming down was me.

"Now I'm going to be quiet for a while, because I'm speaking with Musa," Dawn told me. "But if you don't hear anything from me after ten minutes, then we probably got disconnected, and you should call me back."

It felt strangely intimate to be silent on the phone with a stranger. I wondered whether there was some sort of psychic facilitation I should be working on, or whether my attempts to do so would just clutter up the connection. Instead, I closed my eyes and started counting my breaths. After I reached seventeen, Dawn spoke again. "Well, he's a sweet one, isn't he? He says he loves you very much," she said. I might have started crying a little bit; so what if that line is probably the pet psychic's version of telling someone they're an old soul? I believed it, or I needed to believe it, or maybe there wasn't much difference between the two at that point.

Dawn reported that Musa had been freaked out by my departure and the subletter's arrival; even though he knew I'd been back for months, he was still stuck in a bit of a trauma loop, which was triggering his anxiety every time he saw me. He was healthy enough—he told her that one of my neighbors had been feeding him—but he was not at his best. She told me freedom was incredibly important to him, and if he came inside, even if it was just for a second, I had to let him go back out as soon as he asked. She told me that she had gently encouraged him to come home, where it was warm and the food was plentiful.

Our time was up, but I kept trying to think up questions to keep Dawn on the line. I wasn't quite ready to let her go. Our forty-minute conversation had been like one of those particularly intense therapy sessions where you walk out the door with an exhausted, cleaned-out feeling, like your heart has just been power-washed.

You're going to think I'm making this up, but I swear this is what happened: Two days after I talked to Dawn, I was working in my office when I heard a meow. Musa was standing outside, looking expectant, even a little annoyed. I opened the door and let him in, trying not to make any sudden moves. He padded into the house nonchalantly, brushing against me as if he hadn't spent the past two months avoiding any kind of contact. Then he seemed to reconsider, and turned to walk back outside. I left the door open for him. A couple minutes later, he came back in and went right over to his food bowl. I listened to him crunch away on his kibble, a sound I hadn't even realized I'd missed. His presence in the house felt like a minor miracle, one of those small wonders credited to lesser-known saints.

That was at the end of December; from that day since, we've picked up where we left off. Musa sleeps on my bed, curled into himself like a Junebug. In the morning he complains until I let him outside; he still likes to go watch the chickens get fed. When the evenings are warm, I'll sit on the porch and drink a beer while Musa keeps an eye on the birds.

About a hundred years ago, a German math teacher and mystic named   20
Wilhelm von Osten owned a horse named Clever Hans. Over a period of years, von Osten said, he had patiently given Hans the equivalent of a kindergarten education, including instruction in simple arithmetic. The conversation was two-way; Hans communicated via a kind of hoof language, tapping the ground a specific number of times to indicate a particular number or letter. Fans flocked to von Osten's home in the outskirts of Berlin to see the horse in person; Clever Hans performed before dukes and doctors. Nearly everyone was won over: Von Osten would ask his horse how many ladies were standing in line to see him, and he'd lift his hoof and tap out the correct number. Hans appeared to be able distinguish between gold, silver, and copper. He knew the days of the week and what month it was. He performed simple arithmetic operations and could tell time using a watch. "The versatility of Hans in other directions is astonishing. He can distinguish between straw and felt hats, between canes and umbrellas. He knows the different colors," the *New York Times* reported in 1904.

But not everyone was convinced. In 1907, a group of experts — including psychologists, zoologists, and a circus trainer — known as the Hans Commission devised a series of experiments to try to get to the bottom of Clever Hans's remarkable abilities. They tried putting blinders on the animal, and having someone other than von Osten feed the questions to Clever Hans. Ultimately, the commission determined that there was no such trickery going on with von Osten — but also that the horse wasn't able to understand human language, or at least not in the way von Osten claimed. Instead, he was so tuned in to his handler's body language that he was able to pick up on subtle cues — cues that von Osten didn't even know he was delivering:

The state required for a successful response was not the mere passive expectation that the horse would tap the number demanded of him nor the wish that he might tap it, but rather the determination that he should do it. An inward "Thou shalt," as it were, was spoken to the horse. This affective state was registered in consciousness in terms of sensation of tension in the musculature of the head and neck, by intraorganic sensations, and finally by a steadily rising feeling of unpleasantness. When the final number was reached, the tension would suddenly be released, and a curious feeling of relaxation would ensue.

The public debunking didn't deter Clever Hans's fans, who still flocked to see him. Von Osten was never fully convinced his horse didn't understand him — perhaps because the two *were* communicating in a remarkably attuned way, even if the terms of that conversation weren't what von Osten thought they were.

There are, of course, non-metaphysical explanations for why my cat came back. My father, a stone-cold materialist, believes Musa picked up on the fact that the cat psychic had calmed me down. Some subtle message in my body language must have told him I'd made up my mind to allow him his freedom. In the end, the mechanism of it doesn't matter much to me; whether the credit goes to telepathy or body language or simple luck, I don't see Musa's return as any less of a miracle.

"The word *love* can be found in neither the index of *The Oxford Companion to Animal Behavior* nor the *Encyclopedia of Animal Behavior*," animal behaviorist Jonathan Balcombe writes in *Exultant Ark: A Pictorial Tour of Animal Pleasure* — in part, he theorizes, because "it is difficult, if not impossible, to prove feelings of love in another individual, even a human. This is the challenge of private experiences."

When you're close to someone — cat or human or whoever else — it can be easy to take them for granted, at least until they do a thing that makes you look at them in wonder: Oh! You are a *separate* creature with a *separate* mind! And a chasm opens up between you. Balcombe's "challenge of private experiences" seems to me like a polite phrase for the queasy feeling of peering down into that unbridgeable gulf that exists between all minds. Even so, we keep folding our messages into paper airplanes and trying to fling them across the gap. Some of them, I think, make it over. "The longing to think with animals" isn't always solipsistic, write Daston and Mitman in *Thinking With Animals*. At times, it can even be quite the opposite — "a virtuoso but doomed act of complete empathy." The distance is always there, and we're always reaching across it, in whatever ways we can.

25

Understanding the Text

1. We often think of communication happening through language. Instead, create an expanded definition of communication to account for the relationship Monroe has with Musa and, more generally, the relationships between pets and their owners. You might also include Dawn and her communication with Musa in this definition.

2. Define solipsism, either through a dictionary or through the context of Monroe's usage of the term. What role does solipsism play in the relationship between humans and animals? Offer examples from Monroe's text to support your position.

Reflection and Response

3. Monroe ends with a larger point about the challenges of relating to *any* other being, human or animal. Expand on her discussion about these challenges and the rewards that come from engaging them, of bridging the "unbridgeable gulf that exists between all minds" (p. 49).

4. What does our desire to speak with animals say about us? Start your work with Monroe's discussion of the long history of humans wanting to talk to animals and consider what this history says about the human condition.

Making Connections

5. Philip Sopher ("What Animals Teach Us about Measuring Intelligence," p. 39) also discusses anthropomorphism (and, briefly, pets, too). Synthesize their discussions to make a larger point about what anthropomorphism says about us as human beings.

6. The rise of pet ownership, according to Alicia Puglionesi ("How Counting Horses and Reading Dogs Convinced Us Animals Could Think," p. 51), contributed to shifting conceptions of animal cognition. Use Monroe's discussion of her relationship with Musa to extend this point. In what ways does having very personal relationships with animals change our approaches to larger issues of animals' minds?

How Counting Horses and Reading Dogs Convinced Us Animals Could Think

Alicia Puglionesi

Alicia Puglionesi, who holds a doctorate in the history of science, medicine, and technology from Johns Hopkins University, researches the history of knowledge in the sciences. She contributed this piece to *Atlas Obscura*, an online magazine that indexes unusual or obscure travel destinations through user contributions while offering editorial pieces on subjects ranging from history to food to travel. In this essay, Puglionesi looks at the historical incident of a horse named Clever Hans and how that horse influenced our conceptions about animal cognition.

Inky the octopus, who made a crafty escape from his tank in New Zealand a few months ago, joined a continuous stream of headline-grabbing creatures whose antics, especially when captured on video and shared online, tap into a popular fascination with animal minds.

Although metro-riding beavers, militarized dolphins, and their canny ilk seem to pop up almost weekly now, it wasn't until the early twentieth century that psychologists and the general public began seriously considering whether animals had consciousness, emotions, and intelligence. This was due in part to the fin de siècle° fad for "wonder animals," domesticated critters that solved math problems, answered riddles, and discoursed on philosophy, often using a code to communicate with their handlers.

The catalyst for this wonder animal fad was Clever Hans, a mathematically-inclined German horse who gained notoriety in the early 1900s. He could apparently solve math problems—he even did square roots—and carry on simple conversations by tapping his hooves. When Hans started performing for an amazed German public, he amplified a growing interest in animal intelligence that had the potential to transform science and society. Perhaps animals, long regarded as mindless automata, actually had the capacity for reason and language—which meant they might even possess consciousness and something like a soul.

Clever Hans was not the first "wonder animal" to astound crowds with apparently human abilities. Magicians and traveling showmen had long trained horses, dogs, and more exotic creatures to perform feats like reading and arithmetic—a "learned English dog" discoursed on ancient Greek poetry in the 1750s, while the French lecturer Perrin employed a "little savant dog" for physics demonstrations a few decades a later. The

___

fin de siècle: end of the century, especially the 19th century.

original sense of "wonder" referred to something that didn't fit within the divine order of creation—perhaps miraculous, perhaps diabolical.

> **"Perhaps animals actually had the capacity for reason and language."**

On the stage, wonder animals straddled a line between freak and fraud, but were seldom taken seriously as a scientific phenomenon.

Wilhelm von Osten, a retired high 5 school math instructor in nineteenth-century Berlin, held a different view. He felt that some animals possessed real intelligence and capacity for abstract thought—not just a love of tasty rewards. Asserting that animal minds were similar to those of human children, he used classroom methods to "teach" rather than "train" his Arabian stallion Hans.

Within a few years, Hans learned to count and then perform basic arithmetic using a system of hoof-taps. In 1904, the *New York Times* declared that he could "do almost everything but talk," including telling the time and discriminating between gold and silver coins.

Rather than a wonder or curiosity, von Osten saw this as proof that animals think, learn, and reason, and he intended to make his case to the scientific establishment. The time was ripe for such a radical assertion. Charles Darwin's theory of evolution was still rippling through the Western world, breaking down the categorical distinction between humans and animals. In 1872, Darwin proposed that emotions like surprise, grief, and pain were part of a shared evolutionary inheritance. This paved the way for the emerging discipline of comparative psychology, and threatened humans' special status as the only earthly creatures with thoughts and feelings.

Another factor that primed audiences for a serious encounter with the animal minds was the rise of pet ownership. People had long used animals for food and labor, but only the elite had the luxury of keeping pets as companions. This began to change in the eighteenth and nineteenth centuries, when pets became a middle-class trend. As people formed emotional attachments to their furry friends, they observed qualities like loyalty, love, and intelligence in dogs and, to a lesser extent, cats.

Stories about remarkable pets proliferated in the press. The "incredible journey" tale, in which devoted pets travel vast distances to reunite with their masters, originated around this time. Its heroes included Victor Hugo's poodle, who supposedly trekked from Moscow back to Paris.

Pet owners like Paula Moekel of Mannheim, Germany, invited scien- 10 tists to confirm their ambitious claims. Moekel believed that her terrier Rolf could discourse on philosophy in multiple languages. However, when investigators arrived they had an unsatisfactory experience—Rolf suffered from seizures, and was unable to show off for his guests. This cycle repeated in numerous cases: wonder animals, much like human psychic mediums, could rarely perform under the scrutiny of a skeptical audience.

Clever Hans, however, was not just any coddled pet. Von Osten insisted on the scientific importance of the phenomenon, and invited psychologists and physiologists to examine his equine pupil under controlled conditions. A committee of experts from Berlin scrutinized Hans in 1904 and concluded that his accomplishments were genuine—they ruled out the use of secret signals by von Osten. One of these experts, however, was not entirely satisfied, and persisted in a solo investigation.

The dissenter, a young psychologist named Oskar Pfungst, came out with a devastating critique of Hans and von Osten in 1907. He found that Hans could not produce correct answers if he couldn't see his human questioner or an audience member. Suspecting that the horse relied on physical gestures, Pfungst experimented with shrugging his shoulders or changing his posture during tests—and his subtle movements ruined Hans' performance.

Like so many other wonder animals, the horse merely "read" human cues. Previous investigators had refused to believe that they could send such cues unintentionally, but Pfungst made a firm case, carefully correlating Hans' hoof taps with the twitches and fidgeting of his handlers.

The legacy of Hans and Pfungst lives on today in psychology textbooks. The "Clever Hans effect" is when an experimenter elicits correct answers from an animal subject by giving the subject unconscious cues, creating a persuasive illusion of intelligent thought. This is where the story traditionally stops, with the debunking of Clever Hans and the moral that psychologists must rule out unconscious experimenter bias in their studies.

This was certainly not the end of the line for discussions of animal   15
intelligence, however. Despite scientists' best efforts to curtail it, popular interest in thinking animals remained vigorous throughout the twentieth century. The Hans phenomenon inspired countless imitators, including "Lady Wonder," a mare purported to have telepathic powers. During World War II, Nazi scientists tried training dogs to read and speak in code, hoping to find military applications for these talents. Even within professional psychology there were supporters of animal intelligence (among them Margaret Floy Washburn, the first American woman to receive a doctorate in psychology), but their work was often minimized or dismissed.

Over the past thirty years, though, the old guard of psychology—which saw human mental faculties as distinct from those of animals—has given way to outspoken researchers like primatologist Frans de Waal, who place humans and animals on a mental continuum. Modern celebrity animals like John W. Pilley's dog Chaser and Irene Pepperberg's parrot Alex, who both appear to understand thousands of words and basic grammatical structures, may be the heirs of Clever Hans, but their handlers' scientific respectability makes them harder to dismiss.

Indeed, Hans himself was never as marginal as many textbooks made him seem. Von Osten, who died in 1909 a disappointed man, might be pleased to see that animal intelligence has made a comeback in psychology—scientists are even returning to calculating horses, this time to study how animals make decisions that aid their survival, rather than whether they understand math.

The fate of Clever Hans raises questions about how we define and value intelligence. What, after all, makes figuring square roots more important than reading body language with incredible acuity? Recent work in human psychology is revealing how unconscious cues and impulses actually determine most people's everyday decision-making.

In the past, we've called animals "clever" when they conform to our ideal of rational, calculating intellect—even when we can't uphold that ideal ourselves. Perhaps neither humans nor horses are as clever as we might like to believe.

Understanding the Text

1. What were some of the historical developments that primed people to reconsider animal intelligence at the start of the twentieth century? Summarize these using quotations from Puglionesi's text.

2. Define "wonder" by using Puglionesi's essay. What role does it play in animal intelligence? How are the dual meanings of "wonder" identified by Puglionesi reflected in approaches to animal cognition?

Reflection and Response

3. What is the legacy, for better and worse, of Clever Hans? Trace how it continues to influence animal intelligence discussions.

4. Puglionesi focuses most her discussion of animal intelligence on psychology. Why? What does this discipline do, and how is it relevant to animal cognition?

Making Connections

5. Philip Sopher ("What Animals Teach Us about Measuring Intelligence," p. 39) discusses the many challenges scientists face when trying to study animal intelligence accurately. Use Puglionesi to extend Sopher's discussion. How do Clever Hans and other wonder animals compound these problems?

6. In some essays in this chapter, Clever Hans is used an example of a hoax that shows the problems with animal intelligence. Puglionesi, though, suggests at the end that perhaps we should reconsider this thinking, that perhaps Clever Hans was, in a way, clever after all. Extend that point by using one of the other essays. How might we instead redefine intelligence to account for the skills Clever Hans had?

Do Fish Suffer?

John Horgan

Noted science writer John I Iorgan is the director of the Center for Science Writings at Stevens Institute of Technology in New Jersey and the author of several books, including *The End of Science: Facing the Limits of Science in the Twilight of the Scientific Age* (1996), *Rational Mysticism: Dispatches from the Border between Science and Spirituality* (2003), and *The End of War* (2012). He has also written for *Time*, *Newsweek*, and *National Geographic*. He was a senior writer for *Scientific American*, where he now writes a blog called Cross-Check, which offers critical views of science in the news. This selection was taken from the *Scientific American Blog Network*, a collection of blogs affiliated with the magazine's coverage of science and technology.

Years ago I was surfcasting on an ocean beach and caught a big, beautiful striped bass. My daughter and son, who were eight and ten, respectively, were nearby. I held the fish up and yelled, Look kids, I caught dinner! Skye, my daughter, burst into tears and pleaded with me to let the fish go.

I tried to josh her out of her mood, in vain. I assured her that I'd been catching fish like this since I was a boy, fish don't really feel pain, they're just fish, they're like swimming machines. Skye was unconvinced. I said I would stick a knife into the fish's brain now to put it out of its misery. Dumb move! Skye shrieked in horror and begged me not to kill the fish. By now, other people on the beach, attracted by the commotion, had gathered around the weeping girl and mean man.

This traumatic—for me!—scene came back to me when I attended "Animal Consciousness" at New York University last weekend. I'm trying to wrap up a book on the mind-body problem, so I really didn't have the time to attend the meeting. But I couldn't resist going, and now I can't resist firing off a quick report.

Philosopher David Chalmers, one of the conference organizers, kicked the meeting off by noting that many researchers are investigating whether non-human animals are conscious. If animals are capable of consciousness, he said, they can suffer, and that should matter to us.

Chalmers noted that in 2012 a group of prominent scientists issued 5 the so-called Cambridge Declaration on Consciousness. It stated that "the weight of evidence indicates that humans are not unique in possessing the neurological substrates that generate consciousness. Non-human animals, including all mammals and birds, and many other creatures, including octopuses, also possess these neurological substrates." Octopi are hot now. Research has shown them to be extremely clever, that's why they're mentioned in the Declaration.

Fish should be on included too, according to one speaker at the NYU conference, biologist Victoria Braithwaite. Fish are a lot smarter than we give them credit for, she said. Gobies who live in tidal pools get a sense of the local topography while the tide is high and they can swim freely. When the tide goes out, if they find themselves chased by a predator in one pool, they know in which direction to jump to escape to a nearby pool. Fish from different species have surprisingly complex relationships with each other, Braithwaite said, showing us a film of an adorable grouper and moray eel teaming up to hunt other fish.

Braithwaite, author of the 2010 book *Do Fish Feel Pain?*, has also investigated whether fish can suffer. She has injected irritating chemicals, such as vinegar and bee venom, under the skin of trout and other fish. Here's how she describes her experiments in the *Los Angeles Times*:

> If you've ever felt the nip of vinegar on an open cut or the sting of a bee, you will recognize these feelings as painful. Well, fish find these naturally irritating chemicals unpleasant too. Their gills beat faster, and they rub the affected area on the walls of their tank, lose interest in food and have problems making decisions.

When she gave the fish painkillers, their behavior returned to normal, just as that of a human would. Her research, she writes, "opens a can of worms—so to speak—and begs the question of where do we draw the line. Crustacean welfare? Slug welfare? And if not fish, why birds? Is there a biological basis for drawing a line?"

Psychologist Stuart Derbyshire, who spoke after Braithwaite, dumped cold water over her premise. He assured us that he had nothing against fish, but he doubted whether they feel pain in a way remotely analogous to ours, given how different their brains are. He asked us to note the pressure being exerted on our backsides by our chairs. Before he drew our attention to this sensation, we weren't aware of it, right? Well, fish probably have this kind of sensation without awareness or comprehension, which means they don't really "feel" pain or anything else.

Derbyshire took a beating during the Q&A. When asked if dogs feel 10 pain, he said it depends on what you mean by "feel pain." If forced to answer that simplistic question, he'd have to say no. Dumb move! An audience member held up an actual, living dog, which had been sitting in her lap. Someone had stepped on her dog's paw earlier, she said, and it yelped. What was the dog feeling then? Derbyshire sighed and said he didn't know.

I felt bad for Derbyshire. He seemed to be suffering. But I was glad when Braithwaite declared that it doesn't matter to her whether a dog or fish suffers in the way that humans do. What matters is whether they suffer at all, and she believes they do. The audience applauded.

This exchange set up a talk by philosopher Peter Singer, who jump-started the modern animal-rights movement with his 1975 book *Animal Liberation*. Singer credited Jeremy Bentham with correctly framing the question of animal rights two centuries ago. Bentham said that "the question is not, Can [animals] reason? nor, Can they talk? but, Can they suffer? Why should the law refuse its protection to any sensitive being?"

> "It doesn't matter to her whether a dog or fish suffers in the way that humans do. What matters is whether they suffer at all."

Determining whether creatures are conscious is hard, Singer acknowledged. But in a rebuke to Derbyshire, Singer said that suffering should not require "reflection" to be morally important. Someone asked Singer if it bothered him that Braithwaite's experiments caused fish pain. No, said Singer, showing his utilitarian colors, because her research might help bring about regulations that alleviate the suffering of countless fish.

Singer has been worrying about fish rights for a while. In 2010 he wrote in *The Guardian* that "the evidence is now accumulating that commercial fishing inflicts an unimaginable amount of pain and suffering. We need to learn how to capture and kill wild fish humanely—or, if that is not possible, to find less cruel and more sustainable alternatives to eating them."

By the way, sitting in the front row watching this debate was Thomas Nagel, author of the famous 1974 paper "What Is It Like to Be a Bat?" [15]

I'm a life-long catcher and eater of fish, so it was hard listening to Braithwaite and Singer dwell on fish pain. But it was hard listening to Derbyshire too. How the hell does he know that fish don't suffer? He doesn't, any more than Braithwaite or Singer know that they do. Singer said we should give fish the benefit of the doubt, and I'm inclined to agree. Am I going to stop eating fish, or fishing? Probably not, but when I do I'll feel bad about it.

You may be wondering what happened to that striped bass all those years ago. I threw it back into the ocean. I don't know if the fish felt joy, but my daughter certainly did.

Understanding the Text

1. Answer Horgan's titular question by using his text to determine whether or not fish suffer.

2. Make a visual map of Horgan's argument. You might choose to use an online tool like Prezi (prezi.com) or Wordclouds.com, or you might instead make a collage of digital or print images. How might you use visual elements, including hierarchies, spatial placement, size, and weight, to illustrate important points in the argument?

Reflection and Response

3. Victoria Braithwaite asks, "Is there a biological basis for drawing a line?" (p. 56) between which animals deserve to have their welfare considered and which do not? Answer her question using Horgan's essay. Why are we concerned about the suffering of some animals and not others?

4. Horgan ends his essay not with the fish's feelings but with his daughter's. How might changing the way we treat animals have more to do with us than with animals? What emotional benefits might we gain from respecting the welfare of more animals, including fish?

Making Connections

5. Horgan shifts the conversation from whether or not animals can think to whether or not they can suffer. What difference does that make in the conversation about either animal cognition or animal welfare? Use one other reading from this chapter to support your response.

6. Some people keep fish as pets, yet that relationship doesn't seem to be the same as the one between Rachel Monroe and her cat Musa ("The Cat Psychic," p. 44). What makes fish different from other pets? Draw support from Monroe's discussion of how she relates to her cat and then use those observations to return to Horgan's argument, suggesting what role your insights might play in the conversation around fish, their suffering, and their welfare.

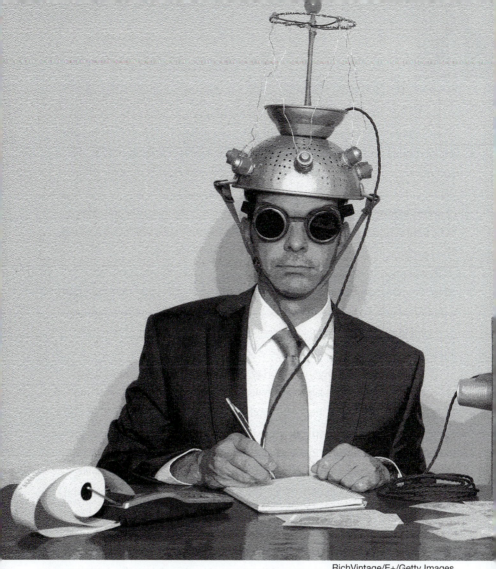

2

Are the Risks of Artificial Intelligence Worth the Rewards?

The term "artificial intelligence" is often associated with the far-off, the futuristic, or other realms of science fiction. But AI is an increasingly prominent part of our daily reality, built into phones, cars, social media, and many other common technologies. Figuring out the risks and rewards of AI is not a question for tomorrow but a question for today. We've come to rely on voice recognition, digital assistants, and any number of smart algorithms that make our lives easier, but perhaps it's time for us to stop and consider the implications of the technologies we love so much. The readings in this section will help you do just that.

In weighing the risks and benefits of AI, you'll also learn more about what we mean when we use the term "intelligence." The test for AI is often whether or not it can do what we do. This test means that creating, defining, or evaluating artificial intelligence requires an understanding of human intelligence, too.

That understanding begins with Ray Kurzweil, who offers some basic definitions of artificial intelligence while placing them in the context of human intelligence. Alan Turing, the first to imagine "thinking machines," adds to the conversation with a description of the process for testing artificial intelligence that served as a standard for years, coming to be known as the "Turing test." While Kurzweil, and to some extent Turing, offers a vision of AI's benefits, Tim Adams shares philosopher Nick Bostrom's serious concerns about the ways in which AI, if not carefully considered and planned, could spell the end of humanity. Adam Elkus discusses the dangers of AI as well, although he does so by looking at the "artificial stupidity" of bots, little snippets of computer code that have swarmed the internet and social media. In doing so, he reminds us that dangers in this area can come from more than one direction. Will Knight focuses instead on one of the most promising directions for artificial intelligence: deep learning systems, which mimic human learning. They can be amazingly accurate and beneficial, but come with plenty of risks and unknown elements. Allie Shaw looks at another risk emerging in AI. the reproduction of existing social injustice through gender bias. Finally, Cade Metz explores the weird and wonderful images produced by Google's DeepDream, an AI system that reflects many of the themes of the other readings.

As an overview of the readings in this chapter might suggest, the question of the risks and rewards of AI doesn't have an easy answer. That's where *your* intelligence comes in. Few questions in life have an easy answer, but when we think about them, when we exercise our own intelligence, we expand that intelligence and expand our skills for navigating a world that is always complex.

What Is AI, Anyway?

Ray Kurzweil

Ray Kurzweil is a prolific inventor who has made major contributions to the fields of document scanning, optical character recognition, music synthesis, and text-to-speech technology. He is an equally prolific author, having published seven books, including *The Age of Spiritual Machines* (1999), *The Singularity Is Near: When Humans Transcend Biology* (2005), and *How to Create a Mind: The Secret of Human Thought Revealed* (2012). Kurzweil is widely known as a futurist, using his familiarity with technology to make predictions about where we are headed; he is also known as a proponent of AI. In the selection offered here, from his 1990 book *The Age of Intelligent Machines*, Kurzweil offers an overview of AI, laying out definitions of both intelligence and artificial intelligence and relating them both to evolutionary processes.

The postindustrial society will be fueled not by oil but by a new commodity called artificial intelligence (AI). We might regard it as a commodity because it has value and can be traded. Indeed, as will be made clear, the knowledge imbedded in AI software and hardware architectures will become even more salient as a foundation of wealth than the raw materials that fueled the first Industrial Revolution. It is an unusual commodity, because it has no material form. It can be a flow of information with no more physical reality than electrical vibrations in a wire.

If artificial intelligence is the fuel of the second industrial revolution, then we might ask what it is. One of the difficulties in addressing this issue is the amount of confusion and disagreement regarding the definition of the field. Other fields do not seem to have this problem. Books on biology do not generally begin with the question, What is biology, anyway? Predicting the future is always problematic, but it will be helpful if we attempt to define what it is we are predicting the future of.

One view is that AI is an attempt to answer a central question that has been debated by scientists, philosophers, and theologians for thousands of years. How does the human brain — three pounds of "ordinary" matter — give rise to thoughts, feelings, and consciousness? While certainly very complex, our brains are clearly governed by the same physical laws as our machines.

> "The human brain may be regarded as a very capable machine."

Viewed in this way, the human brain may be regarded as a very capable machine. Conversely, given sufficient capacity and the right techniques, our machines may ultimately be able to replicate human intelligence. Some philosophers and even a few AI scientists are offended by this characterization of the human mind as a machine, albeit an immensely complicated one. Others find the view inspiring: it means that we will ultimately be able to understand our minds and how they work.

One does not need to accept fully the notion that the human mind is "just" 5 a machine to appreciate both the potential for machines to master many of our intellectual capabilities and the practical implications of doing so.

The Usual Definition

Artificial Stupidity (AS) may be defined as the attempt by computer scientists to create computer programs capable of causing problems of a type normally associated with human thought.

WALLACE MARSHAL, *JOURNAL OF IRREPRODUCIBLE RESULTS (1987)*

Probably the most durable definition of artificial intelligence, and the one most often quoted, states that: Artificial Intelligence is the art of creating machines that perform functions that require intelligence when performed by people. It is reasonable enough as definitions go, although it suffers from two problems. First, it does not say a great deal beyond the words "artificial intelligence." The definition refers to machines and that takes care of the word "artificial." There is no problem here: we have never had much difficulty defining artificial. For the more problematic word "intelligence" the definition provides only a circular definition: an intelligent machine does what an intelligent person does.

A more serious problem is that the definition does not appear to fit actual usage. Few AI researchers refer to the chess-playing machines that one can buy in the local drug store as examples of true artificial intelligence, yet chess is *still* considered an intellectual game. Some equation-manipulation packages perform transformations that would challenge most college students. We consider these to be quite useful packages, but again, they are rarely pointed to as examples of artificial intelligence.

The Moving-Frontier Definition

Mr. Jabez Wilson laughed heavily. "Well, I never!" said he. "I thought at first that you had done something clever, but I see that there was nothing in it, after all?" "I began to think, Watson," said Holmes, "that I made a mistake in explaining. 'Omne ignatum pro magnifico°,' you know, and my poor little reputation, such as it is, will suffer shipwreck if I am so candid."

SIR ARTHUR CONAN DOYLE, *THE COMPLETE SHERLOCK HOLMES*

Omne ignatum pro magnifco: a Latin phrase meaning that something unknown is imagined to be better than it really is.

---

[1]Similar definitions are found in many standard textbooks on AI.

The extent to which we regard something as behaving in an intelligent manner is determined as much by our own state of mind and training as by the properties of the object under consideration. If we are able to explain and predict its behaviour or if there seems to be little underlying plan, we have little temptation to imagine intelligence. With the same object, therefore, it is possible that one man would consider it as intelligent and another would not; the second man would have found out the rules of its behaviour.

ALAN TURING (1947)

AI is the study of how to make computers do things at which, at the moment, people are better.

ELAINE RICH

This leads us to another approach, which I like to call the "moving frontier" definition: artificial intelligence is the study of computer problems that have not yet been solved. This definition, which Marvin Minsky has been advocating since the 1960s, is unlike those found in other fields. A gene-splicing technique does not stop being part of bioengineering the moment it is perfected. Yet, if we examine the shifting judgments as to what has qualified as "true artificial intelligence" over the years, we find this definition has more validity than one might expect.

When the artificial intelligence field was first named at a now famous conference held in 1956 at Dartmouth College, programs that could play chess or checkers or manipulate equations, even at crude levels of performance, were very much in the mainstream of AI.[2] As I noted above, we no longer consider such game-playing programs to be prime examples of AI, although perhaps we should.

One might say that this change in perception simply reflects a tightening of standards. I feel that there is something more profound going on. We are of two minds when it comes to thinking. On the one hand, there is the faith in the AI community that most definable problems (other than the so-called "unsolvable" problems) can be solved, often by successively breaking them down into hierarchies of simpler problems. While some problems will take longer to solve than others, we presently have no clear limit to what can be achieved.

On the other hand, coexisting with the faith that most cognitive problems can be solved is the feeling that thinking or true intelligence is not an

10

---

[2]This conference was originally called the Dartmouth Summer Research Project on Artificial Intelligence; for a full account of this landmark event, see Pamela McCorduck, *Machines Who Think*.

automatic technique. In other words, there is something in the concept of thinking that goes beyond the automatic opening and closing of switches. Thus, when a method has been perfected in a computerized system, we see it as just another useful technique, not as an example of true artificial intelligence. We know exactly how the system works, so it does not seem fundamentally different from any other computer program.

A problem that has *not yet* been solved, on the other hand, retains its mystique. While we may have confidence that such a problem will eventually be solved, we do not yet know its solution. So we do not yet think of it as just an automatic technique and thus allow ourselves to view it as true cybernetic cognition.[3]

Consider as a current example the area of artificial intelligence known as expert systems. Such a system consists of a data base of facts about a particular discipline, a *knowledge base* of codified rules for drawing inferences from the data base, and a high-speed *inference engine* for systematically applying the rules to the facts to solve problems.[4] Such systems have been successfully used to locate fuel deposits, design and assemble complex computer systems, analyze electronic circuits, and diagnose diseases. The judgments of expert systems are beginning to rival those of human experts, at least within certain well-defined areas of expertise.

Today expert systems are widely regarded as a central part of artificial intelligence, and hundreds of projects exist today to apply this set of techniques to dozens of fields. It seems likely that expert systems will become within the next ten years as widespread as computer spreadsheet programs and data-base management systems are today. I predict that when this happens, AI researchers will shift their attention to other issues, and we will no longer consider expert systems to be prime examples of AI technology. They will probably be regarded as just obvious extensions of data-base–management techniques.

Roger Schank uses the example of a pool sweep, a robot pool cleaner, to   15
illustrate our tendency to view an automatic procedure as not intelligent.[5] When we first see a pool sweep mysteriously weaving its way around the

---

[3]Norbert Weiner, the famous mathematician who coined this term (later supplanted by the term "artificial intelligence"), was clearly fond of the meaning of its Greek root, "kubernetes": pilot or governor.

[4]These terms were introduced by Edward Feigenbaum; see his "Art of Artificial Intelligence: Themes and Case Studies in Knowledge Engines," in *AFIPS Conference Proceedings of the 1978 National Computer Conference* 47: 227–240.

[5]Roger Schank, *The Cognitive Computer*, pp. 49–51.

bottom of a pool, we are impressed with its apparent intelligence in systematically finding its way around. When we figure out the method or pattern behind its movements, which is a deceptively simple algorithm of making preprogrammed changes in direction every time it encounters a wall of the pool, we realize that it is not very intelligent after all.

Another example is a computer program named ELIZA designed in 1966 by Joseph Weizenbaum to simulate a psychotherapist.[6] When interacting with ELIZA, users type statements about themselves and ELIZA responds with questions and comments. Many persons have been impressed with the apparent appropriateness and insight of ELIZA's ability to engage in psychoanalytic dialogue. Those users who have been given the opportunity to examine ELIZA's algorithms have been even more impressed at how simple some of its methods are.

We often respond to people the same way. When we figure out how an expert operates and understand his or her methods and rules of thumb, what once seemed very intelligent somehow seems less so.

It will be interesting to see what our reaction will be when a computer takes the world chess championship. Playing a master game of chess is often considered an example of high intellectual (even creative) achievement. When a computer does become the chess champion, which I believe will happen before the end of the century, we will either think more of computers, less of ourselves, or less of chess.[7]

Our ambivalence on the issue of the ability of a machine to truly emulate human thought tends to regard a *working* system as possibly useful but not truly intelligent. Computer-science problems are only AI problems until they are solved. This could be seen to be a frustrating state of affairs. As with the carrot on a stick, the AI practitioner can never quite achieve the goal.

What Is Intelligence, Anyway?

It could be simply an accident of fate that our brains are too weak to understand themselves. Think of the lowly giraffe, for instance, whose brain is obviously far below the level required for self-understanding—yet it is remarkably similar to our own brain. In fact,

---

[6]The layman may also want to see Susan J. Shepard, "Conversing with Tiny ELIZA," *Computer Language* 4 (May 1987).

[7]See Hans Berliner, "New Hitech Computer Chess Success," *AI Magazine* 9 (Summer 1988): 133. And, for a brilliant discussion of machine versus human intelligence in chess and of dangers of rigidity in "learning machines," see Norbert Weiner, discussant, "Scientists and Decision Making," in Martin Greenberger, ed., *Computers and the World of the Future*, pp. 23–28.

the brains of giraffes, elephants, baboons—even the brains of tortoises or unknown beings who are far smarter than we are—probably all operate on basically the same set of principles. Giraffes may lie far below the threshold of intelligence necessary to understand how those principles fit together to produce the qualities of mind; humans may lie closer to that threshold—perhaps just barely below it, perhaps even above it. The point is that there may be no fundamental (i.e., Gödelian°) reason why those qualities are incomprehensible; they may be completely clear to more intelligent beings.

DOUGLAS R. HOFSTADTER, *GÖDEL, ESCHER, BACH: AN ETERNAL GOLDEN BRAID*

A beaver and another forest animal are contemplating an immense man-made dam. The beaver is saying something like, "No, I didn't actually build it. But it's based on an idea of mine."

EDWARD FREDKIN

If we can replace the word "artificial" with "machine," the problem of defining artificial intelligence becomes a matter of defining intelligence. As might be expected, though, defining intelligence is at least as controversial as defining artificial intelligence. One approach is to define intelligence in terms of its constituent processes: *a process comprised of learning, reasoning, and the ability to manipulate symbols.*

Learning is not simply the acquisition of *facts,* which a data-base–management system can do; it is also the acquisition of *knowledge.* Knowledge consists of facts, an understanding of the relationships between the facts, and their implications. One difference between humans and computers lies in the relative strengths in their respective abilities to understand symbolic relationships and to learn facts. A computer can remember billions of facts with extreme precision, whereas we are hard pressed to remember more than a handful of phone numbers. On the other hand, we can read a novel and understand and manipulate the subtle relationships between the characters—something that computers have yet to demonstrate an ability to do. We often use our ability to understand and recall relationships as an aid in remembering simple things, as when we remember names by means of our past associations with each name and when we remember phone numbers in terms of the geometric or numeric patterns they make. We thus use a very complex process to accomplish a very simple task, but it is the only process we have for the job. Computers have been weak in their ability to understand and process information that contains abstractions and complex

20

Gödelian: using Gödel's incompleteness theorems to argue against the possibility of human-level computer intelligence.

webs of relationships, but they are improving, and a great deal of AI research today is directed toward this goal.

Reason is the ability to draw deductions and inferences from knowledge with the purpose of achieving a goal or solving a problem. One of the strengths of human intelligence is its ability to draw inferences from knowledge that is imprecise and incomplete. The very job of a decision maker, whether a national leader or a corporate manager, is to draw conclusions and make decisions based on information that is often contradictory and fragmentary. To date, most computer-based expert systems have used hard rules, which have firm antecedents and certain conclusions. For some problems, such as the job of DEC's XCON, which configures complex computer systems, hard rules make sense. A certain-sized computer board will either fit or not fit in a certain chassis. Other types of decision making, such as the structuring of a marketing program for a product launch or the development of national monetary policy, must take into account incomplete present knowledge and the probabilities of unknown future events. The latest generation of expert systems are beginning to allow rules based on what is called *fuzzy logic*, which provides a mathematical basis for making optimal use of uncertain information.[8] This methodology has been used for years in such pattern-recognition tasks as recognizing printed characters or human speech.

The ability to learn and acquire knowledge and to manipulate it inferentially and deductively is often referred to as symbolic reasoning, the ability to manipulate symbols. A symbol is a name or sign that stands for something else, generally a structure or network of facts and other symbols. Symbols are typically organized in complicated patterns rather than simple lists. Another strength of human intelligence is our ability to recognize the patterns represented by the symbols we know even when they occur in contexts different than the ones in which we originally learned the symbol. One of the reasons that the LISP programming language has been popular in developing AI applications is its strength in manipulating symbols that represent complex patterns and their relationships rather than orderly lists of facts (despite its name, which derives from "list processing").

Rather than defining intelligence in terms of its constituent processes, we might define it in terms of its goal: *the ability to use symbolic reasoning in the pursuit of a goal.* Symbolic reasoning is used to develop and carry out strategies to further the goals of its possessor. A question that then

---

[8]See Lofti Zadeh, "Fuzzy Sets," in *Information and Control* 8: 338–353. See also a fascinating interview with Zadeh published in *Communications of the ACM*, April 1984, pp. 304–311, in which he discusses the inadequacy of precise AI techniques and tools to solve real life ("fuzzy") problems.

arises is, What are the goals? With machine intelligence, the goals have been set by the human designer of each system. The machine may go on to set its own subgoals, but its mission is imbedded in its algorithms. Science-fiction writers, however, have long speculated on a generation of intelligent machines that set their own agendas. With living creatures or species, the goals are often expressed in terms of survival either of the individual or the species. This is consistent with the view of intelligence as the ultimate (most recent) product of evolution.

The evidence does not yet make clear whether intelligence does in fact 25 support the goal of survival. Intelligence has allowed our species to dominate the planet. We have also been sufficiently "intelligent" to unlock the destructive powers that result from manipulating physical laws. Whether intelligence, or at least our version of it, is successful in terms of survival is not yet clear, particularly when viewed from the long time scale of evolution.

Thus far *Homo sapiens* are less than 100,000 years old. Dinosaurs were a successful, surviving class of creatures for 160 million years. They have always been regarded as unintelligent creatures, although recent research has cast doubt on this view. There are, however, many examples of unintelligent creatures that have survived as a species (e.g. palm trees, cockroaches, and horseshoe crabs) for long periods of time.

Humans do use their intelligence to further their goals. Even if we allow for possible cultural bias in intelligence testing, the evidence is convincing that there is a strong correlation between intelligence, as measured by standardized tests, and economic, social, and perhaps even romantic success. A larger question is whether we use our intelligence in setting our goals. Many of our goals appear to stem from desires, fears, and drives from our primitive past.[9]

In summary, there appears to be no *simple* definition of intelligence that is satisfactory to most observers, and most would-be definers of intelligence end up with long checklists of its attributes. Minsky's *Society of Mind* can be viewed as a book-length attempt at such a definition. Allen Newell offers the following list for an intelligent system: it operates in real-time; exploits vast amounts of knowledge; tolerates erroneous, unexpected, and possibly unknown inputs; uses symbols and abstractions; communicates using some form of natural language;

---

[9]See Sigmund Freud, *The Psychopathology of Everyday Life,* in *The Basic Writings of Sigmund Freud;* see also his *Collected Papers;* for another point of view, see Carl Jung et al., *Man and His Symbols;* and for a shorter but broad overview on the subject, see William Kessen and Emily D. Cahan, "A Century of Psychology: From Subject to Object to Agent," *American Scientist,* Nov.–Dec. 1986, pp. 640–650.

learns from the environment; and exhibits adaptive goal-oriented behavior.[10]

The controversy over what intelligence is, is reminiscent of a similar controversy over what life is. Both touch on our vision of who we are. Yet great progress has been made, much of it in recent years, in understanding the structures and methods of life. We have begun to map out DNA, decode some of the hereditary code, and understand the detailed chemistry of reproduction. The concern many have had that understanding these mechanisms would lessen our respect for life has thus far been unjustified. Our increasing knowledge of the mechanisms of life has, if anything, deepened our sense of wonder at the order and diversity of creation.

We are only now beginning to develop a similar understanding of the   30 mechanisms of intelligence. The development of machine intelligence helps us to understand natural intelligence by showing us methods that may account for the many skills that comprise intelligence. The concern that understanding the laws of intelligence will trivialize it and lessen our respect for it may also be unjustified. As we begin to comprehend the depth of design inherent in such "deep" capabilities as intuition and common sense, the awe inherent in our appreciation of intelligence should only be enhanced.

Evolution as an Intelligent Process

God reveals himself in the harmony of what exists.

SPINOZA

A central tenet of AI is that we, an intelligent species, can create intelligent machines. At present the machines we have created, while having better memories and greater speed, are clearly less capable than we are at most intellectual tasks. The gap is shrinking, however. Machine intelligence is rapidly improving. The same cannot be said for human intelligence. A controversial question surrounding AI is whether the gap can ultimately be eliminated. Can machine intelligence ultimately equal that of human intelligence? Can it surpass human intelligence? A broader statement of the question is, Can an intelligent entity be more intelligent than the intelligence that created it?

One way to gain insight into these questions might be to examine the relationship of human intelligence to the intelligent process that

---

[10]Newell's fullest and most current vision can be found in John E. Laird, A. Newell, and Paul S. Rosenbloom, "SOAR: An Architecture for Intelligence" (University of Michigan Cognitive Science and Machine Intelligence Laboratory Technical Report no. 2, 1987).

created it—evolution. Evolution created human and many other forms of intelligence and thus may be regarded as an intelligent process itself.[11]

One attribute of intelligence is its ability to create and design. The results of an intelligent design process—to wit, intelligent designs—have the characteristics of being aesthetically pleasing and functionally effective. It is hard to imagine designs that are more aesthetically pleasing or functionally effective than the myriad of life forms that have been produced by the process we call evolution. Indeed, some theories of aesthetics define aesthetic quality or beauty as the degree of success in emulating the natural beauty that evolution has created.[12]

Evolution can be considered the ultimate in intelligence—it has created designs of indescribable beauty, complexity, and elegance. Yet, it is considered to lack consciousness and free will—it is just an "automatic" process. It is what happens to swirling matter given enough time and the right circumstances.

Evolution is often pitted against religious theories of creation. The religious theories do share one thing in common with the theory of evolution—both attribute creation to an ultimate intelligent force. The most basic difference is that in the religious theories this intelligent force *is* conscious and does have free will, although some theologies, such as Buddhism, conceive of God as an ultimate force of creativity and intelligence and not as a personal willful consciousness.[13]

The theory of evolution can be simply expressed as follows. Changes in the genetic code occur through random mutation; beneficial changes are retained, whereas harmful ones are discarded through the "survival of the fittest."[14] In some ways it makes sense that the survival of the fittest would retain good changes and discard bad ones, since we define "good" to mean more survivable.

Yet let us consider the theory from another perspective. The genetic code is similar to an extraordinarily large computer program, about six

---

[11]See Richard Dawkins's defense of Darwinism in *The Blind Watchmaker: Why the Evidence of Evolution Reveals a Universe without Design*; for some classic arguments on design versus necessity, also see A. Hunter Dupree, in Ada Gray, ed., *Darwiniana*, pp. 51–71.

[12]This subject is eloquently addressed in a slim volume (23 pages) by S. Alexander, *Art and Instinct*.

[13]To some, of course, the concept of God is not applicable to Buddhism; see William James, *The Varieties of Religious Experience*, pp. 42–44 and 315.

[14]Charles Darwin, *The Origin of the Species*. In this, his classic work on natural selection and evolution, Darwin states, "If it could be demonstrated that any complex Organ[ism] existed, which could not possibly have been formed by numerous, successive, slight modifications, my theory would absolutely break down" (p. 229).

billion bits to describe a human, in contrast to a few tens of millions of bits in the most complex computer programs. It is indeed a binary code, and we are slowly learning its digital language.[15] The theory says that changes are introduced essentially randomly, and the changes are evaluated for retention by survival of the entire organism and its ability to reproduce. Yet a computer program controls not just the one characteristic that is being changed but literally millions of other characteristics. Survival of the fittest appears to be a rather crude technique capable of concentrating on at most a few fundamental characteristics at a time. While a few characteristics were being optimized, thousands of others could degrade through the increasing entropy of random change.[16] If we attempted to improve our computer programs in this way, they would surely disintegrate.

The method we use to improve the programs we create is not the introduction of random code changes but carefully planned and designed changes and experiments designed to focus in on the changes just introduced. It has been proposed that evolution itself has evolved to where changes are not entirely random but in some way planned, and that changes are "tested" in some way other than overall survival, in which a change just introduced would be competing with thousands or even millions of other factors.[17]

Yet no one can describe a mechanism in which such planning and isolated evaluation could take place in the process of evolution. There appears, therefore, to be a gap in the theory of evolution. Clearly, the fossil and biochemical evidence is overwhelming that species have indeed undergone a slow but dramatic evolution in complexity and sophistication, yet we do not fully understand the mechanism. The proposed mechanism seems unlikely to work; its designs should disintegrate through increasing entropy.

One possible perspective would state that the creator of an intelligence is inherently superior to the intelligence it creates. The first step of this perspective seems to be well supported in that the intelligence of evolution appears vast. Yet is it?

While it is true that evolution has created some extraordinary designs; it is also true that it took an extremely long period of time to do so. Is the

---

[15]Richard Dawkins, *The Blind Watchmaker,* pp. 112–113.

[16]Note, for *example,* a compelling argument *against* this notion (which instead champions the notion of hierarchy in evolution) in Stephen Jay Gould. "Is a New and General Theory of Evolution Emerging?" *Paleobiology* 6 (1979): 119–130.

[17]See Gould, *Paleobiology* 6 (1979): 119–130. Also, in Stephen Jay Gould, *The Mismeasure of Man,* pp. 326–334, mention is made of "human nature" in relation to the concept of natural selection. See also Richard Dawkins, *The Blind Watchmaker,* pp. 141–142.

length of time required to solve a problem or create a design relevant to an evaluation of the level of an intelligence? Clearly it is. We recognize this by timing our intelligence tests. If someone can solve a problem in a few minutes, we consider that better than solving the same problem in a few hours or a few years. With regard to intelligence as an aid to survival, it is clearly better to solve problems quickly than slowly. In a competitive world we see the benefits of solving problems quickly.

Evolution has achieved intelligent work on an extraordinarily high level yet has taken an extraordinarily long period of time to do so. It is very slow. If we factor its achievements by its ponderous pace, I believe we shall find that its intelligence quotient is only infinitesimally greater than zero. An IQ of only slightly greater than zero is enough for evolution to beat entropy and create extraordinary designs, given enough time, in the same way that an ever so slight asymmetry in the physical laws may have been enough to allow matter to almost completely overtake antimatter.

The human race, then, may very well be smarter than its creator, evolution. If we look at the speed of human progress in comparison to that of evolution, a strong case can be made that we are far more intelligent than the ponderously slow process that created us. Consider the sophistication of *our* creations over a period of only a few thousand years. In another few thousand years our machines are likely to be at least comparable to human intelligence or even surpass it in all likelihood, and thus humans will have clearly beaten evolution, achieving in a matter of thousands of years as much or more than evolution achieved in several billion years. From this perspective, human intelligence may be greater than its creator.[18]

So what about the intelligence that we are in turn creating? It too could be greater than its creator. That is not the case today. While computers have a superiority in certain *idiot savant* types of thinking, our thinking is today significantly superior to that of our machines. Yet the intelligence of our machines is improving at a very rapid pace. Within a matter of years or decades it appears that computers will compete successfully with human intelligence in many spheres. If we extrapolate a sufficient number of decades or centuries into the future, it appears likely that human intelligence will be surpassed.[19] In contrast to what one might intuitively conclude, this perspective points consistently to the possibility that an intelligence may ultimately outperform its creator.

---

[18]This idea is supported, at least in theory, by some pioneers of AI; see, for example, Lawrence Fogel, Alvin Owens, and Michael Walsh, *Artificial Intelligence through Simulated Evolution*, pp. viii and 112.

[19]Edward Fredkin of MIT is credited with saying, "Artificial intelligence is the next step in evolution" in Sherry Turkle, *The Second Self*, p. 242.

Understanding the Text

1. Kurzweil offers multiple definitions of artificial intelligence. Synthesize them into a working definition of AI.

2. Similarly, use Kurzweil to define intelligence, supporting your definition with quotations from his text.

3. Kurzweil often uses quotations at the start of his sections. When quotations are used in this way, they're called *epigraphs*. Convert his epigraphs into actual graphs by drawing the relation between these quotations and his points. You may want to select a particular section, listing his main ideas in the section, and then place the epigraph in relation to these concepts, drawing lines to highlight the connections.

Reflection and Response

4. Kurzweil, writing in 1990, is trying to predict the future in which we now live. How accurate are his predictions? Evaluate his forecast using your experience with technology today.

5. Kurzweil suggests that evolution itself is an intelligence. Extend this discussion by examining the role intelligence plays in evolution. What role does intelligence play in survival? How does evolution select for intelligence? What implications do these processes have when we consider the potential evolution of artificial intelligence?

Making Connections

6. Will Knight ("The Dark Secret at the Heart of AI," p. 100) explores deep learning, a different kind of artificial intelligence, and its mysterious inner workings. Apply Kurzweil to Knight's essay by first determining which of Kurzweil's definitions of AI applies to deep learning, then by modifying his definitions if you do not think any single one accounts for what deep learning does, and finally by reconciling Knight's concerns with deep learning and Kurzweil's discussion of AI in relation to evolution. Does deep learning represent a new evolution of intelligence? At what point does the intelligence we create become more intelligent than us?

7. According to Tim Adams ("Like Children Playing with a Bomb," p. 85), one of Nick Bostrom's concerns about artificial intelligence is an "intelligence explosion" (p. 86). That phenomenon seems strikingly similar to Kurzweil's discussion of intelligence and evolution. Reevaluate Kurzweil's argument through the lens provided by Adams and his representation of Nick Bostrom. Does the development of artificial intelligence represent our doom or our salvation?

Computing Machinery and Intelligence

Alan Turing

British mathematician and computer scientist Alan Turing is widely considered to be the father of artificial intelligence and theoretical computer science. Turing played a crucial role in World War II working as a codebreaker for British military intelligence, where his work enabled the Allied forces to defeat the Nazis in multiple important engagements. After the war, he continued his work of developing computers, which at that time were embryonic machines far from what we are used to today. In 1952, he was convicted of gross indecency because he was a homosexual, and he was ordered to undergo chemical castration. He died two years later of cyanide poisoning, which some believe to have been suicide, some an accident, and some a malicious conspiracy. In this essay excerpted from his landmark 1950 paper, Turing presents for the first time what would come to be known as the "Turing test," which long operated as the gold standard for evaluating artificial intelligence.

The Imitation Game

I propose to consider the question, "Can machines think?" This should begin with definitions of the meaning of the terms "machine" and "think." The definitions might be framed so as to reflect so far as possible the normal use of the words, but this attitude is dangerous. If the meaning of the words "machine" and "think" are to be found by examining how they are commonly used it is difficult to escape the conclusion that the meaning and the answer to the question, "Can machines think?" is to be sought in a statistical survey such as a Gallup poll. But this is absurd. Instead of attempting such a definition I shall replace the question by another, which is closely related to it and is expressed in relatively unambiguous words.

The new form of the problem can be described in terms of a game which we call the "imitation game." It is played with three people, a man (A), a woman (B), and an interrogator (C) who may be of either sex. The interrogator stays in a room apart from the other two. The object of the game for the interrogator is to determine which of the other two is the man and which is the woman. He knows them by labels X and Y, and at the end of the game he says either "X is A and Y is B" or "X is B and Y is A." The interrogator is allowed to put questions to A and B thus:

C : Will X please tell me the length of his or her hair?

Now suppose X is actually A, then A must answer. It is A's object in the game to try and cause C to make the wrong identification. His answer might therefore be

"My hair is shingled, and the longest strands are about nine inches long."   5

In order that tones of voice may not help the interrogator the answers should be written, or better still, typewritten. The ideal arrangement is to have a teleprinter communicating between the two rooms. Alternatively the question and answers can be repeated by an intermediary. The object of the game for the third player (B) is to help the interrogator. The best strategy for her is probably to give truthful answers. She can add such things as "I am the woman, don't listen to him!" to her answers, but it will avail nothing as the man can make similar remarks.

We now ask the question, "What will happen when a machine takes the part of A in this game?" Will the interrogator decide wrongly as often when the game is played like this as he does when the game is played between a man and a woman? These questions replace our original, "Can machines think?"

Contrary Views on the Main Question

We may now consider the ground to have been cleared and we are ready to proceed to the debate on our question, "Can machines think?" It will simplify matters for the reader if I explain first my own beliefs in the matter. I believe that in about fifty years' time it will be possible to pro-gramme computers, with a storage capacity of about 10^9, to make them play the imitation game so well that an average interrogator will not have more than 70 percent chance of making the right identification after five minutes of questioning. The original question, "Can machines think?" I believe to be too meaningless to deserve discussion. Neverthe-less I believe that at the end of the century the use of words and general educated opinion will have altered so much that one will be able to speak of machines thinking without expecting to be contradicted. I believe further that no useful purpose is served by concealing these beliefs. The popular view that scientists proceed inexorably from well-established fact to well-established fact, never being influenced by any unproved conjec-ture, is quite mistaken. Provided it is made clear which are proved facts and which are conjectures, no harm can result. Conjectures are of great importance since they suggest useful lines of research.

I now proceed to consider opinions opposed to my own.

(1) *The Theological Objection.* Thinking is a function of man's immor-   10
tal soul. God has given an immortal soul to every man and woman, but not to any other animal or to machines. Hence no animal or machine can think.

I am unable to accept any part of this, but will attempt to reply in theological terms. I should find the argument more convincing if ani-mals were classed with men, for there is a greater difference, to my mind, between the typical animate and the inanimate than there is between man and the other animals. The arbitrary character of the orthodox view becomes clearer if we consider how it might appear to a member of some other religious community. How do Christians regard the Moslem view that women have no souls? But let us leave this point aside and return to the main argument. It appears to me that the argument quoted above implies a serious restriction of the omnipotence of the Almighty. It is admitted that there are certain things that He cannot do such as making one equal to two, but should we not believe that He has freedom to confer a soul on an elephant if He sees fit? We might expect that He would only exercise this power in conjunction with a mutation which provided the elephant with an appropriately improved brain to minister to the needs of this soul. An argument of exactly similar form may be made for the case of machines. It may seem different because it is more difficult to "swallow." But this really only means that we think it would be less likely that He would consider the circumstances suitable for conferring a soul.[1] The circumstances in question are discussed in the rest of this paper. In attempting to construct such machines we should not be irreverently usurping His power of creating souls, any more than we are in the procreation of children: rather we are, in either case, instruments of His will providing mansions for the souls that He creates.

However, this is mere speculation. I am not very impressed with theological arguments whatever they may be used to support. Such arguments have often been found unsatisfactory in the past. In the time of Galileo it was argued that the texts, "And the sun stood still . . . and hasted not to go down about a whole day" (Joshua x. 13) and "He laid the foundations of the earth, that it should not move at any time" (Psalm cv. 5) were an adequate refutation of the Copernican theory. With our present knowledge such an argument appears futile. When that knowledge was not available it made a quite different impression.

(2) *The "Heads in the Sand" Objection.* "The consequences of machines thinking would be too dreadful. Let us hope and believe that they cannot do so."

This argument is seldom expressed quite so openly as in the form above. But it affects most of us who think about it at all. We like to believe that Man is in some subtle way superior to the rest of creation. It is best if he can be shown to be *necessarily* superior, for then there is no danger of him losing his commanding position. The popularity of the

---

[1] Possibly this view is heretical. St. Thomas Aquinas (*Summa Theologica*, quoted by Bertrand Russell, p. 480) states that God cannot make a man to have no soul. But this may not be a real restriction on His powers, but only a result of the fact that men's souls are immortal, and therefore indestructible.

theological argument is clearly connected with this feeling. It is likely to be quite strong in intellectual people, since they value the power of thinking more highly than others, and are more inclined to base their belief in the superiority of Man on this power.

> "We like to believe that Man is in some subtle way superior to the rest of creation."

I do not think that this argument is sufficiently substantial to require refutation. Consolation would be more appropriate: perhaps this should be sought in the transmigration of souls.

(3) *The Mathematical Objection.* There are a number of results of mathematical logic which can be used to show that there are limitations to the powers of discrete-state machines. The best known of these results is known as Gödel's theorem,[2] and shows that in any sufficiently powerful logical system statements can be formulated which can neither be proved nor disproved within the system, unless possibly the system itself is inconsistent. There are other, in some respects similar, results due to *Church, Kleene, Rosser,* and *Turing.* The latter result is the most convenient to consider, since it refers directly to machines, whereas the others can only be used in a comparatively indirect argument: for instance if Gödel's theorem is to be used we need in addition to have some means of describing logical systems in terms of machines, and machines in terms of logical systems. The result in question refers to a type of machine which is essentially a digital computer with an infinite capacity. It states that there are certain things that such a machine cannot do. If it is rigged up to give answers to questions as in the imitation game, there will be some questions to which it will either give a wrong answer, or fail to give an answer at all however much time is allowed for a reply. There may, of course, be many such questions, and questions which cannot be answered by one machine may be satisfactorily answered by another. We are of course supposing for the present that the questions are of the kind to which an answer "Yes" or "No" is appropriate, rather than questions such as "What do you think of Picasso?" The questions that we know the machines must fail on are of this type, "Consider the machine specified as follows. . . . Will this machine ever answer 'Yes' to any question?" The dots are to be replaced by a description of some machine in a standard form. When the machine described bears a certain comparatively simple relation to the machine which is under interrogation, it can be shown that the answer is either wrong or not forthcoming. This is the

---

[2]Author's names in italics refer to the Bibliography.

mathematical result: it is argued that it proves a disability of machines to which the human intellect is not subject.

The short answer to this argument is that although it is established that there are limitations to the powers of any particular machine, it has only been stated, without any sort of proof, that no such limitations apply to the human intellect. But I do not think this view can be dismissed quite so lightly. Whenever one of these machines is asked the appropriate critical question, and gives a definite answer, we know that this answer must be wrong, and this gives us a certain feeling of superiority. Is this feeling illusory? It is no doubt quite genuine, but I do not think too much importance should be attached to it. We too often give wrong answers to questions ourselves to be justified in being very pleased at such evidence of fallibility on the part of the machines. Further, our superiority can only be felt on such an occasion in relation to the one machine over which we have scored our petty triumph. There would be no question of triumphing simultaneously over *all* machines. In short, then, there might be men cleverer than any given machine, but then again there might be other machines cleverer again, and so on.

Those who hold to the mathematical argument would, I think, mostly be willing to accept the imitation game as a basis for discussion. Those who believe in the two previous objections would probably not be interested in any criteria.

(4) *The Argument from Consciousness.* This argument is very well expressed in Professor Jefferson's Lister Oration for 1949, from which I quote. "Not until a machine can write a sonnet or compose a concerto because of thoughts and emotions felt, and not by the chance fall of symbols, could we agree that machine equals brain—that is, not only write it but know that it had written it. No mechanism could feel (and not merely artificially signal, an easy contrivance) pleasure at its successes, grief when its valves fuse, be warmed by flattery, be made miserable by its mistakes, be charmed by sex, be angry or depressed when it cannot get what it wants."

This argument appears to be a denial of the validity of our test. 20 According to the most extreme form of this view the only way by which one could be sure that a machine thinks is to *be* the machine and to feel oneself thinking. One could then describe these feelings to the world, but of course no one would be justified in taking any notice. Likewise according to this view the only way to know that a *man* thinks is to be that particular man. It is in fact the solipsist point of view. It may be the most logical view to hold but it makes communication of ideas difficult. A is liable to believe "A thinks but B does not" whilst B believes "B thinks but A does not." Instead of arguing continually over this point it is usual to have the polite convention that everyone thinks.

I am sure that Professor Jefferson does not wish to adopt the extreme and solipsist point of view. Probably he would be quite willing to accept the imitation game as a test. The game (with the player B omitted) is frequently used in practice under the name of *viva voce*° to discover whether some one really understands something or has "learnt it parrot fashion." Let us listen in to a part of such a *viva voce*:

INTERROGATOR: In the first line of your sonnet which reads "Shall I compare thee to a summer's day," would not "a spring day" do as well or better?

WITNESS: It wouldn't scan.

INTERROGATOR: How about "a winter's day" That would scan all right.

WITNESS: Yes, but nobody wants to be compared to a winter's day.

INTERROGATOR: Would you say Mr. Pickwick reminded you of Christmas?

WITNESS: In a way.

INTERROGATOR: Yet Christmas is a winter's day, and I do not think Mr. Pickwick would mind the comparison.

WITNESS: I don't think you're serious. By a winter's day one means a typical winter's day, rather than a special one like Christmas.

And so on. What would Professor Jefferson say if the sonnet-writing machine was able to answer like this in the *viva voce*? I do not know whether he would regard the machine as "merely artificially signalling" these answers, but if the answers were as satisfactory and sustained as in the above passage I do not think he would describe it as "an easy contrivance." This phrase is, I think, intended to cover such devices as the inclusion in the machine of a record of someone reading a sonnet, with appropriate switching to turn it on from time to time.

In short then, I think that most of those who support the argument from consciousness could be persuaded to abandon it rather than be forced into the solipsist position. They will then probably be willing to accept our test.

I do not wish to give the impression that I think there is no mystery about consciousness. There is, for instance, something of a paradox connected with any attempt to localise it. But I do not think these mysteries

---

viva voce: an oral examination, as opposed to a written exam.

necessarily need to be solved before we can answer the question with which we are concerned in this paper.

(5) *Arguments from Various Disabilities.* These arguments take the form, 25 "I grant you that you can make machines do all the things you have mentioned but you will never be able to make one to do X." Numerous features X are suggested in this connexion. I offer a selection:

> *Be kind, resourceful, beautiful, friendly, have initiative, have a sense of humour, tell right from wrong, make mistakes, fall in love, enjoy strawberries and cream, make some one fall in love with it, learn from experience, use words properly, be the subject of its own thought, have as much diversity of behaviour as a man, do something really new.*

No support is usually offered for these statements. I believe they are mostly founded on the principle of scientific induction. A man has seen thousands of machines in his lifetime. From what he sees of them he draws a number of general conclusions. They are ugly, each is designed for a very limited purpose, when required for a minutely different purpose they are useless, the variety of behaviour of any one of them is very small, etc., etc. Naturally he concludes that these are necessary properties of machines in general. Many of these limitations are associated with the very small storage capacity of most machines. (I am assuming that the idea of storage capacity is extended in some way to cover machines other than discrete-state machines. The exact definition does not matter as no mathematical accuracy is claimed in the present discussion.) A few years ago, when very little had been heard of digital computers, it was possible to elicit much incredulity concerning them, if one mentioned their properties without describing their construction. That was presumably due to a similar application of the principle of scientific induction. These applications of the principle are of course largely unconscious. When a burnt child fears the fire and shows that he fears it by avoiding it, I should say that he was applying scientific induction. (I could of course also describe his behaviour in many other ways.) The works and customs of mankind do not seem to be very suitable material to which to apply scientific induction. A very large part of space-time must be investigated, if reliable results are to be obtained. Otherwise we may (as most English children do) decide that everybody speaks English, and that it is silly to learn French.

There are, however, special remarks to be made about many of the disabilities that have been mentioned. The inability to enjoy strawberries and cream may have struck the reader as frivolous. Possibly a machine might be made to enjoy this delicious dish, but any attempt to make one do so would be idiotic. What is important about this disability is that it contributes to some of the other disabilities, e.g. to the difficulty of the same kind of friendliness occurring between man and machine as between white man and white man, or between black man and black man.

The claim that "machines cannot make mistakes" seems a curious one. One is tempted to retort, "Are they any the worse for that ?" But let us adopt a more sympathetic attitude, and try to see what is really meant. I think this criticism can be explained in terms of the imitation game. It is claimed that the interrogator could distinguish the machine from the man simply by setting them a number of problems in arithmetic. The machine would be unmasked because of its deadly accuracy. The reply to this is simple. The machine (programmed for playing the game) would not attempt to give the *right* answers to the arithmetic problems. It would deliberately introduce mistakes in a manner calculated to confuse the interrogator. A mechanical fault would probably show itself through an unsuitable decision as to what sort of a mistake to make in the arithmetic. Even this interpretation of the criticism is not sufficiently sympathetic. But we cannot afford the space to go into it much further. It seems to me that this criticism depends on a confusion between two kinds of mistake. We may call them "errors of functioning" and "errors of conclusion." Errors of functioning are due to some mechanical or electrical fault which causes the machine to behave otherwise than it was designed to do. In philosophical discussions one likes to ignore the possibility of such errors; one is therefore discussing "abstract machines." These abstract machines are mathematical fictions rather than physical objects. By definition they are incapable of errors of functioning. In this sense we can truly say that "machines can never make mistakes." Errors of conclusion can only arise when some meaning is attached to the output signals from the machine. The machine might, for instance, type out mathematical equations, or sentences in English. When a false proposition is typed we say that the machine has committed an error of conclusion. There is clearly no reason at all for saying that a machine cannot make this kind of mistake. It might do nothing but type out repeatedly "$0 = 1$." To take a less perverse example, it might have some method for drawing conclusions by scientific induction. We must expect such a method to lead occasionally to erroneous results.

The claim that a machine cannot be the subject of its own thought can of course only be answered if it can be shown that the machine has *some* thought with *some* subject matter. Nevertheless, "the subject matter of a machine's operations" does seem to mean something, at least to the people who deal with it. If, for instance, the machine was trying to find a solution of the equation $x^2 - 40x - 11 = 0$ one would be tempted to describe this equation as part of the machine's subject matter at that moment. In this sort of sense a machine undoubtedly can be its own subject matter. It may be used to help in making up its own programmes, or to predict the effect of alterations in its own structure. By observing the results of its own behaviour it can modify its own programmes so as to achieve some purpose more effectively. These are possibilities of the near future, rather than Utopian dreams.

The criticism that a machine cannot have much diversity of 30 behaviour is just a way of saying that it cannot have much storage capacity. Until fairly recently a storage capacity of even a thousand digits was very rare.

The criticisms that we are considering here are often disguised forms of the argument from consciousness. Usually if one maintains that a machine *can* do one of these things, and describes the kind of method that the machine could use, one will not make much of an impression. It is thought that the method (whatever it may be, for it must be mechanical) is really rather base.

Bibliography

Samuel Butler, Erewhon, London, 1865. Chapters 23, 24, 25, *The Book of the Machines*.

Alonzo Church, "An Unsolvable Problem of Elementary Number Theory," *American J. of Math.*, 58 (1936), 345–363.

K. Gödel, "Über formal unentscheidbare Sätze der Principia Mathematica und verwandter Systeme, I," *Monatshefte für Math. und Phys.*, (1931), 173–189.

D. R. Hartree, *Calculating Instruments and Machines*, New York, 1949.

S. C. Kleene, "General Recursive Functions of Natural Numbers," *American J. of Math.*, 57 (1935), 153–173 and 219–244.

G. Jefferson, "The Mind of Mechanical Man." Lister Oration for 1949. *British Medical Journal*, vol. i (1949), 1105–1121.

Countess of Lovelace, "Translator's notes to an article on Babbage's Analytical Engine," *Scientific Memoirs* (ed. by R. Taylor), vol. 3 (1842), 691–731.

Bertrand Russell, *History of Western Philosophy*, London, 1940.

A. M. Turing, "On Computable Numbers, with an Application to the Entscheidungsproblem," *Proc. London Math. Soc.* (2), 42 (1937), 230–265.

Understanding the Text

1. In the first section of this essay, Turing describes the Imitation Game. After reviewing this section, explain the game in your own words and explain how it relates to the question, "Can machines think?"

2. Turing explores several objections to artificial intelligence. Summarize the two that you think are the most persuasive. How effectively does Turing counter these two objections?

Reflection and Response

3. Turing repeatedly rejects the question "Can machines think?" for alternate forms that he believes are more accurate. How does he reconfigure this question and, more importantly, why does he do so? What problems does he solve by reframing it, and what new avenues does he open?

4. One consistent theme behind the various objections Turing examines is a sense of human superiority, whether based on consciousness, a love of strawberries and cream, or a divinely ordained natural order. In what ways does a thinking machine threaten human superiority? Why should that be something we should preserve? Consider how Turing would respond to these questions as well.

Making Connections

5. One of the objections to thinking machines that Turing examines is the Argument from Consciousness, which in part involves human creativity. However, Cade Metz ("Google's Artificial Brain Is Pumping Out Trippy — and Pricey — Art," p. 116) shows that Google's DeepDream is participating in a sort of creative process in the images it creates. Make a visual argument that applies Metz's essay to Turing's text and to the Argument from Consciousness in particular. Does the existence of DeepDream suggest that artificial intelligence has started to develop some of the unique features of human consciousness, like creativity? You might work through photo collage or digital images to make your visual argument, but be sure to consider how all elements—including size, color, and placement—support the larger argument you're trying to make.

6. Allie Shaw ("Alexa, Siri, Sophia: Deconstructing AI's Subliminal Gender Bias," p. 111) reveals the ways in which gender bias persists in artificial intelligence. Use Shaw's analysis to complicate Turing's discussion of thinking machines. Will a future with AI be different if it reproduces existing social inequalities? Are there parts of Turing's essay that suggest a different path forward, one that moves into AI with a greater sense of social justice? How does the time period in which Turing writes limit his ability to see and address these issues?

Like Children Playing with a Bomb

Tim Adams

Tim Adams is a staff writer for the British newspaper *The Guardian* and a former literary editor for its sister paper *The Observer*. He is also the author of the book *On Being John McEnroe* (2003).

In this piece from *The Guardian*, Adams profiles Nick Bostrom, a Swedish-born philosopher whose work spans multiple fields, including theoretical physics and computational neuroscience. Bostrom is the head of the Future of Humanity Institute at Oxford University, an interdisciplinary institute focused on humanity's future and any threats to it. Bostrom has been quite vocal in expressing concerns about the development of artificial intelligence, including his book-length examination of the subject, *Superintelligence: Paths, Dangers, Strategies* (2014), one of his four published books. This essay profiles Bostrom and his concerns with AI.

You'll find the Future of Humanity Institute down a medieval back-street in the center of Oxford. It is beside St. Ebbe's church, which has stood on this site since 1005, and above a Pure Gym, which opened in April. The institute, a research faculty of Oxford University, was established a decade ago to ask the very biggest questions on our behalf. Notably: what exactly are the "existential° risks" that threaten the future of our species; how do we measure them; and what can we do to prevent them? Or to put it another way: in a world of multiple fears, what precisely should we be most terrified of?

When I arrive to meet the director of the institute, Professor Nick Bostrom, a bed is being delivered to the second-floor office. Existential risk is a round-the-clock kind of operation; it sleeps fitfully, if at all.

Bostrom, a forty-three-year-old Swedish-born philosopher, has lately acquired something of the status of prophet of doom among those currently doing most to shape our civilization: the tech billionaires of Silicon Valley. His reputation rests primarily on his book *Superintelligence: Paths, Dangers, Strategies*, which was a surprise *New York Times* bestseller last year and now arrives in paperback, trailing must-read recommendations from Bill Gates and Tesla's Elon Musk. (In the best kind of literary review, Musk also gave Bostrom's institute £1m to continue to pursue its inquiries.)

The book is a lively, speculative examination of the singular threat that Bostrom believes—after years of calculation and argument—to be the one most likely to wipe us out. This threat is not climate change, nor

existential: relating to a philosophical theory which emphasizes the existence of the individual person determining their own development through acts of the will.

pandemic, nor nuclear winter; it is the possibly imminent creation of a general machine intelligence greater than our own.

The cover of Bostrom's book is dominated by a mad-eyed, pen-and-ink 5 picture of an owl. The owl is the subject of the book's opening parable. A group of sparrows are building their nests. "We are all so small and weak," tweets one, feebly. "Imagine how easy life would be if we had an owl who could help us build our nests!" There is general twittering agreement among sparrows everywhere; an owl could defend the sparrows! It could look after their old and their young! It could allow them to live a life of leisure and prosperity! With these fantasies in mind, the sparrows can hardly contain their excitement and fly off in search of the swivel-headed savior who will transform their existence.

There is only one voice of dissent: "Scronkfinkle, a one-eyed sparrow with a fretful temperament, was unconvinced of the wisdom of the endeavor. Quoth he: 'This will surely be our undoing. Should we not give some thought to the art of owl-domestication and owl-taming first, before we bring such a creature into our midst?'" His warnings, inevitably, fall on deaf sparrow ears. Owl-taming would be complicated; why not get the owl first and work out the fine details later? Bostrom's book, which is a shrill alarm call about the darker implications of artificial intelligence, is dedicated to Scronkfinkle.

Bostrom articulates his own warnings in a suitably fretful manner. He has a reputation for obsessiveness and for workaholism; he is slim, pale, and semi-nocturnal, often staying in the office into the early hours. Not surprisingly, perhaps, for a man whose days are dominated by whiteboards filled with formulas expressing the relative merits of fifty-seven varieties of apocalypse, he appears to leave as little as possible to chance. In place of meals he favors a green-smoothie elixir involving vegetables, fruit, oat milk, and whey powder. Other interviewers have remarked on his avoidance of handshakes to guard against infection. He does proffer a hand to me, but I have the sense he is subsequently isolating it to disinfect when I have gone. There is, perhaps as a result, a slight impatience about him, which he tries hard to resist.

In his book he talks about the "intelligence explosion" that will occur when machines much cleverer than us begin to design machines of their own. "Before the prospect of an intelligence explosion, we humans are like small children playing with a bomb," he writes. "We have little idea when the detonation will occur, though if we hold the device to our ear we can hear a faint ticking sound." Talking to Bostrom, you have a feeling that for him that faint ticking never completely goes away.

We speak first about the success of his book, the way it has squarely hit a nerve. It coincided with the open letter signed by more than one-thousand eminent scientists—including Stephen Hawking, Apple co-founder Steve Wozniak, and Musk—and presented at last year's International Joint Conference on Artificial Intelligence, urging a ban on the use and development of fully autonomous weapons (the "killer robots" of science fiction that are very close to reality). Bostrom, who is both aware of his own capacities and modest about his influence, suggests it was a happy accident of timing.

"Machine learning and deep learning [the pioneering 'neural' computer algorithms that most closely mimic human brain function] have over the last few years moved much faster than people anticipated," he says. "That is certainly one of the reasons why this has become such a big topic just now. People can see things moving forward in the technical field, and they become concerned about what next." 10

Bostrom sees those implications as potentially Darwinian. If we create a machine intelligence superior to our own, and then give it freedom to grow and learn through access to the internet, there is no reason to suggest that it will not evolve strategies to secure its dominance, just as in the biological world. He sometimes uses the example of humans and gorillas to describe the subsequent one-sided relationship and that is never going to end well. An inferior intelligence will always depend on a superior one for its survival.

There are times, as Bostrom unfolds various scenarios in *Superintelligence*, when it appears he has been reading too much of the science fiction he professes to dislike. One projection involves an AI system eventually building covert "nanofactories producing nerve gas or target-seeking mosquito-like robots [which] might then burgeon forth simultaneously from every square metre of the globe" in order to destroy meddling and irrelevant humanity. Another, perhaps more credible vision, sees the superintelligence "hijacking political processes, subtly manipulating financial markets, biasing information flows, or hacking human-made weapons systems" to bring about the extinction.

Does he think of himself as a prophet?

He smiles. "Not so much. It is not that I believe I know how it is going to happen and have to tell the world that information. It is more I feel quite ignorant and very confused about these things but by working for many years on probabilities you can get partial little insights here and there. And if you add those together with insights many other people might have, then maybe it will build up to some better understanding."

Bostrom came to these questions by way of the transhumanist movement, which tends to view the digital age as one of unprecedented potential for optimising our physical and mental capacities and transcending the limits of our mortality. Bostrom still sees those possibilities 15 as the best case scenario in the superintelligent future, in which we will harness technology to overcome disease and illness, feed the world, create a utopia of fulfilling creativity, and perhaps eventually overcome death. He has been identified in the past as a member of Alcor, the cryogenic initiative that promises to freeze mortal remains in the hope that, one day, minds can be reinvigorated and uploaded in digital form to live in perpetuity. He is coy about this when I ask directly what he has planned.

"I have a policy of never commenting on my funeral arrangements," he says.

But he thinks there is a value in cryogenic research?

"It seems a pretty rational thing for people to do if they can afford it," he says. "When you think about what life in the quite near future could be like, trying to store the information in your brain seems like a conservative option as opposed to burning the brain down and throwing it away. Unless you are really confident that the information will never be useful. . . ."

I wonder at what point his transhumanist optimism gave way to his more nightmarish visions of superintelligence. He suggests that he has not really shifted his position, but that he holds the two possibilities—the heaven and hell of our digital future—in uneasy opposition.

"I wrote a lot about human enhancement ethics in the mid-90s, when it   20 was largely rejected by academics," he says. "They were always like, 'Why on earth would anyone want to cure ageing?' They would talk about over-population and the boredom of living longer. There was no recognition that this is why we do any medical research: to extend life. Similarly with cognitive enhancement—if you look at what I was writing then, it looks more on the optimistic side—but all along I was concerned with existential risks too."

There seems an abiding unease that such enhancements—pills that might make you smarter, or slow down aging—go against the natural order of things. Does he have a sense of that?

"I'm not sure that I would ever equate natural with good," he says. "Cancer is natural, war is natural, parasites eating your insides are natural. What is natural is therefore never a very useful concept to figure out what we should do. Yes, there are ethical considerations but you have to judge them on a case-by-case basis. You must remember I am a transhumanist. I want my life extension pill now. And if there were a pill that could improve my cognition by 10 percent, I would be willing to pay a lot for that."

Has he tried the ones that claim to enhance concentration?

"I have, but not very much. I drink coffee, I have nicotine chewing gum, but that is about it. But the only reason I don't do more is that I am not yet convinced that anything else works."

He is not afraid of trying. When working, he habitually sits in the cor- 25
ner of his office surrounded by a dozen lamps, apparently in thrall to the
idea of illumination.

Bostrom grew up an only child in the coastal Swedish town of Hels-
ingborg. Like many gifted children, he loathed school. His father worked
for an investment bank, his mother for a Swedish corporation. He doesn't
remember any discussion of philosophy—or art or books—around the
dinner table. Wondering how he found himself obsessed with these large
questions, I ask if he was an anxious child: did he always have a powerful
sense of mortality?

"I think I had it quite early on," he says. "Not because I was on the
brink of death or anything. But as a child I remember thinking a lot that
my parents may be healthy now but they are not always going to be
stronger or bigger than me."

That thought kept him awake at nights?

"I don't remember it as anxiety, more as a melancholy sense."

And was that ongoing desire to live for ever rooted there too? 30

"Not necessarily. I don't think that there is any particularly different
desire that I have in that regard to anyone else. I don't want to come
down with colon cancer—who does? If I was alive for five-hundred years
who knows how I would feel? It is not so much fixated on immortality,
just that premature death seems prima facie° bad."

A good deal of his book asks questions of how we might make superintelligence—whether it comes in fifty years or five-hundred years—"nice",
congruent with our humanity. Bostrom sees this as a technical challenge
more than a political or philosophical one. It seems to me, though, that a
good deal of our own ethical framework, our sense of goodness, is based
on an experience and understanding of suffering, of our bodies. How
could a non-cellular intelligence ever "comprehend" that?

"There are a lot of things that machines can't understand currently
because they are not that smart," he says, "but once they become so,
I don't think there would be any special difficulty in understanding
human suffering and death." That understanding might be one way they
could be taught to respect human value, he says. "But it depends what
your ethical theory is. It might be more about respecting others' autonomy, or striving to achieve beautiful things together." Somehow, and
he has no idea how really, he thinks those things will need to be hard-
wired from the outset to avoid catastrophe. It is no good getting your owl
first then wondering how to train it. And with artificial systems already
superior to the best human intelligence in many discrete fields, a conversation about how that might be done is already overdue.

prima facie: based on the first impression; accepted as correct until proved otherwise.

The sense of intellectual urgency about these questions derives in part from what Bostrom calls an "epiphany experience", which occurred when he was in his teens. He found himself in 1989 in a library and picked up at random an anthology of nineteenth-century German philosophy, containing works by Nietzsche and Schopenhauer. Intrigued, he read the book in a nearby forest, in a clearing that he used to visit to be alone and write poetry. Almost immediately he experienced a dramatic sense of the possibilities of learning. Was it like a conversion experience?

"More an awakening," he says. "It felt like I had sleepwalked through 35 my life to that point and now I was aware of some wider world that I hadn't imagined."

Following first the leads and notes in the philosophy book, Bostrom set about educating himself in fast forward. He read feverishly, and in spare moments he painted and wrote poetry, eventually taking degrees in philosophy and mathematical logic at Gothenburg university, before completing a Ph.D. at the London School of Economics, and teaching at Yale.

Did he continue to paint and write?

"It seemed to me at some point that mathematical pursuit was more important," he says. "I felt the world already contained a lot of paintings and I wasn't convinced it needed a few more. Same could be said for poetry. But maybe it did need a few more ideas of how to navigate the future."

One of the areas in which AI is making advances is in its ability to compose music and create art, and even to write. Does he imagine that sphere too will quickly be colonised by a superintelligence, or will it be a last redoubt of the human?

"I don't buy the claim that the artificial composers currently can com- 40 pete with the great composers. Maybe for short bursts but not over a whole symphony. And with art, though it can be replicated, the activity itself has value. You would still paint for the sake of painting."

Authenticity, the man-made, becomes increasingly important?

"Yes and not just with art. If and when machines can do everything better than we can do, we would continue to do things because we enjoy doing them. If people play golf it is not because they need the ball to reside in successive holes efficiently, it is because they enjoy doing it. The more machines can do everything we can do the more attention we will give to these things that we value for their own sake."

Early in his intellectual journey, Bostrom did a few stints as a philosophical standup comic in order to improve his communication skills. Talking to him, and reading his work, an edge of knowing absurdity at the sheer scale of the problems is never completely absent from his arguments. The axes of daunting-looking graphs in his papers will be calibrated on closer inspection in terms of "endurable", "crushing" and "hellish." In his introduction to *Superintelligence*, the observation "Many of the points made in this book are probably wrong" typically leads to a footnote that reads: "I don't know which ones." Does he sometimes feel he is morphing into Douglas Adams?

"Sometimes the work does seem strange," he says. "Then from another point it seems strange that most of the world is completely oblivious to the most major things that are going to happen in the 21st century. Even people who talk about global warming never mention any threat posed by AI."

Because it would dilute their message?

"Maybe. At any time in history it seems to me there can only be one official global concern. Now it is climate change, or sometimes terrorism. When I grew up it was nuclear Armageddon. Then it was overpopulation. Some are more sensible than others, but it is really quite random."

> "Even people who talk about 45 global warming never mention any threat posed by AI."

Bostrom's passion is to attempt to apply some maths to that randomness. Does he think that concerns about AI will take over from global warming as a more imminent threat any time soon?

"I doubt it," he says. "It will come gradually and seamlessly without us really addressing it."

If we are going to look anywhere for its emergence, Google, which is throwing a good deal of its unprecedented resources at deep learning technology (not least with its purchase in 2014 of the British pioneer DeepMind) would seem a reasonable place to start. Google apparently has an AI ethics board to confront these questions, but no one knows who sits on it. Does Bostrom have faith in its "Don't be evil" mantra?

"There is certainly a culture among tech people that they want to feel 50 they are doing something that is not just to make money but that it has some positive social purpose. There is this idealism."

Can he help shape the direction of that idealism?

"It is not so much that one's own influence is important," he says. "Anyone who has a role in highlighting these arguments will be valuable. If the human condition really were to change fundamentally in our century, we find ourselves at a key juncture in history." And if Bostrom's more nihilistic° predictions are correct, we will have only one go at getting the nature of the new intelligence right.

---

nihilistic: rejecting all religious and moral principles in the belief that life is meaningless.

Last year Bostrom became a father. (Typically his marriage is conducted largely by Skype—his wife, a medical doctor, lives in Vancouver.) I wonder, before I go, if becoming a dad has changed his sense of the reality of these futuristic issues?

"Only in the sense that it emphasises this dual perspective, the positive and negative scenarios. This kind of intellectualizing, that our world might be transformed completely in this way, always seems a lot harder to credit at a personal level. I guess I allow both of these perspectives as much room as I can in my mind."

At the same time as he entertains those thought experiments, I suggest, half the world remains concerned where its next meal is coming from. Is the threat of superintelligence quite an elitist anxiety? Do most of us not think of the longest-term future because there is more than enough to worry about in the present? 55

"If it got to the point where the world was spending hundreds of billions of dollars on this stuff and nothing on more regular things then one might start to question it," he says. "If you look at all the things the world is spending money on, what we are doing is less than a pittance. You go to some random city and you travel from the airport to your hotel. Along the highway you see all these huge buildings for companies you have never heard of. Maybe they are designing a new publicity campaign for a razor blade. You drive past hundreds of these buildings. Any one of those has more resources than the total that humanity is spending on this field. We have half a floor of one building in Oxford, and there are two or three other groups doing what we do. So I think it is OK."

And how, I ask, might we as individuals and citizens think about and frame these risks to the existence of our species? Bostrom shrugs a little. "If we are thinking of this very long time frame, then it is clear that very small things we do now can make a significant difference in that future."

A recent paper of Bostrom's, which I read later at home, contains a little rule of thumb worth bearing in mind. Bostrom calls it "maxipok." It is based on the idea that "the objective of reducing existential risks should be a dominant consideration whenever we act out of an impersonal concern for humankind as a whole." What does maxipok involve? Trying to "maximize the probability of an 'OK outcome' where an OK outcome is any outcome that avoids existential catastrophe."

It certainly sounds worth a go.

Understanding the Text

1. Language shapes our perceptions. What if Bostrom's intelligence "explosion" were called something else? His use of the term leads directly into an analogy of children playing with a bomb. Imagine an alternate term for the same growth in intelligence. How would naming it differently remove some of the bias inherent in the term "explosion"?

2. Bostrom is a transhumanist and therefore is deeply invested in overcoming the limits of being human and human mortality. Review the sections of the text that discuss his transhumanism. How does he reconcile this approach to life with his concerns about AI?

3. Using Adams's text, define "maxipok." What steps might we take to reach "maxipok" with AI?

Reflection and Response

4. According to Adams, Bostrom "holds the two possibilities — the heaven and hell of our digital future — in uneasy opposition" (p. 88). How does he accomplish that balance?

5. Developing an ethical system for AI seems integral to avoiding the kinds of existential risks to humanity that concern Bostrom the most. How can we promote the development of such a system?

Making Connections

6. According to Adam Elkus ("Meet the Bots," p. 94), we don't have to wait for some superintelligence to be concerned; simple bots are just as troublesome — and dangerous. Synthesize his position with what Adams represents from Bostrom. How does Elkus illustrate the danger of any sort of artificial intelligence, even a simple one?

7. Adams asks, "Is the threat of superintelligence quite an elitist anxiety?" (p. 92). Extend Bostrom's answer to Adams's question by using Alan Turing ("Computing Machinery and Intelligence," p. 75), particularly since both Bostrom and Turing are well-respected, well-positioned, white, first world men. Is it a luxury to think about artificial intelligence when there is so much suffering in the world? Are these questions that instead must be answered for everyone's safety?

Meet the Bots

Adam Elkus

Adam Elkus, a doctoral student in computational social science at George Mason University, has published articles on technology, defense, and international security in *The Atlantic*, *Foreign Policy*, *Small Wars Journal*, and the *Armed Forces Journal*. He also served as a fellow in the Cybersecurity Initiative of the centrist think tank New America. Elkus wrote this essay for *Slate* in 2015 as part of its Future Tense series, a collaboration between *Slate*, New America, and Arizona State University. As part of that series, Elkus has also published articles on robots, artificial intelligence, and Amazon's Echo device.

The day that science fiction writers have feared for so long has finally come—the machines have risen up. There is nowhere you can run and nowhere you can hide. The software "bot" onslaught is here, and every *Homo sapien* is a target of the limitless legions of unceasing, unemotional, and untiring automatons. Resistance is futile, silly human—the bots are on the march. To get a scale of the size of the automated army arrayed against us, consider that a 2014 story reported that one-third of all web traffic is considered to be fake. The bots are pretending to be us.

Bots, like rats, have colonized an astounding range of environments. Play online video games? That dude with seemingly superhuman reflexes that keeps pwning° you is probably a bot. Go on the online dating platform Tinder and you will be targeted by wave after wave of these rapacious robotic creatures as you search for love and companionship. Want to have a conversation with people on Twitter? Some of them are probably not human. Have the temerity to go up against the Kremlin or even the Mexican government with an opposing point of view? Call John Connor, because here come the bots—bots that try to relentlessly remind you of things favorable to the regime, bots that try to stop protests, and many other automated instruments of political repression. And, if that weren't enough, hackers may use bots to automate a variety of dastardly deeds.

Tesla's Elon Musk and the famous astrophysicist Stephen Hawking have become standard-bearers for the growing fear over artificial intelligence—but perhaps the most fascinating element here is that their warnings focus on hypothetical malicious automatons while ignoring real ones. Musk, in a recent interview, mused about whether we would be lucky

pwning: utterly defeating (especially in video games).

if future robots enslaved us as pets. Yet today humankind is imperiled by a different type of bot onslaught from which there is no escaping, and Musk has not sounded the alarm. Perhaps that is due to the fact that the artificial menace behind this rise of the machines is not really anything we would consider to be "artificial intelligence." Instead, to survey the bot armies marching across the internet is to marvel at the power of artificial stupidity. Despite bots' crudely coded, insectoid simplicity, they have managed to make a lot of people's live miserable.

So what's a bot? Despite the name *bot*, these nonhuman internet entities are not (contra to stock art in tech articles), literally robots typing on keyboards with metallic fingers. They are crude computer programs, ably defined by James Gleick in a *New York Review of Books* piece:

> *It's understood now that, beside what we call the "real world," we inhabit a variety of virtual worlds. Take Twitter. Or the Twitterverse. Twittersphere. You may think it's a stretch to call this a "world," but in many ways it has become a toy universe, populated by millions, most of whom resemble humans and may even, in their day jobs, be humans. But increasing numbers of Twitterers don't even pretend to be human. Or worse, do pretend, when they are actually bots. "Bot" is of course short for robot. And bots are very, very tiny, skeletal, incapable robots—usually little more than a few crude lines of computer code. The scary thing is how easily we can be fooled.*

So why is it called a "bot" despite the fact that it is far simpler than 5 most real-world robots, which have complex software architectures? To answer this question is to go to some foundational debates about what machine intelligence really represents. In their textbook on artificial intelligence, David Poole and Alan Mackworth delineate several approaches to building artificial agents. One is to make a complex computer program that functions well in an environment simplified for the agent. For example, a factory robot can do well in its industrial home but might very well be lost outside that context. The other is to make a simple, buglike agent with limited abilities to reason and act but the ability to function in a complex and interactive environment. Many bio-inspired robots fit this design paradigm.

The simplest way to understand a bot, as computer security researcher David Geer notes, is as an "agent for a user or another program." Although bots have a lot in common with Poole and Mackworth's second, agent design paradigm, it is also fair to say that they sidestep artificial intelligence and its debates altogether. If artificial intelligences are surprisingly primitive and fragile, difficult to generalize to new environments, and based on a contradictory set of scientific assumptions, bots have no such problems. A.I. programs are the majestic lions and eagles of the artificial ecosystem, bots the disgusting yet evolutionarily successful cockroaches and termites. Many bots amount to automatic control programs roughly as sophisticated as a thermostat. Interested readers who want to make themselves a Reddit bot to help them read and reply to posts, for example, may consult this handy guide in the Python scripting language. But not all bots are even programmed in a high-level programming language. Take many game bots, for example. Third-party bots for the game *Counter-Strike: Global Offensive* just amount to configuration files that customize existing game opponents, and you can write bots for many games with the Windows program AutoHotkey.

Bots are easy to make, require a minimum of programming experience and software engineering knowledge, and can be tremendously profitable. And that is a large part of what makes botting serious business. This may seem like an exaggeration, given how frivolous Tinder bots, Twitter auto-trolls, and gamebots may seem. For example, I like to break up the monotony of grad school by trolling a Twitter bot by telling it to do better at passing its Turing test. I've even facetiously suggested setting up a bot school with fellow *Slate* Future Tense contributor Miles Brundage to help it gain some "intelligence."

However, the toll that bots have exacted is no laughing matter. The Gameover Zeus botnet, for example, cost its small-business targets about $100 million in losses in the United States and infected about 1 million computers worldwide. And when the aim is using bots to suppress political speech, the damage is difficult to quantify but meaningful all the same. The trouble with bots lies in the implications of their capacity to fool, and their sheer numbers.

When the filmmakers behind the new artificial intelligence movie *Ex Machina* went to the drawing board for an attention-grabbing guerrilla ad campaign to promote their flick, they didn't build a robot of their own. Instead, they made a Tinder bot. Lonely SXSW festivalgoers on the online dating platform interacted with an alluring woman who asked them what it meant to be human . . . only to find out that "she" was a scripted computer program with the face of *Ex Machina*'s lead actress preprogrammed to flirt with them. While scripted chatbots are as old as A.I. itself, this fake SXSW temptress is emblematic of a larger, worrying trend.

> "Bots succeed or fail based on how well their creators understand the art of creating the "illusion of intelligence.""

Skilled Tinder bot programmers, for example, can fool gullible users by designing and scripting their bots to mimic the proverbial girl next door. Bots have suggestive pictures of normal girls a male Tinder user would run across, respond to messages relatively slowly to mimic a real-world online dating interaction, and incorporate deceptively real features of dating site conversation, such as compliments and flirting, to entice would-be suitors to send them phone texts. Bots succeed or fail based on how well their creators understand the art of creating the "illusion of intelligence," a kind of computational con game that uses the least "intelligent" of artificial agents to nonetheless project humanity to web surfers going about their business.

What's the harm, beyond broken hearts? Bot scammers on dating sites are out to directly get money from lovesick targets or utilize them to install malware on unsuspecting users' computers. Spammers have proved remarkably creative and adaptive. Perhaps the most pernicious form of Tinder-botting is "sextortion," the act of luring unsuspecting users into webcam sessions with a seemingly innocent hottie only to be recorded and blackmailed. Unless they pay up, the fraudster will ensure the video is either posted online or sent directly to their loved ones.

Criminal botting, however, goes far beyond just online dating sites; bots are a time-honored hacker tool. You're probably familiar with *botnets*, groups of bots networked together to simultaneously execute a distributed denial-of-service attack by sending large numbers of messages to a target system. But that doesn't scratch the surface of the various malicious means available to bot programmers. Bots can generate new encryption to fool security software, be equipped with programmable attack mechanisms, and cooperate with one another in a distributed system to generate complex attacks. Bots may even be combined with computer worms to create hybrid threats. While bots do not replicate or spread on their own, they may piggyback off worms to do so. The 2004 Witty worm, which infected and crashed tens of thousands of servers, is believed to have been launched by a botnet.

But the problematic implications of bots are by no means limited to the criminal domain. Since current Mexican President Enrique Peña Nieto's election, the Mexican government, for example, has used swarms of bots to censor political discourse. Over the last year in particular, online activism campaigns against the unpopular president disappeared after the Mexican government unleashed bots to crowd out the protest hashtag #YaSeQueNoAplauden as a trending topic. If online campaigns rely on critical mass, judicious deployment of large groups of bots can squash them.

Ukrainian Facebook users also recently requested that Facebook CEO Mark Zuckerberg do something about a "bot army" of Kremlin-controlled bots that spam Facebook with complaints about pro-Ukraine activists' Facebook pages. As a result, even though they're not violating FB's terms of service, activists sometimes find their pages banned. In general, Russia has proved particularly adept at marrying the illusory humanity of spambots and the brute force attack of bot swarms in its own propaganda campaigns. A recent social network analysis of the Kremlin's bot ecology revealed an extensive array of bots disguised as real users that took to Twitter in an attempt to sway the narrative mere hours after Russian opposition dissident Boris Nemtsov was shot under suspicious circumstances.

While it is important to have those, like philosopher Nick Bostrom   15 or the Future of Life Institute, that plan ahead for both near- and long-term policy contingencies arising from artificial intelligence, it speaks volumes that the real-world bot onslaught seems secondary to strange and impossibly convoluted scenarios like Roko's Basilisk. Not all bots are bad; there's a curious and playful side to bot-making seen in ingenious hacks like Twitch Plays Pokémon and "What If" experiments like *Civilization* botfights. Bots have also, amusingly enough, been incorporated into the time-honored battle to get a reservation at high-end San Francisco restaurants. One may also protest with activist bots preprogrammed to fight the power. But there is also no mistaking the power of bots to harm, whether the aim is scamming, political repression, or criminal bothacking.

Let us not mince words—we are being besieged by the bot hordes. Who can save humanity from the bot menace? All is not lost; the challenge of bot detection drives some of the most interesting research in computer science. This has resulted in tools like Indiana University's 2014 BotOrNot bot spotter. But bot finding is an arms race; just when companies think they've outwitted the botters, the bots adapt. Unfortunately, our twilight struggle against the bots will likely be a long one.

Understanding the Text

1. Elkus uses a number of animal metaphors to describe bots and other artificial intelligences. Analyze the impact of these metaphors. How does his choice of metaphor shape his argument and the way his readers respond to it?

2. Elkus also uses a number of military metaphors in this essay. Extend these metaphors to complicate Elkus's argument. Are bots the enemy or just a weapon? What are the two sides in this war, and what does each side want? Is a truce possible? What would that look like?

Reflection and Response

3. Elkus claims that bots are able to "project humanity to web surfers" (p. 97). If humanity is so easily imitated, what does that say about us? Why are we so easily fooled? What does it take to be "human"?

4. How can we beat the bots? Work from Elkus's essay to extrapolate strategies we can use to overcome this challenge. Should it take place through policies on social media sites like Tinder or Twitter? Should we act differently online? Can educating internet users avoid the problem? Your work on the military metaphor in question 2 might also be useful in making your response.

Making Connections

5. Ray Kurzweil ("What Is AI, Anyway?," p. 62) offers several definitions of artificial intelligence. Apply these definitions to Elkus's discussion of bots. How would we need to modify our definition of "artificial intelligence" to account for bots?

6. Elkus suggests that bots represent not artificial intelligence, but "artificial stupidity" (p. 95). Working from Elkus's text, develop a definition of this term and then apply this concept to one of the other readings in this chapter. Is artificial stupidity simply a different kind of artificial intelligence? What aspects of AI does it illuminate that might otherwise be obscured?

The Dark Secret at the Heart of AI

Will Knight

Will Knight is the senior editor for artificial intelligence at *MIT Technology Review*. Previously, he wrote for *New Scientist* magazine. Knight's work focuses on robotics, machine learning, neural networks, deep learning, and automated driving. *MIT Technology Review*, where this essay was published, is a magazine owned by, but independent of, the Massachusetts Institute of Technology, where it has been published since 1899.

Last year, a strange self-driving car was released onto the quiet roads of Monmouth County, New Jersey. The experimental vehicle, developed by researchers at the chip maker Nvidia, didn't look different from other autonomous cars, but it was unlike anything demonstrated by Google, Tesla, or General Motors, and it showed the rising power of artificial intelligence. The car didn't follow a single instruction provided by an engineer or programmer. Instead, it relied entirely on an algorithm that had taught itself to drive by watching a human do it.

Getting a car to drive this way was an impressive feat. But it's also a bit unsettling, since it isn't completely clear how the car makes its decisions. Information from the vehicle's sensors goes straight into a huge network of artificial neurons that process the data and then deliver the commands required to operate the steering wheel, the brakes, and other systems. The result seems to match the responses you'd expect from a human driver. But what if one day it did something unexpected—crashed into a tree, or sat at a green light? As things stand now, it might be difficult to find out why. The system is so complicated that even the engineers who designed it may struggle to isolate the reason for any single action. And you can't ask it: there is no obvious way to design such a system so that it could always explain why it did what it did.

The mysterious mind of this vehicle points to a looming issue with artificial intelligence. The car's underlying AI technology, known as deep learning, has proved very powerful at solving problems in recent years, and it has been widely deployed for tasks like image captioning, voice recognition, and language translation. There is now hope that the same techniques will be able to diagnose deadly diseases, make million-dollar trading decisions, and do countless other things to transform whole industries.

But this won't happen—or shouldn't happen—unless we find ways of making techniques like deep learning more understandable to their creators and accountable to their users. Otherwise it will be hard to predict when failures might occur—and it's inevitable they will. That's one reason Nvidia's car is still experimental.

Already, mathematical models are being used to help determine who 5
makes parole, who's approved for a loan, and who gets hired for a job.
If you could get access to these mathematical models, it would be possible to understand their reasoning. But banks, the military, employers,
and others are now turning their attention to more complex
machine-learning approaches that could make automated decision-
making altogether inscrutable. Deep learning, the most common of
these approaches, represents a fundamentally different way to program
computers. "It is a problem that is already relevant, and it's going to be
much more relevant in the future," says Tommi Jaakkola, a professor at
MIT who works on applications of machine learning. "Whether it's an
investment decision, a medical decision, or maybe a military decision,
you don't want to just rely on a 'black box' method."

There's already an argument that
being able to interrogate an AI system
about how it reached its conclusions is a
fundamental legal right. Starting in the
summer of 2018, the European Union
may require that companies be able to
give users an explanation for decisions that automated systems reach.
This might be impossible, even for systems that seem relatively simple
on the surface, such as the apps and websites that use deep learning to
serve ads or recommend songs. The computers that run those services
have programmed themselves, and they have done it in ways we cannot understand. Even the engineers who build these apps cannot fully
explain their behavior.

> "Deep learning represents a fundamentally different way to program computers."

This raises mind-boggling questions. As the technology advances, we
might soon cross some threshold beyond which using AI requires a leap
of faith. Sure, we humans can't always truly explain our thought processes
either—but we find ways to intuitively trust and gauge people. Will that
also be possible with machines that think and make decisions differently
from the way a human would? We've never before built machines that
operate in ways their creators don't understand. How well can we expect
to communicate—and get along with—intelligent machines that could
be unpredictable and inscrutable? These questions took me on a journey
to the bleeding edge of research on AI algorithms, from Google to Apple
and many places in between, including a meeting with one of the great
philosophers of our time.

In 2015, a research group at Mount Sinai Hospital in New York was
inspired to apply deep learning to the hospital's vast database of patient
records. This data set features hundreds of variables on patients, drawn
from their test results, doctor visits, and so on. The resulting program,

Adam Ferriss's Google DeepDream artwork.
Adam Ferriss

which the researchers named Deep Patient, was trained using data from about 700,000 individuals, and when tested on new records, it proved incredibly good at predicting disease. Without any expert instruction, Deep Patient had discovered patterns hidden in the hospital data that seemed to indicate when people were on the way to a wide range of ailments, including cancer of the liver. There are a lot of methods that are "pretty good" at predicting disease from a patient's records, says Joel Dudley, who leads the Mount Sinai team. But, he adds, "this was just way better."

At the same time, Deep Patient is a bit puzzling. It appears to antici-pate the onset of psychiatric disorders like schizophrenia surprisingly well. But since schizophrenia is notoriously difficult for physicians to predict, Dudley wondered how this was possible. He still doesn't know. The new tool offers no clue as to how it does this. If something like Deep Patient is actually going to help doctors, it will ideally give them the rationale for its prediction, to reassure them that it is accurate and to justify, say, a change in the drugs someone is being prescribed. "We can build these models," Dudley says ruefully, "but we don't know how they work."

Artificial intelligence hasn't always been this way. From the outset, there were two schools of thought regarding how understandable, or explainable, AI ought to be. Many thought it made the most sense to build machines that reasoned according to rules and logic, making their inner workings transparent to anyone who cared to examine some code. Others felt that intelligence would more easily emerge if machines took inspira-tion from biology, and learned by observing and experiencing. This meant turning computer programming on its head. Instead of a programmer writ-ing the commands to solve a problem, the program generates its own algo-rithm based on example data and a desired output. The machine-learning techniques that would later evolve into today's most powerful AI systems followed the latter path: the machine essentially programs itself.

At first this approach was of limited practical use, and in the 1960s and '70s it remained largely confined to the fringes of the field. Then the computerization of many industries and the emergence of large data sets renewed interest. That inspired the development of more powerful machine-learning techniques, especially new versions of one known as the artificial neural network. By the 1990s, neural networks could auto-matically digitize handwritten characters.

But it was not until the start of this decade, after several clever tweaks and refinements, that very large—or "deep"—neural networks demon-strated dramatic improvements in automated perception. Deep learning is responsible for today's explosion of AI. It has given computers extraor-dinary powers, like the ability to recognize spoken words almost as well as a person could, a skill too complex to code into the machine by hand. Deep learning has transformed computer vision and dramatically improved machine translation. It is now being used to guide all sorts of key decisions in medicine, finance, manufacturing—and beyond.

The workings of any machine-learning technology are inherently more opaque, even to computer scientists, than a hand-coded system. This is not to say that all future AI techniques will be equally unknow-able. But by its nature, deep learning is a particularly dark black box.

You can't just look inside a deep neural network to see how it works. A network's reasoning is embedded in the behavior of thousands of

Adam Ferriss's Google DeepDream artwork.
Adam Ferriss

simulated neurons, arranged into dozens or even hundreds of intricately interconnected layers. The neurons in the first layer each receive an input, like the intensity of a pixel in an image, and then perform a calculation before outputting a new signal. These outputs are fed, in a complex web, to the neurons in the next layer, and so on, until an overall output is produced. Plus, there is a process known as back-propagation that tweaks the calculations of individual neurons in a way that lets the network learn to produce a desired output.

The many layers in a deep network enable it to recognize things at   15
different levels of abstraction. In a system designed to recognize dogs, for
instance, the lower layers recognize simple things like outlines or color;
higher layers recognize more complex stuff like fur or eyes; and the top-
most layer identifies it all as a dog. The same approach can be applied,
roughly speaking, to other inputs that lead a machine to teach itself: the
sounds that make up words in speech, the letters and words that create
sentences in text, or the steering-wheel movements required for driving.

Ingenious strategies have been used to try to capture and thus explain
in more detail what's happening in such systems. In 2015, researchers at
Google modified a deep-learning-based image recognition algorithm so
that instead of spotting objects in photos, it would generate or modify
them. By effectively running the algorithm in reverse, they could discover
the features the program uses to recognize, say, a bird or building. The
resulting images, produced by a project known as DeepDream, showed
grotesque, alien-like animals emerging from clouds and plants, and hal-
lucinatory pagodas blooming across forests and mountain ranges. The
images proved that deep learning need not be entirely inscrutable; they
revealed that the algorithms home in on familiar visual features like a
bird's beak or feathers. But the images also hinted at how different deep
learning is from human perception, in that it might make something out
of an artifact that we would know to ignore. Google researchers noted
that when its algorithm generated images of a dumbbell, it also generated a human arm holding it. The machine had concluded that an arm
was part of the thing.

Further progress has been made using ideas borrowed from neuroscience and cognitive science. A team led by Jeff Clune, an assistant
professor at the University of Wyoming, has employed the AI equivalent
of optical illusions to test deep neural networks. In 2015, Clune's group
showed how certain images could fool such a network into perceiving
things that aren't there, because the images exploit the low-level patterns
the system searches for. One of Clune's collaborators, Jason Yosinski, also
built a tool that acts like a probe stuck into a brain. His tool targets any
neuron in the middle of the network and searches for the image that
activates it the most. The images that turn up are abstract (imagine an
impressionistic take on a flamingo or a school bus), highlighting the
mysterious nature of the machine's perceptual abilities.

We need more than a glimpse of AI's thinking, however, and there is
no easy solution. It is the interplay of calculations inside a deep neural
network that is crucial to higher-level pattern recognition and complex
decision-making, but those calculations are a quagmire of mathematical
functions and variables. "If you had a very small neural network, you

might be able to understand it," Jaakkola says. "But once it becomes very large, and it has thousands of units per layer and maybe hundreds of layers, then it becomes quite un-understandable."

In the office next to Jaakkola is Regina Barzilay, an MIT professor who is determined to apply machine learning to medicine. She was diagnosed with breast cancer a couple of years ago, at age 43. The diagnosis was shocking in itself, but Barzilay was also dismayed that cutting-edge statistical and machine-learning methods were not being used to help with oncological research or to guide patient treatment. She says AI has huge potential to revolutionize medicine, but realizing that potential will mean going beyond just medical records. She envisions using more of the raw data that she says is currently underutilized: "imaging data, pathology data, all this information."

After she finished cancer treatment last year, Barzilay and her stu- 20 dents began working with doctors at Massachusetts General Hospital to develop a system capable of mining pathology reports to identify patients with specific clinical characteristics that researchers might want to study. However, Barzilay understood that the system would need to explain its reasoning. So, together with Jaakkola and a student, she added a step: the system extracts and highlights snippets of text that are representative of a pattern it has discovered. Barzilay and her students are also developing a deep-learning algorithm capable of finding early signs of breast cancer in mammogram images, and they aim to give this system some ability to explain its reasoning, too. "You really need to have a loop where the machine and the human collaborate," Barzilay says.

The U.S. military is pouring billions into projects that will use machine learning to pilot vehicles and aircraft, identify targets, and help analysts sift through huge piles of intelligence data. Here more than anywhere else, even more than in medicine, there is little room for algorithmic mystery, and the Department of Defense has identified explainability as a key stumbling block.

David Gunning, a program manager at the Defense Advanced Research Projects Agency, is overseeing the aptly named Explainable Artificial Intelligence program. A silver-haired veteran of the agency who previously oversaw the DARPA project that eventually led to the creation of Siri, Gunning says automation is creeping into countless areas of the military. Intelligence analysts are testing machine learning as a way of identifying patterns in vast amounts of surveillance data. Many autonomous ground vehicles and aircraft are being developed and tested. But soldiers probably won't feel comfortable in a robotic tank that doesn't explain itself to them, and analysts will be reluctant to act on information without some reasoning. "It's often the nature of these machine-learning systems that they produce a lot of false alarms, so an intel analyst really needs extra help to understand why a recommendation was made," Gunning says.

This March, DARPA chose 13 projects from academia and industry for funding under Gunning's program. Some of them could build on work led by Carlos Guestrin, a professor at the University of Washington. He and his colleagues have developed a way for machine-learning systems to provide a rationale for their outputs. Essentially, under this method a computer automatically finds a few examples from a data set and serves them up in a short explanation. A system designed to classify an e-mail message as coming from a terrorist, for example, might use many millions of messages in its training and decision-making. But using the Washington team's approach, it could highlight certain keywords found in a message. Guestrin's group has also devised ways for image recognition systems to hint at their reasoning by highlighting the parts of an image that were most significant.

One drawback to this approach and others like it, such as Barzilay's, is that the explanations provided will always be simplified, meaning some vital information may be lost along the way. "We haven't achieved the whole dream, which is where AI has a conversation with you, and it is able to explain," says Guestrin. "We're a long way from having truly interpretable AI."

It doesn't have to be a high-stakes situation like cancer diagnosis or military maneuvers for this to become an issue. Knowing AI's reasoning is also going to be crucial if the technology is to become a common and useful part of our daily lives. Tom Gruber, who leads the Siri team at Apple, says explainability is a key consideration for his team as it tries to make Siri a smarter and more capable virtual assistant. Gruber wouldn't discuss specific plans for Siri's future, but it's easy to imagine that if you receive a restaurant recommendation from Siri, you'll want to know what the reasoning was. Ruslan Salakhutdinov, director of AI research at Apple and an associate professor at Carnegie Mellon University, sees explainability as the core of the evolving relationship between humans and intelligent machines. "It's going to introduce trust," he says.

Just as many aspects of human behavior are impossible to explain in detail, perhaps it won't be possible for AI to explain everything it does. "Even if somebody can give you a reasonable-sounding explanation [for his or her actions], it probably is incomplete, and the same could very well be true for AI," says Clune, of the University of Wyoming. "It might just be part of the nature of intelligence that only part of it is exposed to rational explanation. Some of it is just instinctual, or subconscious, or inscrutable."

Adam Ferriss's Google DeepDream artwork.

Adam Ferriss

If that's so, then at some stage we may have to simply trust AI's judgment or do without using it. Likewise, that judgment will have to incorporate social intelligence. Just as society is built upon a contract of expected behavior, we will need to design AI systems to respect and fit with our social norms. If we are to create robot tanks and other killing machines, it is important that their decision-making be consistent with our ethical judgments.

To probe these metaphysical concepts, I went to Tufts University to meet with Daniel Dennett, a renowned philosopher and cognitive scientist who studies consciousness and the mind. A chapter of Dennett's latest book, *From Bacteria to Bach and Back*, an encyclopedic treatise on consciousness, suggests that a natural part of the evolution of intelligence itself is the creation of systems capable of performing tasks their creators do not know how to do. "The question is, what accommodations do we have to make to do this wisely—what standards do we demand of them, and of ourselves?" he tells me in his cluttered office on the university's idyllic campus.

He also has a word of warning about the quest for explainability. "I think by all means if we're going to use these things and rely on them, then let's get as firm a grip on how and why they're giving us the answers as possible," he says. But since there may be no perfect answer, we should be as cautious of AI explanations as we are of each other's—no matter how clever a machine seems. "If it can't do better than us at explaining what it's doing," he says, "then don't trust it."

Understanding the Text

1. What are the benefits of deep learning artificial intelligence, and what are the risks? Review Knight's essay to locate places where he discusses each and then summarize both the advantages and disadvantages of using neural networks in AI.

2. The word "inscrutable" appears a surprising number of times in this piece. What does this word mean, and how does it apply to Knight's overall argument?

Reflection and Response

3. Given the challenges Knight describes, but given, too, the potential of deep learning's abilities to solve problems, automate processes, and improve quality of life, how should we proceed? What steps are necessary to minimize risks? What strategies have researchers already implemented, and can they be expanded to resolve the problems with neural networks?

4. Part of what's at stake in deep learning is our ability to trust AI, which is to say our ability to form a relationship with it. What elements are necessary for us to create such a relationship? What role does communication or explainability play in creating trust in this kind of relationship?

Making Connections

5. One of the deep learning projects that Knight examines is Google's DeepDream. Cade Metz ("Google's Artificial Brain Is Pumping Out Trippy — and Pricey — Art," p. 116) examines DeepDream in more detail. Synthesize these two essays to suggest the relationship between intelligence and creativity. Is AI creative? What kind of creativity do programmers need to create deep learning? What role does each of these qualities play in being human, and what does that say about the future of AI?

6. Knight discusses some of the military applications of deep learning. This discussion recalls Adam Elkus's ("Meet the Bots," p. 94) use of military terminology in discussing bots. Working from both their essays, discuss the challenges we must overcome before further implementing military use of artificial intelligence.

Alexa, Siri, Sophia: Deconstructing AI's Subliminal Gender Bias

Allie Shaw

Allie Shaw is a freelance writer specializing in consumer technology, connectivity, and lifestyle topics, with bylines at a variety of publications. This particular essay was published in 2019 on SWAAY, an online journal highlighting the voices of women in an effort to shift cultural narratives and promote meaningful conversation. SWAAY was founded by Iman Oubou, an entrepreneur whose career spans science and beauty pageants.

For women in artificial intelligence research, gender bias is a major barrier to success. Silicon Valley's gender problem isn't just a social justice issue however. Should the top positions in tech continue to go to men only, the tech world could be stifling its own capacity for innovation and threatening the future of AI research. The world's top female researchers are redefining the field and enacting a sea-change in the way the AI industry think about gender.

The Tech World's Gender Problem

Gender bias in the tech industry dates back to its inception. The historically male-dominated industry has long possessed an almost cult-like meritocracy[9], where employees are often encouraged to devote their entire lives to the success of the product. This creates an environment where discriminatory practices remain pervasive under the guise of a reward system; employees outside the standard masculine mold are often denied the same pay or promotion pathways as male employees, even when they meet or exceed job expectations.

In 2015, tech investor Trae Vassallo and several colleagues coauthored a survey titled "The Elephant in the Valley." The survey investigated the experiences of female leaders and innovators in the tech industry, and the results were bleak; 84 percent of interviewees were told they were "too aggressive," 66 percent experienced exclusionary practices, and a shocking 60 percent experienced sexual harassment. Just 18 percent of undergraduates in computer science in 2011 were women, down from 37 percent in 1985.

meritocracy: the holding of power by people selected on the basis of their ability.

Gender Bias in Artificial Intelligence

Like the rest of the tech industry, AI's gender bias is similarly pervasive. The artificial intelligence sector is expected to grow from $21 billion to $190 billion between 2018 and 2025, and the employment demographic is overwhelmingly male. The field has had a difficult time developing its female workforce, potentially due to the nature of AI research itself.

"Research has become very narrowly focused on solving technical 5 problems and not on the big questions," says Marie desJardins, Professor of Computer Science at the University of Maryland. Also, desJardins notes the distance between the work being done in AI and the betterment of society in general. That gap could be turning women away from the field, since women tend to value their work's contribution to their community higher than men.

AI's diversity issues affect women as well as other gender minorities like transgender and non-binary individuals, and these diversity issues also continue beyond gender. "Cultural diversity is big too," says Heather Knight, founder of Marilyn Monrobot Labs in New York City. Racial underrepresentation in the tech world compounds issues for women from minority ethnic groups. Gender and racial bias in AI are significant enough to have an effect on the way the algorithms themselves are developed, which could have lasting consequences for society if the problem isn't met head-on.

AI Algorithms Reflect Gender Bias

If researchers use biased datasets to train AIs, gender bias may become embedded in the technology itself. A study conducted on image-recognition software in 2016 found patterns that reinforced gender stereotypes. When asked to associate images with either men or women, the algorithm consistently linked women to images of kitchens, reflecting or exaggerating the gender biases it perceived.

Since the 100,000 images used were collected broadly from the web, biases in media were reflected in the AI's analysis. In a similar case, Microsoft's conversational AI "Tay" took in data from Twitter conversations and began repeating racist and misogynist phrases in less than twenty-four hours.

AIs will need to be closely managed to avoid mirroring the gender biases present in today's society.

Biases in Technology and Media

The link between gender discrimination and artificial intelligence doesn't 10 end in employment statistics. Gender bias is implicit in AI itself. "There's a clear bias in the way women are depicted in science fiction," says Alex Haslam, media relations specialist for HowtoWatch.com. "AIs are overwhelmingly female, and are often depicted as dangerous."

Many critics have also found it problematic that almost every digital assistant uses a female name and voice. Siri, Google Assistant, Cortana, and Alexa all reinforce the stereotype of the female administrator. "It's much easier to find a female voice that everyone likes than a male voice that everyone likes," Stanford communications professor Clifford Nass tells CNN. Whether psychological or cultural, the presence of female AIs helps these stereotypes persist.

> "Gender bias is implicit in AI itself."

Women Shaping the Future of AI

New efforts to close the gender gap in the sciences are charting a new course for those who have often been marginalized in the AI industry. Female professors, researchers, investors, and scientists are tackling gender bias in AI using innovative applications of technology, education, and more than a little common sense.

"The field of AI has traditionally been focused on computational intelligence, not on social or emotional intelligence," explains Rana el Kaliouby, cofounder of the AI research firm Affectiva. Kaliouby and other AI experts are looking to develop a social conscience for the AI algorithms of tomorrow, embedding moral and ethical principles into the technology.

Other female leaders in the AI field are addressing enrollment issues by designing education programs specifically for young girls. Millions of individuals have enrolled in AI and machine learning courses through programs like Coursera, with disadvantaged or underrepresented groups reporting the most benefit.

Addressing Gender Bias Through AI Technology

The incredible capacity of artificial intelligence is also addressing gender bias in society directly. A new AI algorithm developed by Google and The Geena Davis Institute on Gender in Media uses AI to detect male and female faces in popular films. The AI algorithm logs screen-time and speaking time for characters of different genders.

In the top films of the past three years, the algorithm found discouraging gaps; female characters received roughly half of the screen and speaking time of male characters. In the future, this data could assist filmmakers in avoiding techniques or casting selections that reinforce biases, encouraging stronger gender diversity in film.

15

Conclusion

The embedded nature of gender bias in today's society makes progress towards equality difficult, but burgeoning fields like artificial intelligence have a higher potential for social progress. Top computer scientists and AI experts have turned their attention to addressing gender bias in AI. If artificial intelligence lives up to its expectations as a game-changing technology, a more socially responsible foundation today could have a big influence on our future.

Understanding the Text

1. Shaw explores the problem of gender bias in artificial intelligence at a number of levels, ranging from jobs in the industry to the structure and perception of AI itself. Using PowerPoint or some other presentation software, summarize Shaw's arguments. Consider how aspects of your presentation, including fonts, colors, transitions, and images, can enhance Shaw's argument.

2. What strategies might we pursue to address this gender bias? Begin with the strategies Shaw presents and then expand them with your own ideas.

Reflection and Response

3. Shaw looks at the default voice of apps and devices like Alexa and Siri. Users can, however, make some changes on many devices. For example, you can select a different key word for Amazon's devices, such as "Computer," "Amazon," or "Echo." Similarly, you can select a different voice for Apple's Siri, male or female, Australian, British, Irish, South African, or American. How might enacting any of these changes intervene in gender bias? What other kinds of biases remain, even within these selections?

4. Shaw briefly mentions the impact of other biases, including the impact of gender bias on transgender and nonbinary people as well as separate cultural and racial bias in AI. Expand on her work by unearthing some of the biases you see in your use of AI, ranging from automatic translation programs to virtual and digital assistants to image tagging programs.

5. Shaw quotes Rana el Kaliouby, who suggests that women bring "social or emotional intelligence" to AI (p. 113). Complicate el Kaliouby's statement and Shaw's implicit endorsement of it. Can't women also participate in "computational intelligence" (p. 113)? How does assigning social and emotional intelligence along gender lines reinforce existing stereotypes? What other kinds of intelligence might we bring to AI? If you've worked in Chapters 3 or 4, you might want to bring your insights from there to your response.

Making Connections

6. Gender bias, Shaw suggests, goes back to the very beginning of the technology industry, but does it go back to the beginning of artificial intelligence as well? Review Alan Turing's essay ("Computing Machinery and Intelligence," p. 75) with Shaw's observations in mind. Does Turing reflect a strong gender bias? Does the "Turing test" for AI reflect a gender bias?

7. Nick Bostrom, in Tim Adams's profile ("Like Children Playing with a Bomb," p. 85), discusses any number of catastrophic dangers from AI. How might gender bias be even more dangerous? Synthesize Shaw's essay with Bostrom's concerns. How might subtle biases, like the one around gender, do more damage than an outright destructive AI?

Google's Artificial Brain Is Pumping Out Trippy—and Pricey—Art

Cade Metz

Cade Metz is journalist with the *New York Times*, where he writes on technology topics ranging from artificial intelligence to automated cars to robotics. He has also written for *PC Magazine* and *The Register*. Currently, Metz is working on a book on AI; he is also the author of a number of plays. This selection is from his time as a writer for *Wired*, a magazine that focuses on the impact that emerging technologies have on our world.

On Friday evening, inside an old-movie-house-cum-art-gallery at the heart of San Francisco's Mission district, Google graphics guru Blaise Agüera y Arcas delivered a speech to an audience of about eight hundred geek hipsters.

He spoke alongside a series of images projected onto the wall that once held a movie screen, and at one point, he showed off a nearly 500-year-old double portrait by German Renaissance painter Hans Holbein. The portrait includes a strangely distorted image of a human skull, and as Agüera y Arcas explained, it's unlikely that Holbein painted this by hand. He almost certainly used mirrors or lenses to project the image of a skull onto a canvas before tracing its outline. "He was using state-of-the-art technologies," Agüera y Arcas told his audience.

His point was that we've been using technology to create art for centuries—that the present isn't all that different from the past. It was his way of introducing the gallery's latest exhibit, in which every work is the product of artificial neural networks—networks of computer hardware and software that approximate the web of neurons in the human brain. Last year, researchers at Google created a new kind of art using neural nets, and this weekend, the tech giant put this machine-generated imagery on display in a two-day exhibit that raised roughly $84,000 for the Gray Area Foundation for the Arts, a San Francisco nonprofit devoted to the confluence of art and tech.

The night was one of those uniquely hip yet wonderfully geeky Silicon Valley scenes. "Look! There's Clay Bavor, the head of Google's suddenly enormous virtual reality project." "There's TechCrunch's Josh Constine!" "And there's MG Siegler, who used to write for TechCrunch but now, um, goes to neural network art shows. Or, at least, I think that's him." But it was also a night to reflect on the rapid and unceasing rise of artificial intelligence. Technology has now reached the point where neural networks are not only driving the Google search engine, but spitting out art for which some people will pay serious money.

For Agüera y Arcas, this is just a natural progression—part of the 5 traditional that extends through Hans Holbein and back to, well, the first art ever produced. For others, it's a rather exciting novelty. "This is the first time I've seen art that works more like a science project," said Alexander Lloyd, a regular patron of the Gray Area Foundation, after he spent a few thousand dollars on one piece of neural network art. But Friday's show was also a reminder that we're careening towards a new world where machines are more autonomous than they have ever been, where they do even more of the work, where they can transport us to places beyond even our own analog imaginations.

Deep (Learning) Dreams

Today, inside big online services like Google and Facebook and Twitter, neural networks automatically identify photos, recognize commands spoken in smartphones, and translate conversations from one language to another. If you feed enough photos of your uncle to a neural net, it can learn to recognize your uncle. That's how Facebook identifies faces in all those photos you upload. Now, with an art "generator" it calls DeepDream, Google has turned these neural nets inside out. They're not recognizing images. They're creating them.

> "Google has turned neural nets inside out. They're not recognizing images. They're creating them."

Google calls this "Inceptionism," a nod to the 2010 Leonardo DiCaprio movie, *Inception*, that imagines a technology capable of inserting us into each other's dreams. But that may not be the best analogy. What this tech is really doing is showing us the dreams of a machine.

To peer into the brain of DeepDream, you start by feeding it a photo or some other image. The neural net looks for familiar patterns in the image. It enhances those patterns. And then it repeats the process with the same image. "This creates a feedback loop: if a cloud looks a little bit like a bird, the network will make it look more like a bird," Google said in a blog post when it first unveiled this project. "This in turn will make the network recognize the bird even more strongly on the next pass and so forth, until a highly detailed bird appears, seemingly out of nowhere."

The result is both fascinating and a little disturbing. If you feed a photo of yourself into the neural net and it finds something that kinda looks like a dog in the lines of your faces, it turns that part of your face into a dog. "It's almost like the neural net is hallucinating," says Steven

Hansen, who recently worked as an intern at Google's DeepMind AI lab in London. "It sees dogs everywhere!" Or, if you feed the neural net an image of random noise, it may produce a tree or a tower or a whole city of towers. In that same noise, it might find the faint images of a pig and a snail, creating a rather frightening new creature by combining the two. Think: machines on LSD.

Virtually Art

Created by a Google engineer named Alexander Mordvintsev, this tech- 10
nique began as a way of better understanding the way neural networks behave. Though neural nets are enormously powerful, they're still a bit of a mystery. We can't completely grasp what goes on inside this web of hardware and software. Mordvintsev and others are still reaching for this understanding. But in the meantime, another Google engineer, Mike Tyka, seized on the technique as a way of creating art. Tyka works with neural networks at Google, but he's also a sculptor. He saw the technique as a way of combining his two interests.

Artists like Tyka choose the images that get fed into the neural nets. And they can tune the neural nets to behave in certain ways. They may even *retrain* them to recognize new patterns, unleashing seemingly limitless possibilities. Some of this artwork looks quite similar, with their spirals and dogs and trees. But many pieces venture in their own directions, across bleaker and more mechanical landscapes.

Four of Tyka's neural net creations were auctioned off on Friday. *Castles in the Sky With Diamonds. Ground Still State of God's Original Brigade. Carboniferous Fantasy.* And *The Babylon of the Blue Sun.* Across the gallery, the names matched the strange visual splendor of the images. And that's not surprising. Joshua To, who curated the show, says that many of the titles were also chosen by neural networks, feeding off the images themselves. An NYU grad student named Ross Goodwin used this technique to generate the titles for Tyka's work.

For Hansen, these auto-generated works aren't a big leap from what we've had before. "I feels like an advanced version of PhotoShop," he says. But at the very least, DeepDream serves a symbol for a much bigger change.

Machines are doing so much more *on their own.* You see this, most notably, in the Google Search engine, where the rise of neural networks means that humans play less of a role—or, at least, humans are farther removed from the engine's final decisions. It's not just following rules that human engineers tell it to follow.

And that gap will only grow, not just in Google's search engine but across so many other services and technologies. On Friday, at the edges of the gallery, Google invited visitors to strap on its Cardboard virtual reality headsets to venture even deeper into DeepDream. For now, Cardboard stops a little short of a true alternate universe. But the technology is rapidly improving. It's no stretch to predict that on day, machines will create these virtual worlds largely on their own. Clay Bavor, Google's head of VR, wasn't just a guest as the exhibit. He was a sponsor of this weekend's show and one of driving forces behind it. Joshua To also works on VR at Google. Yes, Hans Holbien used technology to make his art. But this is going somewhere else entirely. 15

Understanding the Text

1. Draw a diagram of the process that DeepDream uses to create images. To make the diagram, you may use a digital tool, a collage, or a free-hand drawing. Consider making it as artistic as possible.

2. According to Metz, what is the relation between technology and art? Engage his position by articulating your own sense of that relationship. Be sure to use specific passages from Metz that support your sense or where your position diverges from Metz's.

Reflection and Response

3. What is art? Form your own definition of art and then apply it to Metz's discussion of DeepDream. Does DeepDream create art?

4. Who creates the art — DeepDream or the programmers? Support your argument with quotations from Metz and then consider the implications of your position for artificial intelligence. If the programmers create the art, does all AI similarly come back to human beings?

Making Connections

5. To what extent does DeepDream represent a kind of artificial intelligence? Apply the definitions of AI offered by Ray Kurzweil ("What Is AI, Anyway?," p. 62). Does DeepDream reflect the "moving frontier" (p. 63)? Does it show signs of intelligence?

6. Allie Shaw ("Alexa, Siri, Sophia: Deconstructing AI's Subliminal Gender Bias," p. 111) warns us of the gender bias that seems to permeate AI. Apply her essay to Metz's discussion of DeepDream. Does art escape gender bias? Consider not only the products of DeepDream but also those working on and around it.

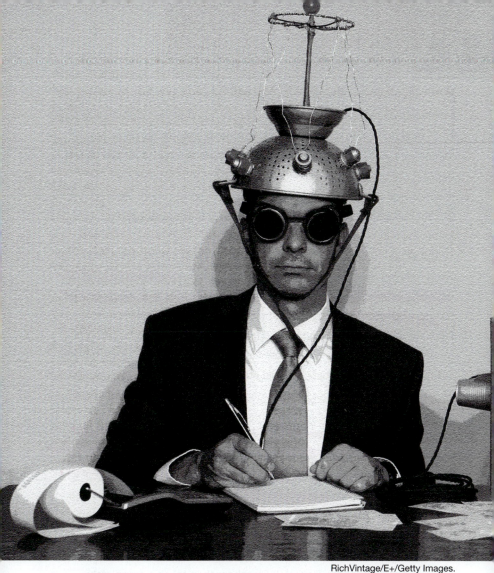

3

Is There More Than One Kind of Intelligence?

For many of us, being "smart" has to do with the kinds of skills valued in school, like a strong memory, great writing skills, following directions, and the ability to do well on exams. These ideas are reinforced by any number of tests in and around schools, such as the SAT, the ACT, or Advanced Placement exams. Given that you are most likely in school right now, that understanding of intelligence might feel relevant to your current experiences, whether you are excelling, struggling, or somewhere in between.

But what if there was more to intelligence? What if there were other ways of being smart? The readings in this chapter challenge that limited understanding of intelligence by introducing new kinds of intelligence that broaden the conversation. The authors presented here, experts from the fields of psychology, education, and human development, offer different models of what intelligence is, what it does, and who has it. These models will help you question our traditional notion of intelligence, and along the way, you may also find out you're smart in ways you never thought of before.

Howard Gardner opens this conversation by exploring the long history of our typical understanding of intelligence and proposing instead that there are multiple intelligences. Daniel Goleman offers a specific example of what that might mean by looking at emotional intelligence while also critiquing the assumption that cognitive intelligence—the kind of intelligence that schools usually value—is the key to success in life. Although emotional intelligence is a useful concept, Adam Grant complicates it by pointing out some of its dangers. Robert J. Sternberg then takes a completely different tack by suggesting something he calls "successful intelligence," a kind of creative and practical intelligence that works in conjunction with analytical intelligence—something like street smarts, as opposed to book smarts. Yet another model is proposed by Ross Alloway and Tracy Alloway, whose research into working memory suggests that the ability to hold and work with lots of information in your head is a better approach to thinking

photo: RichVintage/E+/Getty Images.

about intelligence. All these models focus on individuals. Philip Ball, on the other hand, looks at the "wisdom of crowds," or group intelligence, and its uncanny ability to make good decisions and accurate predictions, often better than the ones given by the smartest individual in the group. Given all these approaches to intelligence, John D. Mayer suggests that instead of abandoning the SAT for admissions, colleges and universities should test students even more, using the kinds of instruments developed to measure these various other kinds of intelligence, which often predict a person's success in life better than grades or the SAT.

These readings also demonstrate that knowledge is a constantly evolving domain. Researchers are continually developing new theories, testing them, revising them, and moving toward better understandings of intelligence and everything else. You're participating in that process too as you read and write about these ideas, and you'll grow in that process as you move beyond this class and into your discipline. That's what universities are about: not grades, but the never-ending pursuit of a better understanding of our world.

The Idea of Multiple Intelligences

Howard Gardner

Howard Gardner is the John H. and Elisabeth A. Hobbs Research Professor of Cognition and Education at the Harvard Graduate School of Education; a member of Harvard's Project Zero, which focuses on education in and through the arts; and a director at the Good Project, which prepares students to be good citizens by promoting ethics and thoughtful decision-making. He is the recipient of a MacArthur Prize Fellowship and a fellowship from the John S. Guggenheim Memorial Foundation. Gardner has authored more than thirty books, including *The Unschooled Mind: How Children Think and How Schools Should Teach* (1991), *Creating Minds: An Anatomy of Creativity Seen Through the Lives of Freud, Einstein, Picasso, Stravinsky, Eliot, Graham, and Gandhi* (1993), and *Changing Minds: The Art and Science of Changing Our Own and Other People's Minds* (2004). Gardner is best known for his theory of multiple intelligences, which fundamentally changed conversations around intelligence and how it is measured. Gardner proposed that theory in *Frames of Mind: The Theory of Multiple Intelligences* (1983), from which this selection is taken.

A young girl spends an hour with an examiner. She is asked a number of questions that probe her store of information (Who discovered America? What does the stomach do?), her vocabulary (What does *nonsense* mean? What does *belfry* mean?), her arithmetic skills (At eight cents each, how much will three candy bars cost?), her ability to remember a series of numbers (5,1,7,4,2,3,8), her capacity to grasp the similarity between two elements (elbow and knee, mountain and lake). She may also be asked to carry out certain other tasks — for example, solving a maze or arranging a group of pictures in such a way that they relate a complete story. Some time afterward, the examiner scores the responses and comes up with a single number — the girl's intelligence quotient, or IQ. This number (which the little girl may actually be told) is likely to exert appreciable effect upon her future, influencing the way in which her teachers think of her and determining her eligibility for certain privileges. The importance attached to the number is not entirely inappropriate: after all, the score on an intelligence test does predict one's ability to handle school subjects, though it foretells little of success in later life.

The preceding scenario is repeated thousands of times every day, all over the world; and, typically, a good deal of significance is attached to the single score. Of course, different versions of the test are used for various ages and in diverse cultural settings. At times, the test is administered with paper and pencil rather than as an interchange with an examiner. But the broad outlines—an hour's worth of questions yielding one round number—are pretty much the way of intelligence testing the world around.

Many observers are not happy with this state of affairs. There must be more to intelligence than short answers to short questions—answers that predict academic success; and yet, in the absence of a better way of thinking about intelligence, and of better ways to assess an individual's capabilities, this scenario is destined to be repeated universally for the foreseeable future.

But what if one were to let one's imagination wander freely, to consider the wider range of performances that are in fact valued throughout the world? Consider, for example, the twelve-year-old male Puluwat in the Caroline Islands, who has been selected by his elders to learn how to become a master sailor. Under the tutelage of master navigators, he will learn to combine knowledge of sailing, stars, and geography so as to find his way around hundreds of islands. Consider the fifteen-year-old Iranian youth who has committed to heart the entire Koran and mastered the Arabic language. Now he is being sent to a holy city, to work closely for the next several years with an ayatollah, who will prepare him to be a teacher and religious leader. Or, consider the fourteen-year-old adolescent in Paris, who has learned how to program a computer and is beginning to compose works of music with the aid of a synthesizer.

A moment's reflection reveals that each of these individuals is attaining a   5 high level of competence in a challenging field and should, by any reasonable definition of the term, be viewed as exhibiting intelligent behavior. Yet it should be equally clear that current methods of assessing the intellect are not sufficiently well honed to allow assessment of an individual's potentials or achievements in navigating by the stars, mastering a foreign tongue, or composing with a computer. The problem lies less in the technology of testing than in the ways in which we customarily think about the intellect and in our ingrained views of intelligence. Only if we expand and reformulate our view of what counts as human intellect will we be able to devise more appropriate ways of assessing it and more effective ways of educating it.

Around the world many individuals involved in education are reaching similar conclusions. There is interest in new programs (some of them grandiose) which seek to develop human intelligence for a whole culture, to train individuals in such general skills as "anticipatory learning," to help individuals to realize their human potential. Intriguing experiments, ranging from the Suzuki method of training violin to the LOGO method of introducing the fundamentals of computer programming, seek to elicit accomplished performances from young children. Some of these experiments have had demonstrated success, while others are still in the pilot phase. Yet it is probably just to say that the successes as well as the failures have occurred in the absence of an adequate framework for thinking about intelligences. Certainly in no case does there exist a view of intelligence which incorporates the range of abilities I have just surveyed. To arrive at such a formulation is the purpose of the present book.

In the chapters that follow, I outline a new theory of human intellectual competences. This theory challenges the classical view of intelligence that most of us have absorbed explicitly (from psychology or education texts) or implicitly (by living in a culture with a strong but possibly circumscribed view of intelligence). So that the new features of this theory can be more readily identified, I will in these introductory pages consider some facts of the traditional view: where it came from, why it has become entrenched, what are some of the outstanding issues that remain to be resolved. Only then will I turn to the characteristics of the revisionist theory that I am propounding here.

For well over two thousand years, at least since the rise of the Greek city-state, a certain set of ideas has dominated discussions of the human condition in our civilization. This collection of ideas stresses the existence and the importance of mental powers—capacities that have been variously termed *rationality, intelligence,* or the deployment of *mind.* The unending search for an essence of humanity has led, with seeming ineluctability,° to a focus upon our species's quest for knowledge; and those capacities that figure in knowing have been especially valued. Whether it be Plato's philosopher-king, the Hebrew prophet, the literate scribe in a medieval monastery, or the scientist in a laboratory, the individual capable of using his* mental powers has been singled out. Socrates' "Know thyself," Aristotle's "All men by Nature desire to know," and Descartes's "I think: therefore I am" provide epigraphs that frame an entire civilization.

Even in that dark millennium that intervened between Classical times and the Renaissance, the ascendancy of intellectual factors was rarely challenged. Early in the medieval period, St. Augustine, the very father of faith, declared:

> *The prime author and mover of the universe is intelligence. Therefore, the final cause of the universe must be the good of the intelligence and that is truth. . . . Of all human pursuits, the pursuit of wisdom is the most perfect, the most sublime, the most useful, and the most agreeable. The most perfect, because in so far as a man gives himself up to the pursuit of wisdom, to that extent he enjoys already some portion of true happiness.*

ineluctability: inevitability; inability to avoid.

---

*For ease of exposition, the pronoun "he" will be used in its generic sense throughout this piece.

At the height of the Middle Ages, Dante put forth his view that "the 10
proper function of the human race, taken in the aggregate, is to actualize
continually the entire capacity possible to the intellect, primarily in speculation, then through its extension and for its sake, secondarily in action."
And then, at the dawn of the Renaissance, a century before Descartes's time,
Francis Bacon described the English ship in New Atlantis which comes upon
a Utopian island whose chief institution is a great establishment devoted to
scientific research. The ruler of this realm declares to visiting travelers:

> *I will give the greatest jewel I have. For I will impart unto thee, for the*
> *love of God and men, a relation of the true state of Solomon's house. . . .*
> *The end of our foundation is the knowledge of causes, and secret motions*
> *of things; and the enlarging of the bounds of human empire, to the*
> *effecting of all things possible.*

Of course, esteem for knowledge—and for those who appear to possess it—is not the only theme that haunts what we have come to term (somewhat inexactly) the "Western world." The virtues of feeling, faith, and

"Reason, intelligence, logic, knowledge are not synonymous."

courage have also been leitmotifs° over the centuries and, in fact, have
sometimes (if not always justifiably) been contrasted with the quest for
knowledge. What is instructive is that, even when faith or love is extolled
above all else, each is typically opposed to the powers of reason. In a parallel vein, when leaders of a totalitarian bent have sought to remake their
societies in the light of a new vision, they have typically "put away" those
rationalists or intellectuals whom they could not co-opt—once again paying a kind of perverse compliment to the powers of reason.

Reason, intelligence, logic, knowledge are not synonymous; and
much of this book constitutes an effort to tease out the various skills and
capacities that have too easily been combined under the rubric of "the
mental." But, first, I must introduce a different kind of distinction—a
contrast between two attitudes toward mind which have competed and
alternated across the centuries. Adopting the appealing distinction of the
Greek poet Archilochus, one can contrast those who view all intellect
as a piece (let us dub them the "hedgehogs"), with those who favor its
fragmentation into several components (the "foxes"). The hedgehogs
not only believe in a singular, inviolable capacity which is the special
property of human beings: often, as a corollary, they impose the conditions that each individual is born with a certain amount of intelligence,

leitmotifs: recurring themes or ideas.

and that we individuals can in fact be rank-ordered in terms of our God-given intellect or I.Q. So entrenched is this way of thinking—and talking—that most of us lapse readily into rankings of individuals as more or less "smart," "bright," "clever," or "intelligent."

An equally venerable tradition of the West glorifies the numerous distinct functions or parts of the mind. In Classical times, it was common to differentiate between reason, will, and feeling. Medieval thinkers had their trivium of grammar, logic, and rhetoric, and their quadrivium of mathematics, geometry, astronomy, and music. As the science of psychology was launched, an even larger array of human mental abilities or faculties was posited. (Franz Joseph Gall, whom I shall formally introduce later, nominated 37 human faculties or powers of the mind; J. P. Guilford, a contemporary figure, favors 120 vectors of mind.) Some of the foxes also tend to the innate and rank-ordering cast of thought, but one can find many among them who believe in the altering (and ameliorating) effects of environment and training.

Dating back many centuries, debate between the hedgehogs and the foxes continues into our own time. In the area of brain study, there have been the *localizers*, who believe that different portions of the nervous system mediate diverse intellectual capacities; and these localizers have been arrayed against the *holists*, who deem major intellectual functions to be the property of the brain as a whole. In the area of intelligence testing, an interminable debate has raged between those (following Charles Spearman) who believe in a general factor of intellect; and those (following L. L. Thurstone) who posit a family of primary mental abilities, with none pre-eminent among them. In the area of child development, there has been vigorous debate between those who postulate general structures of the mind (like Jean Piaget) and those who believe in a large and relatively unconnected set of mental skills (the environmental-learning school). Echoes in other disciplines are quite audible.

Thus, against a shared belief, over the centuries, in the primacy of intellectual powers, there is continuing debate about the propriety of parceling intellect into parts. As it happens, some long-standing issues in our cultural tradition show no signs of resolution. I doubt that topics like free will or the conflict between faith and reason will ever be resolved to everyone's satisfaction. But, in other cases, there may be hope for progress. Sometimes progress occurs as a consequence of logical clarification, as for instance, when a fallacy is exposed. (No one continues in the mistaken belief that the distorted faces in El Greco's portraits were due to an astigmatic condition, once it has been explained that astigmatism would not lead to the painting of elongated faces. An astigmatic painter would *perceive* the faces on his canvas (and in the everyday world) to be elongated; but, in fact, these faces would appear completely normal to non-astigmatic eyes.) Sometimes progress results from dramatic scientific findings (the discoveries of Copernicus and Kepler radically changed our view about the architecture of the universe). And sometimes progress comes about when a large body of information is woven together in a convincing tapestry of argument (as happened when, in the course of introducing his theory of evolution, Charles Darwin reviewed masses of evidence about the development and differentiation of species).

The time may be at hand for some clarification about the structure of human intellectual competence. In the present case, there is neither a single scientific breakthrough, nor the discovery of an egregious logical blunder, but rather the confluence of a large body of evidence from a variety of sources. Such a confluence, which has been gathering with even greater force over the past few decades, seems to be recognized (at least in peripheral vision) by those concerned with human cognition. But the lines of convergence have rarely, if ever, been focused on directly and systematically examined in one place; and they certainly have not been shared with the wider public. Such confrontation and collation are the twin purposes of this book.

In what follows, I argue that there is persuasive evidence for the existence of several *relatively autonomous* human intellectual competences, abbreviated hereafter as "human intelligences." These are the "frames of mind" of my title. The exact nature and breadth of each intellectual "frame" has not so far been satisfactorily established, nor has the precise number of intelligences been fixed. But the conviction that there exist at least some intelligences, that these are relatively independent of one another, and that they can be fashioned and combined in a multiplicity of adaptive ways by individuals and cultures, seems to me to be increasingly difficult to deny.

Previous efforts (and there have been many) to establish independent intelligences have been unconvincing, chiefly because they rely on only one or, at the most, two lines of evidence. Separate "minds" or "faculties" have been posited solely on the basis of logical analysis, solely on the history of educational disciplines, solely on the results of intelligence testing, or solely on the insights obtained from brain study. These solitary efforts have rarely yielded the same list of competences and have thereby made a claim for multiple intelligences seem that much less tenable.

My procedure is quite different. In formulating my brief on behalf of multiple intelligences, I have reviewed evidence from a large and hitherto unrelated group of sources: studies of prodigies, gifted individuals, brain-damaged patients, *idiots savants*, normal children, normal adults, experts in different lines of work, and individuals from diverse cultures. A preliminary list of candidate intelligences has been bolstered (and, to my mind, partially validated) by converging evidence from these diverse sources. I have become convinced of the existence of an intelligence to the extent that it can be found in relative isolation in special populations (or absent in isolation in otherwise normal populations); to the extent that it may become highly developed in specific individuals or in specific cultures; and to the extent that psychometricians, experimental researchers, and/or experts in particular disciplines can posit core abilities that, in effect, define the intelligence. Absence of some or all of these indices, of course, eliminates a candidate intelligence. In ordinary life, as I will show, these intelligences typically work in harmony, and so their autonomy may be invisible. But when the appropriate observational lenses are donned, the peculiar nature of each intelligence emerges with sufficient (and often surprising) clarity.

The major assignment in this book, then, is to make the case for the existence of multiple intelligences (later abbreviated as "M.I."). Whether or not the case for specific intelligences proves persuasive, I shall at least have gathered between two covers several bodies of knowledge that have hitherto lived in relative segregation. In addition, however, this volume has a number of other, and not wholly subsidiary, purposes — some primarily scientific, others distinctly practical.

First of all, I seek to expand the purviews of cognitive and developmental psychology (the two areas to which, as a researcher, I feel the closest). The expansion that I favor looks, in one direction, toward the biological and evolutionary roots of cognition and, in the other direction, toward cultural variations in cognitive competence. To my mind, visits to the "lab" of the brain scientist and to the "field" of an exotic culture should become part of the training of individuals interested in cognition and development.

Second, I wish to examine the educational implications of a theory of multiple intelligences. In my view, it should be possible to identify an individual's intellectual profile (or proclivities) at an early age and then draw upon this knowledge to enhance that person's educational opportunities and options. One could channel individuals with unusual talents into special programs, even as one could devise prosthetics and special enrichment programs for individuals presenting an atypical or a dysfunctional profile of intellectual competences.

Third, I hope that this inquiry will inspire educationally oriented anthropologists to develop a model of how intellectual competences may be fostered in various cultural settings. Only through such efforts will it be possible to determine whether theories of learning and teaching travel readily across national boundaries or must be continually refashioned in light of the particularities of each culture.

Finally—this is the most important, but also the most difficult, challenge—I hope that the point of view that I articulate here may prove of genuine utility to those policy makers and practitioners charged with "the development of other individuals." Training and heightening of intellect is certainly "in the international air": the World Bank's report on Human Development, the Club of Rome's essay on anticipatory learning, and the Venezuelan Project on Human Intelligence are but three recent visible examples. Too often practitioners involved in efforts of this sort have embraced flawed theories of intelligence or cognition and have, in the process, supported programs that have accomplished little or even proved counterproductive. To aid such individuals, I have developed a framework that, building on the theory of multiple intelligences, can be applied to any educational situation. If the framework put forth here is adopted, it may at least discourage those interventions that seem doomed to failure and encourage those that have a chance for success.

I regard the present effort as a contribution to the emerging science of   25 cognition. To a considerable extent, I am summarizing the work of other scholars; but, to a certain extent (and I intend to make clear where), I am proposing a new orientation. Some of the claims are controversial, and I expect that experts versed in cognitive science will eventually have their say as well. Part II, the "heart" of the book, consists of a description of several intellectual competences of whose existence I feel reasonably certain. But, as befits a potential contribution to science, I shall first (in chapter 2) review other efforts to characterize intellectual profiles and then, after putting forth the evidence in support of my theory, will (in chapter 11) subject that point of view to lines of criticism. As part of my mission to broaden the study of cognition, I adopt a biological and crosscultural perspective throughout part II and also devote a separate chapter each to the biological bases of cognition (chapter 3) and to cultural variations in education (chapter 13). Finally, given the "applied" agenda I have just sketched, I shall in the concluding chapters of the book address more directly questions of education and policy.

A word, finally, about the title of this chapter. As I have indicated, the idea of multiple intelligences is an old one, and I can scarcely claim any great originality for attempting to revive it once more. Even so, by featuring the word *idea* I want to underscore that the notion of multiple intelligences is hardly a proven scientific fact: it is, at most, an idea that has recently regained the right to be discussed seriously. Given the ambition and scope of this book, it is inevitable that this idea will harbor many shortcomings. What I hope to establish is that "multiple intelligences" is an idea whose time has come.

Understanding the Text

1. Make an outline of Gardner's argument. In reviewing the outline, pay attention to the overall structure of his argument but even more to the places where he pivots from, say, an anecdote to a larger history or from what others have said to his own argument. What strategies does he use to make these transitions? How might you do something similar in your own writing?

2. In his last paragraph, Gardner stresses that he is only proposing the *idea* of multiple intelligences. Why do you think he makes this move? What does it do to or for his argument? Why might he wait until the very end of his essay to move into this discussion?

3. Using your smartphone or another video recording device, interview two or three people you know about intelligence. Ask them what they think intelligence is or what it means to be smart and record their responses. Then make your own video reflecting on the answers, incorporating shots from your interviews (if you have those editing skills). Have Gardner's ideas changed the way we think about intelligence? Do people continue to have a "hedgehog" mentality? How is intelligence commonly understood?

Reflection and Response

4. In reviewing the history of how we think about intelligence, Gardner identifies two primary strands of thought, represented variously as "hedgehogs" and "foxes" (p. 127) or "localizers" and "holists" (p. 128) and reappearing in many different fields of study. Using his text, explain what he means by these two approaches and then consider the implications of each approach. Write a response to Gardner that engages these positions through synthesis or by advocating for one or the other. Is one approach more practical than the other? Is the most complete picture achieved by combining them?

5. In making his argument, Gardner states that "the precise number of intelligences [has not] been fixed" (p. 129). Write a paper in which you make an argument for a specific kind of intelligence that differs from the sort of intellectual competence that Gardner associates with intelligence in the Western tradition. Use passages from his text to provide context and support for your intelligence.

Making Connections

6. Daniel Goleman ("When Smart Is Dumb," p. 133) explicitly references Gardner's work while proposing his own idea of emotional intelligence. Apply Gardner's discussion of intelligence to Goleman's work. Does it represent a hedgehog or a fox approach? Does it reflect the kind of multiple intelligences that Gardner wants to propose?

7. Gardner opens his essay with a critique of traditional IQ tests. John D. Mayer ("We Need More Tests, Not Fewer," p. 166) suggests that the limitations of these tests are not a reason to abandon them; instead, we just need more — and different — tests. Synthesize Mayer's position with Gardner's arguments. Would it be sufficient to develop an IQ test for multiple intelligences? Will there always be some residue of smarts that escapes testing?

When Smart Is Dumb

Daniel Goleman

Author and science journalist Daniel Goleman spent more than a decade reporting on the brain and behavioral sciences for the *New York Times*. He is the author of eight books, including *Focus: The Hidden Driver of Excellence* (2013) and *A Force for Good: The Dalai Lama's Vision for Our World* (2015). His 1995 book, *Emotional Intelligence: Why It Can Matter More than IQ*, from which this selection is taken, was a *New York Times* bestseller for more than a year and introduced his best-known concept, emotional intelligence, a kind of emotional smarts. He currently serves as cochair for the Consortium for Research on Emotional Intelligence in Organizations, which promotes research on emotional intelligence in the workplace.

Exactly why David Pologruto, a high-school physics teacher, was stabbed with a kitchen knife by one of his star students is still debatable. But the facts as widely reported are these:

Jason H., a sophomore and straight-A student at a Coral Springs, Florida, high school, was fixated on getting into medical school. Not just any medical school—he dreamt of Harvard. But Pologruto, his physics teacher, had given Jason an 80 on a quiz. Believing the grade—a mere B—put his dream in jeopardy, Jason took a butcher knife to school and, in a confrontation with Pologruto in the physics lab, stabbed his teacher in the collarbone before being subdued in a struggle.

A judge found Jason innocent, temporarily insane during the incident—a panel of four psychologists and psychiatrists swore he was psychotic during the fight. Jason claimed he had been planning to commit suicide because of the test score, and had gone to Pologruto to tell him he was killing himself because of the bad grade. Pologruto told a different story: "I think he tried to completely do me in with the knife" because he was infuriated over the bad grade.

After transferring to a private school, Jason graduated two years later at the top of his class. A perfect grade in regular classes would have given him a straight-A, 4.0 average, but Jason had taken enough advanced courses to raise his grade-point average to 4.614—way beyond A+. Even as Jason graduated with highest honors, his old physics teacher, David Pologruto, complained that Jason had never apologized or even taken responsibility for the attack.

The question is, how could someone of such obvious intelligence 5 do something so irrational—so downright dumb? The answer:

Academic intelligence has little to do with emotional life. The brightest among us can founder on the shoals of unbridled passions and unruly impulses; people with high IQs can be stunningly poor pilots of their private lives.

One of psychology's open secrets is the relative inability of grades, IQ, or SAT scores, despite their popular mystique, to predict unerringly who will succeed in life. To be sure, there is a relationship between IQ and life circumstances for large groups as a whole: many people with very low IQs end up in menial jobs, and those with high IQs tend to become well-paid—but by no means always.

"At best, IQ contributes about 20 percent to the factors that determine life success, which leaves 80 percent to other forces."

There are widespread exceptions to the rule that IQ predicts success—many (or more) exceptions than cases that fit the rule. At best, IQ contributes about 20 percent to the factors that determine life success, which leaves 80 percent to other forces. As one observer notes, "The vast majority of one's ultimate niche in society is determined by non-IQ factors, ranging from social class to luck."

Even Richard Herrnstein and Charles Murray, whose book *The Bell Curve* imputes a primary importance to IQ, acknowledge this; as they point out, "Perhaps a freshman with an SAT math score of 500 had better not have his heart set on being a mathematician, but if instead he wants to run his own business, become a U.S. Senator or make a million dollars, he should not put aside his dreams. . . . The link between test scores and those achievements is dwarfed by the totality of other characteristics that he brings to life."

My concern is with a key set of these "other characteristics," *emotional intelligence*: abilities such as being able to motivate oneself and persist in the face of frustrations; to control impulse and delay gratification; to regulate one's moods and keep distress from swamping the ability to think; to empathize and to hope. Unlike IQ, with its nearly one-hundred-year history of research with hundreds of thousands of people, emotional intelligence is a new concept. No one can yet say exactly how much of the variability from person to person in life's course it accounts for. But what data exist suggest it can be as powerful, and at times more powerful, than IQ. And while there are those who argue that IQ cannot be changed much by experience or education, I will show in Part Five that the crucial emotional competencies can indeed be learned and improved upon by children—if we bother to teach them.

Emotional Intelligence and Destiny

I remember the fellow in my own class at Amherst College who had   10
attained five perfect 800 scores on the SAT and other achievement tests he
took before entering. Despite his formidable intellectual abilities, he spent
most of his time hanging out, staying up late, and missing classes by
sleeping until noon. It took him almost ten years to finally get his degree.

IQ offers little to explain the different destinies of people with roughly
equal promises, schooling, and opportunity. When ninety-five Harvard
students from the classes of the 1940s—a time when people with a wider
spread of IQ were at Ivy League schools than is presently the case—were
followed into middle age, the men with the highest test scores in college
were not particularly successful compared to their lower-scoring peers in
terms of salary, productivity, or status in their field. Nor did they have
the greatest life satisfaction, nor the most happiness with friendships,
family, and romantic relationships.

A similar follow-up in middle age was done with 450 boys, most sons of
immigrants, two thirds from families on welfare, who grew up in Somerville,
Massachusetts, at the time a "blighted slum" a few blocks from Harvard.
A third had IQs below 90. But again IQ had little relationship to how well
they had done at work or in the rest of their lives; for instance, 7 percent of
men with IQs under 80 were unemployed for ten or more years, but so were
7 percent of men with IQs over 100. To be sure, there was a general link (as
there always is) between IQ and socioeconomic level at age forty-seven. But
childhood abilities such as being able to handle frustrations, control emotions, and get on with other people made the greater difference.

Consider also data from an ongoing study of eighty-one valedictorians and salutatorians from the 1981 class in Illinois high schools. All, of
course, had the highest grade-point averages in their schools. But while
they continued to achieve well in college, getting excellent grades, by
their late twenties they had climbed to only average levels of success.
Ten years after graduating from high school, only one in four were at the
highest level of young people of comparable age in their chosen profession, and many were doing much less well.

Karen Arnold, professor of education at Boston University, one of
the researchers tracking the valedictorians, explains, "I think we've discovered the 'dutiful'—people who know how to achieve in the system.
But valedictorians struggle as surely as we all do. To know that a person
is a valedictorian is to know only that he or she is exceedingly good at
achievement as measured by grades. It tells you nothing about how they
react to the vicissitudes° of life."

vicissitudes: changes in fortune or circumstance, most often unfavorable ones.

And that is the problem: academic intelligence offers virtually no   15
preparation for the turmoil—or opportunity—life's vicissitudes bring.
Yet even though a high IQ is no guarantee of prosperity, prestige, or
happiness in life, our schools and our culture fixate on academic abilities, ignoring *emotional* intelligence, a set of traits—some might call it
character—that also matters immensely for our personal destiny. Emotional life is a domain that, as surely as math or reading, can be handled
with greater or lesser skill, and requires its unique set of competencies.
And how adept a person is at those is crucial to understanding why
one person thrives in life while another, of equal intellect, dead-ends:
emotional aptitude is a *meta-ability*, determining how well we can use
whatever other skills we have, including raw intellect.

Of course, there are many paths to success in life, and many domains in
which other aptitudes are rewarded. In our increasingly knowledge-based
society, technical skill is certainly one. There is a children's joke: "What
do you call a nerd fifteen years from now?" The answer: "Boss." But
even among "nerds" emotional intelligence offers an added edge in the
workplace. Much evidence testifies that people who are emotionally
adept—who know and manage their own feelings well, and who read
and deal effectively with other people's feelings—are at an advantage in
any domain of life, whether romance and intimate relationships or picking up the unspoken rules that govern success in organizational politics.
People with well-developed emotional skills are also more likely to be
content and effective in their lives, mastering the habits of mind that
foster their own productivity; people who cannot marshal some control
over their emotional life fight inner battles that sabotage their ability for
focused work and clear thought.

A Different Kind of Intelligence

To the casual observer, four-year-old Judy might seem a wallflower
among her more gregarious° playmates. She hangs back from the action
at playtime, staying on the margins of games rather than plunging into
the center. But Judy is actually a keen observer of the social politics of her
preschool classroom, perhaps the most sophisticated of her playmates in
her insights into the tides of feeling within the others.

Her sophistication is not apparent until Judy's teacher gathers the
four-year-olds around to play what they call the Classroom Game. The
Classroom Game—a dollhouse replica of Judy's own preschool classroom with stick figures who have for heads small photos of the students

gregarious: sociable; fond of company.

and teachers — is a test of social perceptiveness. When Judy's teacher asks her to put each girl and boy in the part of the room they like to play in most — the art corner, the blocks corner, and so on — Judy does so with complete accuracy. And when asked to put each boy and girl with the children they like to play with most, Judy shows she can match best friends for the entire class.

Judy's accuracy reveals that she has a perfect social map of her class, a level of perceptiveness exceptional for a four-year-old. These are the skills that, in later life, might allow Judy to blossom into a star in any of the fields where "people skills" count, from sales and management to diplomacy.

That Judy's social brilliance was spotted at all, let alone this early, was due to her being a student at the Eliot-Pearson Preschool on the campus of Tufts University, where Project Spectrum, a curriculum that intentionally cultivates a variety of kinds of intelligence, was then being developed. Project Spectrum recognizes that the human repertoire of abilities goes far beyond the three R's, the narrow band of word-and-number skills that schools traditionally focus on. It acknowledges that capacities such as Judy's social perceptiveness are talents that an education can nurture rather than ignore or even frustrate. By encouraging children to develop a full range of the abilities that they will actually draw on to succeed, or use simply to be fulfilled in what they do, school becomes an education in life skills.

The guiding visionary behind Project Spectrum is Howard Gardner, a psychologist at the Harvard School of Education. "The time has come," Gardner told me, "to broaden our notion of the spectrum of talents. The single most important contribution education can make to a child's development is to help him toward a field where his talents best suit him, where he will be satisfied and competent. We've completely lost sight of that. Instead we subject everyone to an education where, if you succeed, you will be best suited to be a college professor. And we evaluate everyone along the way according to whether they meet that narrow standard of success. We should spend less time ranking children and more time helping them to identify their natural competencies and gifts, and cultivate those. There are hundreds and hundreds of ways to succeed, and many, many different abilities that will help you get there."

If anyone sees the limits of the old ways of thinking about intelligence, it is Gardner. He points out that the glory days of the IQ tests began during World War I, when two million American men were sorted out through the first mass paper-and-pencil form of the IQ test, freshly developed by Lewis Terman, a psychologist at Stanford. This led to decades of what Gardner calls the "IQ way of thinking": "that people are either smart or not, are born that way, that there's nothing much you can do about it, and that tests can tell you if you are one of the smart ones or not. The SAT test for college admissions is based on the same notion of a single kind of aptitude that determines your future. This way of thinking permeates society."

Gardner's influential 1983 book *Frames of Mind* was a manifesto refuting the IQ view; it proposed that there was not just one, monolithic kind of intelligence that was crucial for life success, but rather a wide spectrum of intelligences, with seven key varieties. His list includes the two standard academic kinds, verbal and mathematical-logical alacrity, but it goes on to include the spatial capacity seen in, say, an outstanding artist or architect; the kinesthetic genius displayed in the physical fluidity and grace of a Martha Graham or Magic Johnson; and the musical gifts of a Mozart or YoYo Ma. Rounding out the list are two faces of what Gardner calls "the personal intelligences": interpersonal skills, like those of a great therapist such as Carl Rogers or a world-class leader such as Martin Luther King Jr., and the "intrapsychic" capacity that could emerge, on the one hand, in the brilliant insights of Sigmund Freud, or, with less fanfare, in the inner contentment that arises from attuning one's life to be in keeping with one's true feelings.

The operative word in this view of intelligences is *multiple*: Gardner's model pushes way beyond the standard concept of IQ as a single, immutable factor. It recognizes that the tests that tyrannized us as we went through school—from the achievement tests that sorted us out into those who would be shunted toward technical schools and those destined for college, to the SATs that determined what, if any, college we would be allowed to attend—are based on a limited notion of intelligence, one out of touch with the true range of skills and abilities that matter for life over and beyond IQ.

Gardner acknowledges that seven is an arbitrary figure for the variety of intelligences; there is no magic number to the multiplicity of human talents. At one point, Gardner and his research colleagues had stretched these seven to a list of twenty different varieties of intelligence. Interpersonal intelligence, for example, broke down into four distinct abilities: leadership, the ability to nurture relationships and keep friends, the ability to resolve conflicts, and skill at the kind of social analysis that four-year-old Judy excels at.

This multifaceted view of intelligence offers a richer picture of a child's ability and potential for success than the standard IQ. When Spectrum students were evaluated on the Stanford-Binet Intelligence Scale—once the gold standard of IQ tests—and again by a battery designed to measure Gardner's spectrum of intelligences, there was no significant relationship between children's scores on the two tests. The five children with the highest IQs (from 125 to 133) showed a variety of profiles on the ten strengths measured by the Spectrum test. For example, of the five "smartest" children according to the IQ tests, one was strong in three areas, three had strengths in two areas, and one "smart" child had just one Spectrum strength. Those strengths were scattered: four of these children's strengths were in music, two in the visual arts, one in social understanding, one in logic, two in language. None of the five high-IQ kids were strong in movement, numbers, or mechanics; movement and numbers were actually weak spots for two of these five.

Gardner's conclusion was that "the Stanford-Binet Intelligence Scale did not predict successful performance across or on a consistent subset of Spectrum activities." On the other hand, the Spectrum scores give parents and teachers clear guidance about the realms that these children will take a spontaneous interest in, and where they will do well enough to develop the passions that could one day lead beyond proficiency to mastery.

Gardner's thinking about the multiplicity of intelligence continues to evolve. Some ten years after he first published his theory, Gardner gave these nutshell summaries of the personal intelligences:

> Inter*personal intelligence is the ability to understand other people: what motivates them, how they work, how to work cooperatively with them. Successful salespeople, politicians, teachers, clinicians, and religious leaders are all likely to be individuals with high degrees of interpersonal intelligence. Intrapersonal intelligence . . . is a correlative ability, turned inward. It is a capacity to form an accurate, veridical° model of oneself and to be able to use that model to operate effectively in life.*

In another rendering, Gardner noted that the core of interpersonal intelligence includes the "capacities to discern and respond appropriately to the moods, temperaments, motivations, and desires of other people." In intrapersonal intelligence, the key to self-knowledge, he included "access to one's own feelings and the ability to discriminate among them and draw upon them to guide behavior."

Spock vs. Data: When Cognition Is Not Enough

There is one dimension of personal intelligence that is broadly pointed 30
to, but little explored, in Gardner's elaborations: the role of emotions. Perhaps this is so because, as Gardner suggested to me, his work is so

---

veridical: truthful.

strongly informed by a cognitive-science model of mind. Thus his view of these intelligences emphasizes cognition—the *understanding* of oneself and of others in motives, in habits of working, and in putting that insight into use in conducting one's own life and getting along with others. But like the kinesthetic realm, where physical brilliance manifests itself nonverbally, the realm of the emotions extends, too, beyond the reach of language and cognition.

While there is ample room in Gardner's descriptions of the personal intelligences for insight into the play of emotions and mastery in managing them, Gardner and those who work with him have not pursued in great detail the role of *feeling* in these intelligences, focusing more on cognitions *about* feeling. This focus, perhaps unintentionally, leaves unexplored the rich sea of emotions that makes the inner life and relationships so complex, so compelling, and so often puzzling. And it leaves yet to be plumbed both the sense in which there is intelligence *in* the emotions and the sense in which intelligence can be brought *to* emotions.

Gardner's emphasis on the cognitive elements in the personal intelligences reflects the zeitgeist of psychology that has shaped his views. Psychology's overemphasis on cognition even in the realm of emotion is, in part, due to a quirk in the history of that science. During the middle decades of this century academic psychology was dominated by behaviorists in the mold of B. F. Skinner, who felt that only behavior that could be seen objectively, from the outside, could be studied with scientific accuracy. The behaviorists ruled all inner life, including emotions, out-of-bounds for science.

Then, with the coming in the late 1960s of the "cognitive revolution," the focus of psychological science turned to how the mind registers and stores information, and the nature of intelligence. But emotions were still off-limits. Conventional wisdom among cognitive scientists held that intelligence entails a cold, hard-nosed processing of fact. It is hyperrational, rather like *Star Trek*'s Mr. Spock, the archetype of dry information bytes unmuddied by feeling, embodying the idea that emotions have no place in intelligence and only muddle our picture of mental life.

The cognitive scientists who embraced this view have been seduced by the computer as the operative model of mind, forgetting that, in reality, the brain's wetware is awash in a messy, pulsating puddle of neurochemicals, nothing like the sanitized, orderly silicon that has spawned the guiding metaphor for mind. The predominant models among cognitive scientists of how the mind processes information have lacked an acknowledgment that rationality is guided by—and can be swamped by—feeling. The cognitive model is, in this regard, an impoverished view of the mind, one that fails to explain the Sturm und Drang° of feelings that brings flavor to the intellect. In order to persist in this view, cognitive scientists themselves have had to ignore the relevance for their models of mind of their personal hopes and fears, their marital squabbles and professional jealousies—the wash of feeling that gives life its flavor and its urgencies, and which in every moment biases exactly how (and how well or poorly) information is processed.

The lopsided scientific vision of an emotionally flat mental life—which   35 has guided the last eighty years of research on intelligence—is gradually changing as psychology has begun to recognize the essential role of feeling in thinking. Rather like the Spockish character Data in *Star Trek: The Next Generation*, psychology is coming to appreciate the power and virtues of emotions in mental life, as well as their dangers. After all, as Data sees (to his own dismay, could he feel dismay), his cool logic fails to bring the right *human* solution. Our humanity is most evident in our feelings; Data seeks to feel, knowing that something essential is missing. He wants friendship, loyalty; like the Tin Man in *The Wizard of Oz*, he lacks a heart. Lacking the lyrical sense that feeling brings, Data can play music or write poetry with technical virtuosity, but not feel its passion. The lesson of Data's yearning for yearning itself is that the higher values of the human heart—faith, hope, devotion, love—are missing entirely from the coldly cognitive view. Emotions enrich; a model of mind that leaves them out is impoverished.

When I asked Gardner about his emphasis on thoughts about feelings, or metacognition, more than on emotions themselves, he acknowledged that he tended to view intelligence in a cognitive way, but told me, "When I first wrote about the personal intelligences, I *was* talking about emotion, especially in my notion of intrapersonal intelligence—one component is emotionally tuning in to yourself. It's the visceral-feeling signals you get that are essential for interpersonal intelligence. But as it has developed in practice, the theory of multiple intelligence has evolved to focus more on metacognition"—that is, awareness of one's mental processes—"rather than on the full range of emotional abilities."

Even so, Gardner appreciates how crucial these emotional and relationship abilities are in the rough-and-tumble of life. He points out that "many people with IQs of 160 work for people with IQs of 100, if the former have poor intrapersonal intelligence and the latter have a high one. And in the day-to-day world no intelligence is more important than the interpersonal. If you don't have it, you'll make poor choices about who to marry, what job to take, and so on. We need to train children in the personal intelligences in school."

Sturm und Drang: raging turmoil.

Can Emotions Be Intelligent?

To get a fuller understanding of just what such training might be like, we must turn to other theorists who are following Gardner's intellectual lead—most notably a Yale psychologist, Peter Salovey, who has mapped in great detail the ways in which we can bring intelligence to our emotions. This endeavor is not new; over the years even the most ardent theorists of IQ have occasionally tried to bring emotions within the domain of intelligence, rather than seeing "emotion" and "intelligence" as an inherent contradiction in terms. Thus E. L. Thorndike, an eminent psychologist who was also influential in popularizing the notion of IQ in the 1920s and 1930s, proposed in a *Harper's Magazine* article that one aspect of emotional intelligence, "social" intelligence—the ability to understand others and "act wisely in human relations"—was itself an aspect of a person's IQ. Other psychologists of the time took a more cynical view of social intelligence, seeing it in terms of skills for manipulating other people—getting them to do what you want, whether they want to or not. But neither of these formulations of social intelligence held much sway with theorists of IQ, and by I960 an influential textbook on intelligence tests pronounced social intelligence a "useless" concept.

But personal intelligence would not be ignored, mainly because it makes both intuitive and common sense. For example, when Robert Sternberg, another Yale psychologist, asked people to describe an "intelligent person," practical people skills were among the main traits listed. More systematic research by Sternberg led him back to Thorndike's conclusion: that social intelligence is both distinct from academic abilities and a key part of what makes people do well in the practicalities of life. Among the practical intelligences that are, for instance, so highly valued in the workplace is the kind of sensitivity that allows effective managers to pick up tacit messages.

In recent years a growing group of psychologists has come to similar   40
conclusions, agreeing with Gardner that the old concepts of IQ revolved around a narrow band of linguistic and math skills, and that doing well on IQ tests was most directly a predictor of success in the classroom or as a professor but less and less so as life's paths diverged from academe. These psychologists—Sternberg and Salovey among them—have taken a wider view of intelligence, trying to reinvent it in terms of what it takes to lead life successfully. And that line of enquiry leads back to an appreciation of just how crucial "personal" or emotional intelligence is.

Salovey subsumes Gardner's personal intelligences in his basic definition of emotional intelligence, expanding these abilities into five main domains:

1 *Knowing one's emotions.* Self-awareness—recognizing a feeling *as it happens*—is the keystone of emotional intelligence. As we will see in Chapter 4, the ability to monitor feelings from moment to moment is crucial to psychological insight and self-understanding. An inability to notice our true feelings leaves us at their mercy. People with greater certainty about their feelings are better pilots of their lives, having a surer sense of how they really feel about personal decisions from whom to marry to what job to take.

2. *Managing emotions.* Handling feelings so they are appropriate is an ability that builds on self-awareness. Chapter 5 will examine the capacity to soothe oneself, to shake off rampant anxiety, gloom, or irritability—and the consequences of failure at this basic emotional skill. People who are poor in this ability are constantly battling feelings of distress, while those who excel in it can bounce back far more quickly from life's setbacks and upsets.

3. *Motivating oneself.* As Chapter 6 will show, marshaling emotions in the service of a goal is essential for paying attention, for self-motivation and mastery, and for creativity. Emotional self-control—delaying gratification and stifling impulsiveness—underlies accomplishment of every sort. And being able to get into the "flow" state enables outstanding performance of all kinds. People who have this skill tend to be more highly productive and effective in whatever they undertake.

4. *Recognizing emotions in others.* Empathy, another ability that builds on emotional self-awareness, is the fundamental "people skill." Chapter 7 will investigate the roots of empathy, the social cost of being emotionally tone-deaf, and the reasons empathy kindles altruism. People who are empathic are more attuned to the subtle social signals that indicate what others need or want. This makes them better at callings such as the caring professions, teaching, sales, and management.

5. *Handling relationships.* The art of relationships is, in large part, skill in managing emotions in others. Chapter 8 looks at social competence and incompetence, and the specific skills involved. These are the abilities that undergird popularity, leadership, and interpersonal effectiveness. People who excel in these skills do well at anything that relies on interacting smoothly with others; they are social stars.

Of course, people differ in their abilities in each of these domains; some of us may be quite adept at handling, say, our own anxiety, but relatively inept at soothing someone else's upsets. The underlying basis for our level of ability is, no doubt, neural, but as we will see, the brain is remarkably plastic, constantly learning. Lapses in emotional skills can be remedied: to a great extent each of these domains represents a body of habit and response that, with the right effort, can be improved on.

IQ and Emotional Intelligence: Pure Types

IQ and emotional intelligence are not opposing competencies, but rather separate ones. We all mix intellect and emotional acuity; people with a high IQ but low emotional intelligence (or low IQ and high emotional intelligence) are, despite the stereotypes, relatively rare. Indeed, there is a slight correlation between IQ and some aspects of emotional intelligence—though small enough to make clear these are largely independent entities.

Unlike the familiar tests for IQ, there is, as yet, no single paper-and-pencil test that yields an "emotional intelligence score" and there may never be one. Although there is ample research on each of its components, some of them, such as empathy, are best tested by sampling a person's actual ability at the task—for example, by having them read a person's feelings from a video of their facial expressions. Still, using a measure for what he calls "ego resilience" which is quite similar to emotional intelligence (it includes the main social and emotional competences), Jack Block, a psychologist at the University of California at Berkeley, has made a comparison of two theoretical pure types: people high in IQ versus people high in emotional aptitudes. The differences are telling.

The high-IQ pure type (that is, setting aside emotional intelligence) 45 is almost a caricature of the intellectual, adept in the realm of mind but inept in the personal world. The profiles differ slightly for men and women. The high-IQ male is typified—no surprise—by a wide range of intellectual interests and abilities. He is ambitious and productive, predictable and dogged, and untroubled by concerns about himself. He also tends to be critical and condescending, fastidious and inhibited, uneasy with sexuality and sensual experience, unexpressive and detached, and emotionally bland and cold.

By contrast, men who are high in emotional intelligence are socially poised, outgoing and cheerful, not prone to fearfulness or worried rumination. They have a notable capacity for commitment to people or causes, for taking responsibility, and for having an ethical outlook; they are sympathetic and caring in their relationships. Their emotional life is rich, but appropriate; they are comfortable with themselves, others, and the social universe they live in.

Purely high-IQ women have the expected intellectual confidence, are fluent in expressing their thoughts, value intellectual matters, and have a wide range of intellectual and aesthetic interests. They also tend to be introspective, prone to anxiety, rumination, and guilt, and hesitate to express their anger openly (though they do so indirectly).

Emotionally intelligent women, by contrast, tend to be assertive and express their feelings directly, and to feel positive about themselves; life holds meaning for them. Like the men, they are outgoing and gregarious, and express their feelings appropriately (rather than, say, in outbursts they later regret); they adapt well to stress. Their social poise lets them easily reach out to new people; they are comfortable enough with themselves to be playful, spontaneous, and open to sensual experience. Unlike the women purely high in IQ, they rarely feel anxious or guilty, or sink into rumination.

These portraits, of course, are extremes — all of us mix IQ and emotional intelligence in varying degrees. But they offer an instructive look at what each of these dimensions adds separately to a person's qualities. To the degree a person has both cognitive and emotional intelligence, these pictures merge. Still, of the two, emotional intelligence adds far more of the qualities that make us more fully human.

Understanding the Text

1. Goleman discusses emotional intelligence at length, but he doesn't offer an explicit definition of the term. Read back through his text to formulate a definition of this concept, supported with passages from Goleman's text.

2. In considering the different kinds of emotional intelligence, Goleman references the work of Peter Salovey, who offers five domains for these abilities. Select one of these domains and create a visual representation of it, through images found on the internet, through a collage of print images, or using a graphics program.

Reflection and Response

3. Grades, Goleman argues, do not predict success in life and only reflect success in school. Expand on Goleman's argument by first crafting your own definition of success and then synthesize it with Goleman's argument. What do you think it takes to be successful? How might cognitive or emotional intelligence play a role in that? Does being successful require some sort of smarts, either in terms of intellectual or emotional facility?

4. In considering Jack Block's "pure types" of people with high IQ or high emotional aptitude (p. 144), Goleman splits the discussion along gender lines. Why? What's gained by a discussion of pure types by gender? In what ways might organizing the discussion in this way be detrimental? Does this part of his argument affect his overall argument in any way?

Making Connections

5. Adam Grant ("The Dark Side of Emotional Intelligence," p. 147) suggests that Goleman's concept can actually be quite dangerous because people with high emotional intelligence have the capacity to manipulate others. Consider the claims of both authors and then stipulate your own position on the risks and rewards of emotional intelligence, supported with quotations from the authors.

6. In focusing on group intelligence, Philip Ball ("'Wisdom of the Crowd': The Myths and Realities," p. 162) also focuses on a traditional notion of cognitive intelligence. Expand Ball's discussion by using Goleman's concept to consider the emotional wisdom of crowds. Is such a thing possible? What would it look like? Does Goleman's discussion suggest that emotional intelligence is a trait only for individuals? Would the diversity that Ball examines be important?

The Dark Side of Emotional Intelligence

Adam Grant

Adam Grant is the Saul P. Steinberg Professor of Management and Professor of Psychology at the University of Pennsylvania's Wharton School of Business, where his research and teaching focus on organizational psychology, management, and workplace dynamics. He is the author of several bestselling books, including *Give and Take: A Revolutionary Approach to Success* (2013), *Originals: How Non-Conformists Move the World* (2016), and, with Sheryl Sandberg, *Option B: Facing Adversity, Building Resilience, and Finding Joy* (2017). His research has received awards from the Academy of Management, the American Psychological Association, the Society for Industrial Organization and Psychology, and the National Science Foundation. In the selection here, published online in *The Atlantic*, Grant separates the notion of emotional intelligence from moral good by looking at the ways in which this valued skill can be used to manipulate others.

Some of the greatest moments in human history were fueled by emotional intelligence. When Martin Luther King Jr. presented his dream, he chose language that would stir the hearts of his audience. "Instead of honoring this sacred obligation" to liberty, King thundered, "America has given the Negro people a bad check." He promised that a land "sweltering with the heat of oppression" could be "transformed into an oasis of freedom and justice," and envisioned a future in which "on the red hills of Georgia sons of former slaves and the sons of former slave-owners will be able to sit down together at the table of brotherhood."

Delivering this electrifying message required emotional intelligence—the ability to recognize, understand, and manage emotions. Dr. King demonstrated remarkable skill in managing his own emotions and in sparking emotions that moved his audience to action. As his speechwriter Clarence Jones reflected, King delivered "a perfectly balanced outcry of reason and emotion, of anger and hope. His tone of pained indignation matched that note for note."

Recognizing the power of emotions, another one of the most influential leaders of the 20th century spent years studying the emotional effects of his body language. Practicing his hand gestures and analyzing images of his movements allowed him to become "an absolutely spellbinding public speaker," says the historian Roger Moorhouse—"it was something he worked very hard on." His name was Adolf Hitler.

Since the 1995 publication of Daniel Goleman's bestseller, emotional intelligence has been touted by leaders, policymakers, and educators as the solution to a wide range of social problems. If we can teach our children to manage emotions, the argument goes, we'll have less bullying and more cooperation. If we can cultivate emotional intelligence among leaders and doctors, we'll have more caring workplaces and more compassionate healthcare. As a result, emotional intelligence is now taught widely in secondary schools, business schools, and medical schools.

"Emotional intelligence is important, but the unbridled enthusiasm has obscured a dark side."

Emotional intelligence is important, but the unbridled enthusiasm has obscured a dark side. New evidence shows that when people hone their emotional skills, they become better at manipulating others. When you're good at controlling your own emotions, you can disguise your true feelings. When you know what others are feeling, you can tug at their heartstrings and motivate them to act against their own best interests.

Social scientists have begun to document this dark side of emotional intelligence. In emerging research led by University of Cambridge professor Jochen Menges, when a leader gave an inspiring speech filled with emotion, the audience was less likely to scrutinize the message and remembered less of the content. Ironically, audience members were so moved by the speech that they claimed to recall more of it.

The authors call this the awestruck effect, but it might just as easily be described as the dumbstruck effect. One observer reflected that Hitler's persuasive impact came from his ability to strategically express emotions—he would "tear open his heart"—and these emotions affected his followers to the point that they would "stop thinking critically and just emote."

Leaders who master emotions can rob us of our capacities to reason. If their values are out of step with our own, the results can be devastating. New evidence suggests that when people have self-serving motives, emotional intelligence becomes a weapon for manipulating others. In a study led by the University of Toronto psychologist Stéphane Côté, university employees filled out a survey about their Machiavellian° tendencies, and took a test measuring their knowledge about effective strategies for managing emotions. Then, Côté's team assessed how often the employees deliberately undermined their colleagues. The employees who engaged in the most harmful behaviors were Machiavellians with high emotional intelligence. They used their emotional skills to demean and embarrass

Machiavellian: cunning or scheming in an unscrupulous way, so named for cunning Italian diplomat Niccolò Machiavelli.

their peers for personal gain. In one computer company studied by Tel Aviv University professor Gideon Kunda, a manager admitted to telling a colleague "how excited we all are with what he is doing," but at the same time, "distancing my organization from the project," so "when it blows up," the company's founder would blame the colleague.

Shining a light on this dark side of emotional intelligence is one mission of a research team led by University College London professor Martin Kilduff. According to these experts, emotional intelligence helps people disguise one set of emotions while expressing another for personal gain. Emotionally intelligent people "intentionally shape their emotions to fabricate favorable impressions of themselves," Professor Kilduff's team writes. "The strategic disguise of one's own emotions and the manipulation of others' emotions for strategic ends are behaviors evident not only on Shakespeare's stage but also in the offices and corridors where power and influence are traded."

Of course, people aren't always using emotional intelligence for nefarious° ends. More often than not, emotional skills are simply instrumental tools for goal accomplishment. In a study of emotions at the Body Shop, a research team led by Stanford professor Joanne Martin discovered that founder Anita Roddick leveraged emotions to inspire her employees to fundraise for charity. As Roddick explained, "Whenever we wanted to persuade our staff to support a particular project we always tried to break their hearts." However, Roddick also encouraged employees to be strategic in the timing of their emotion expressions. In one case, after noticing that an employee often "breaks down in tears with frustration," Roddick said it was acceptable to cry, but "I told her it has to be used. I said, 'Here, cry at this point in the . . . meeting.'" When viewing Roddick as an exemplar of an emotionally intelligent leader, it becomes clear that there's a fine line between motivation and manipulation. Walking that tightrope is no easy task.

In settings where emotions aren't running high, emotional intelligence may have hidden costs. Recently, psychologists Dana Joseph of the University of Central Florida and Daniel Newman of the University of Illinois comprehensively analyzed every study that has ever examined the link between emotional intelligence and job performance. Across hundreds of studies of thousands of employees in 191 different jobs, emotional intelligence wasn't consistently linked with better performance. In jobs that required extensive attention to emotions, higher emotional intelligence translated into better performance. Salespeople, real-estate agents, call-center representatives, and counselors all excelled

10

nefarious: wicked or criminal.

at their jobs when they knew how to read and regulate emotions—they were able to deal more effectively with stressful situations and provide service with a smile.

However, in jobs that involved fewer emotional demands, the results reversed. The more emotionally intelligent employees were, the *lower* their job performance. For mechanics, scientists, and accountants, emotional intelligence was a liability rather than an asset. Although more research is needed to unpack these results, one promising explanation is that these employees were paying attention to emotions when they should have been focusing on their tasks. If your job is to analyze data or repair cars, it can be quite distracting to read the facial expressions, vocal tones, and body languages of the people around you. In suggesting that emotional intelligence is critical in the workplace, perhaps we've put the cart before the horse.

Instead of assuming that emotional intelligence is always useful, we need to think more carefully about where and when it matters. In a recent study at a healthcare company, I asked employees to complete a test about managing and regulating emotions, and then asked managers to evaluate how much time employees spent helping their colleagues and customers. There was no relationship whatsoever between emotional intelligence and helping: Helping is driven by our motivations and values, not by our abilities to understand and manage emotions. However, emotional intelligence was consequential when examining a different behavior: challenging the status quo by speaking up with ideas and suggestions for improvement.

Emotionally intelligent employees spoke up more often and more effectively. When colleagues were treated unjustly, they felt the righteous indignation to speak up, but were able to keep their anger in check and reason with their colleagues. When they went out on a limb to advocate for gender equity, emotional intelligence helped them keep their fear at bay. When they brought ideas for innovation to senior leaders, their ability to express enthusiasm helped them avoid threatening leaders. On a much smaller scale, they were able to follow Martin Luther King Jr.'s lead in rocking the boat while keeping it steady.

More than two decades have passed since psychologists Peter Salovey 15 at Yale and John Mayer at the University of New Hampshire introduced the concept of emotional intelligence in 1990. Why has it taken us so long to develop a more nuanced view? After Daniel Goleman popularized the idea in 1995, many researchers—perhaps awestruck themselves by enthusiasm for the concept of emotional intelligence—proceeded to conduct studies that were fatally flawed. As University of Lausanne professor John Antonakis observed, "practice and voodoo science is running way ahead of rigorous research."

One of the most persistent problems was the use of self-report measures, which asked employees to rate their own emotional abilities on items like "I can tell how people are feeling even if they never tell me" and "I am generally very good at calming someone down when he or she is upset." Abilities cannot be accurately measured with self-reports. As emotion experts Sigal Barsade of Wharton and Donald Gibson of Fairfield University lament, "One might compare this approach to assessing mathematical skills by asking respondents, 'How good are you at solving algebraic equations?' rather than asking the person to actually solve an algebraic equation."

Thanks to more rigorous research methods, there is growing recognition that emotional intelligence—like any skill—can be used for good or evil. So if we're going to teach emotional intelligence in schools and develop it at work, we need to consider the values that go along with it and where it's actually useful. As Professor Kilduff and colleagues put it, it is high time that emotional intelligence is "pried away from its association with desirable moral qualities."

Understanding the Text

1. What exactly is the dark side of emotional intelligence? Expound on Grant's title by offering a definition of this concept drawn from his text and supported with quotations.

2. Grant doesn't want to dismiss emotional intelligence altogether. What does he ask us to do instead? Review his text and compile the responses he'd like us to have to emotional intelligence.

Reflection and Response

3. Grant writes that "there's a fine line between motivation and manipulation" when it comes to using emotional intelligence, using the example of Anita Roddick, founder of the Body Shop (p. 149). Write an essay in which you propose ways we can walk that fine line. When is emotional intelligence useful? When should it not be used? How do we avoid manipulating others? Can we? What are the ethics of emotional intelligence?

4. Grant contrasts reason and emotion throughout his essay. But are they always so separate? Write an essay in which you complicate the relationship between emotion and reason. How might emotions cause us to reason more? Is reason always a reliable way to make decisions?

Making Connections

5. Although he is specifically discussing emotional intelligence, many of Grant's points seem like they could be applied to other kinds of intelligences as well. Expand Grant's argument by applying it to one of the other readings in this section. Can any kind of intelligence be dangerous? Are there certain responsibilities "smart" people have, no matter what kind of intelligence?

6. Near the end of his essay, Grant discusses flaws in the early research around emotional intelligence. Connect this critique to Howard Gardner's ("The Idea of Multiple Intelligences," p. 124) approach to laying out an argument for multiple intelligences. Based on Gardner's rationale for coming to the conclusion that multiple intelligences exist, would he be subject to the same critique? What methods should we use for thinking about and research intelligence?

What Is "Successful" Intelligence?

Robert J. Sternberg

Robert J. Sternberg is a professor of human development in the College of Human Ecology at Cornell University. He has authored more than two dozen books, including *Successful Intelligence: How Practical and Creative Intelligence Determines Success in Life* (1996), *Why Smart People Can Be So Stupid* (2002), and *Wisdom, Intelligence, and Creativity Synthesized* (2003). He is widely recognized for his significant contributions to psychology, including theories on creativity, wisdom, love, and hate. He also contributed the triarchic theory of intelligence, which places book smarts alongside creativity and street smarts. The excerpt presented here is from his early work on successful intelligence, a more approachable version of his triarchic theory.

Jack, who considers himself smartest in his class, likes to make fun of Irvin, the boy he has identified as stupidest in the class. Jack pulls aside his friend Tom and says, "You want to see what 'stupid' means, Tom? Watch this . . . Hey, Irvin. Here are two coins. Take whichever one you want. It's yours."

Irvin looks at the two coins, a nickel and a dime, for a while and then selects the nickel.

"Go ahead, Irv, take it, it's yours." Jack laughs.

Irvin takes the larger coin and walks away. An adult who has been watching the transaction from a distance walks up to Irvin and gently points out that the dime is worth more than the nickel, even though it is smaller, and that Irvin has just cost himself 5 cents.

"Oh, I know that," replies Irvin, "but if I picked the dime, Jack would 5 never ask me to choose between the two coins again. This way, he'll keep asking me again and again. I've already collected over a dollar from him, and all I have to do is keep choosing the nickel."

This apocryphal story points out something we already intuitively know — that someone can be slow in school but think well outside it, and vice-versa. The hoary question "How can someone so smart be so dumb?" reminds us that people can be good or bad thinkers, regardless of how well they may do in a school setting. I found this out the hard way.

My interest in broadening our means of identifying potential high performers in life and not just in school came from an experience in my own career. Because of my wretched performance on IQ tests as a child, I became very interested in psychology. By the time I was in 7th grade, I decided I wanted to study intelligence. I did just that. In carrying out a project on the development of mental tests, I constructed my own test. I also found in my hometown library the Stanford-Binet intelligence test and decided to give it to some of my classmates.

My first subject was a girl in whom I was romantically interested. I figured I would break the ice by giving her the test. Not a good idea. The relationship not only terminated at that point, it never even got started.

My choice of the next subject — a boy I had known from Cub Scouts — was also a mistake. I thought he was a good friend, but he was a fink. He told his mother I had given him the test. She told the junior high school guidance counselor, who reported me to the head school psychologist. The whole affair came to an unpleasant conclusion when the psychologist took me out of social studies class and, after bawling me out for 50 minutes, threatened to personally burn the book containing the test if I ever brought it to school again. He suggested that if I wanted to continue studying intelligence, I should limit my subjects to rats.

Once in college, I was still eager to study intelligence and figure out 10 why I was so stupid, because I knew I had a low IQ. There is a not so hidden point here. Once students get low scores on aptitude tests such as an IQ test, the SAT, or the ACT, they come to think of themselves as dumb. Even if they achieve, they may view themselves as achieving in spite of their being dumb. Society may view them in the same way. They may come to be labeled overachievers, people whose achievements seem to exceed their intelligence and who ought to be pushed down in size.

> "Some societies don't value outstanding performance or, at least, performance that stands out."

Some societies don't value outstanding performance or, at least, performance that stands out. In Norway, they speak of the Law of Jante, according to which if someone's head sticks up over the heads of others, then it should be cut off to get that person down to size. This same mentality is rather common in other parts of the world and is not unknown here. Many people grow up in families or go to schools where what is valued most is *not* standing out from the crowd — at least in unconventional ways. Too often, conformity is the norm.

Pursuing my interest in psychology as a freshman at Yale, I got off to a bad start. I got a grade of C in the introductory psychology course, scarcely an indication of a bright future in the field. It was further confirmation that my IQ scores were right and I didn't have the ability. My psychology professor apparently agreed with me. Handing back a test to me one day, he commented that there was a famous Sternberg in psychology (Saul), and it appeared there wasn't about to be another. I took the message to heart and decided to switch to another major. I chose mathematics, because I thought it was useful. The choice turned out to be fortunate. After receiving a worse grade In the introductory course for math majors than I had received in the introductory psychology course, I decided to switch back to psychology. And I did well in the upper-level courses.

I have now been a psychologist for 21 years, and one thing of which I am certain is that I have never—not even once—had to do in the profession what I needed to do to get an A in the introductory course, as well as in some of the other courses. In particular, I've never had to memorize a book or lecture. If I can't remember something, I just look it up. The way schools set things up, however, they reward with A's the students who are good memorizers, not just at the college level but at many other levels as well. In defense of our schools, the educational systems in many other countries are worse in this regard.

The problem is that, in psychology as in other fields, the demands of the field bear little or no resemblance to the demands of the training needed in order to enter the field. For example, my son once said to me that he hated history and wished he never had to take another history course. I said to him that I, personally, had always found history interesting and I wondered why he didn't. His response was that he hated memorizing dates. Indeed, memorizing dates, battles, and historical documents constitutes the way many history courses are taught. But historians are not experts in their fields by virtue of being walking encyclopedias of dates or names of battles or historical documents.

In general, the same thing is true in the sciences. Often what gets 15 an A is memorizing formulas or solving problems in textbooks and on tests. But scientists don't memorize formulas for a living, nor do they solve textbook problems. Rather, they generate problems for themselves. Indeed, to a large extent they are judged on the importance of the problems they decide to study.

I went to my son's English class one Parents' Day. They were studying the *Odyssey*. A good book—actually, a great one. The teacher read a quote, and the students had to identify who said it, or what was happening at the time. For students who loved to memorize, that was just fine. But no one who excelled in that class was showing the talents of either a writer or a literary critic. And among those who did not do so well was, for all we could tell, one who had the potential talent to be the next Shakespeare. Unlikely, perhaps, but the teacher would never know, given the way the class was taught.

The danger is that we overlook many talented people in any field of study because of the way we measure intelligence, and some of the best potential psychologists, biologists, historians, or whatever may get derailed because they are made to think they don't have the talent to pursue their interests. Clearly, we need to teach in a way that recognizes, develops, and rewards the three aspects of successful intelligence that are important to pursuing a career in any field.

Two boys are walking in a forest. They are quite different. The first boy's teachers think he is smart, his parents think he is smart, and as a result, he thinks he is smart. He has good test scores, good grades, and other good paper credentials that will get him far in his scholastic life. Few people consider the second boy smart. His test scores are nothing great, his grades aren't so good, and his other paper credentials are, in general, marginal. At best, people would call him shrewd or street-smart. As the two boys walk along in the forest, they encounter a problem—a huge, furious, hungry-looking grizzly bear, charging straight at them. The first boy, calculating that the grizzly bear will overtake them in 17.3 seconds, panics. In this state, he looks at the second boy, who is calmly taking off his hiking boots and putting on his jogging shoes.

The first boy says to the second boy, "You must be crazy. There is no way we are going to outrun that grizzly bear!"

The second boy replies, "That's true. But all I have to do is outrun 20 you!"

Both boys in that story are smart, but they are smart in different ways. The first boy quickly analyzed the problem, but that was as far as his intelligence took him. The second boy not only spotted the problem, he came up with a creative and practical solution. He displayed successful intelligence.

To be successfully intelligent is to think well in three different ways: analytically, creatively, and practically. Typically, only analytical intelligence is valued on tests and in the classroom. Yet the style of intelligence that schools most readily recognize as smart may well be less useful to many students in their adult lives than creative and practical intelligence.

The three aspects of successful intelligence are related. Analytical thinking is required to solve problems and to judge the quality of ideas. Creative intelligence is required to formulate good problems and ideas in the first place. Practical intelligence is needed to use the ideas and their analysis in an effective way in one's everyday life.

Successful intelligence is most effective when it balances all three of its analytical, creative, and practical aspects. It is more important to know when and how to use these aspects of successful intelligence than just to have them. Successfully intelligent people don't just have abilities, they reflect on when and how to use these abilities effectively.

Understanding the Text

1. Using Sternberg's text, define successful intelligence and its three aspects.
2. What, according to Sternberg, are the problems with education?
3. Sternberg uses stories to make many of his points. Why do you think he takes this approach? What does it say about his audience? How effective are these stories, and when might you use a similar technique in your writing?

Reflection and Response

4. What are the consequences of being labeled "dumb"? Use Sternberg's text to write an essay about the negative and positive effects of thinking of yourself as not smart. You may want to incorporate your personal experience.
5. Sternberg notes that there is a disjunction between how we teach subjects in school and how professionals in the field actually work in those subjects. Using your smartphone or another video recording device, make a vlog about this problem and then propose changes to education we might make to better prepare students for their lives after school.

Making Connections

6. "Successfully intelligent people don't just have abilities," Sternberg concludes, "they reflect on when and how to use these abilities effectively" (p. 156). Apply Sternberg's conclusion to Adam Grant's ("The Dark Side of Emotional Intelligence," p. 147) discussion of the dangers of emotional intelligence. How can embracing successful intelligence help us use emotional intelligence wisely?
7. In "The End of IQ (and the Dawn of Working Memory)," Ross Alloway and Tracy Alloway (p. 158) advocate for the concept of working memory. Synthesize their ideas with Sternberg's arguments about successful intelligence. Is working memory a component of successful intelligence? What about the other factors?

The End of IQ (and the Dawn of Working Memory)

Ross Alloway and Tracy Alloway

Tracy Packiam Alloway is an associate professor of psychology at the University of North Florida, where her husband. Ross Alloway, also served as a researcher. Together they have authored books on working memory, including *The Working Memory Advantage: Train Your Brain to Function Stronger, Smarter, Faster* (2013) and *Understanding Working Memory* (2014). The Alloways' research has been featured the *Washington Post* and *Newsweek* as well as on Salon.com, and Ross Alloway writes a blog for the *Huffington Post*. The selection featured here was published on the *Huffington Post*.

If you are proud of your high IQ, stop reading now. Your IQ is an anachronism, and its reign is coming to an end. IQ, a measure of intelligence dependent on one's knowledge of specific information, has lost its relevance in the age of information. There is far too much information to know in our global society for any test to measure it adequately. Moreover, IQ won't help you in the things that really matter: it won't help you find happiness, it won't help you make better decisions, and it won't help you manage your kids' homework and the accounts at the same time. It isn't even that useful at its raison d'être°: predicting success.

We know this because we followed school children over a six-year period and found that their IQ score at 5 years old wasn't very helpful in determining their grades at 11 years old. On the one hand, schools that rely on IQ to identify the best students may be missing a lot of them, and on the other hand, students that are rather clever may be missing out on opportunities only available to those with a higher IQ score. Beyond the classroom, employers that rely on IQ scores for hiring or promotion may be hurting the bottom line by overlooking the best candidates.

This begs the question, why do we still use IQ? In our Google Age, where any datum can be had at the tap of a touch-screen, who cares if you know how to assemble blocks in a particular pattern (a key component of IQ testing) or even the answers to the following questions:

- Velvet Joe appears in advertisements of (a) toothpowder (b) dry goods (c) tobacco (d) soap.

---

raison d'être: French phrase meaning the most important reason for someone or something's existence.

158

- What should you do if you lose a friend's ball?
- Define the word "Police"

Each question is from an IQ test: a century ago, 30 years ago, and a current IQ test. Each question draws on very specific cultural knowledge, and that's a problem if your culture doesn't match with the answers in the manual.

We gave the last question to a child whose answer was "I don't like 5 police, they took my dad away." He was supposed to answer along the lines of "they keep people safe" — and was marked wrong. But was he wrong? His answer matched his information. *He* didn't believe that the police kept *him* safe by arresting *his* father.

A measure of intelligence based on culturally-loaded information will exclude those without that information. That doesn't mean they aren't intelligent, and in the postmodern age, when cultures cross-germinate in rapid fashion, defining intelligence according to one's familiarity with a specific cultural domain is behind the times.

> "A measure of intelligence based on culturally-loaded information will exclude those without that information."

The Dawn of Working Memory

So, how should we think about intelligence? There is one thing everyone in the information age has to do: work with information in all its diverse forms. By testing how well someone works with information, rather than how well they know culturally-loaded information, a person from Paris, Texas, is on a level playing field with someone from Paris, France, and vice-versa.

Working memory is our ability to consciously work with information. By *conscious*, we mean you are thinking about the information, concentrating on it, shining a mental spotlight on it, and ignoring everything else. By *work*, we mean that you are manipulating the information, making calculations with it, or reformulating it.

The classic example of a job that requires a strong working memory is that of an air traffic controller, whose responsibility is to maintain the safe and orderly flow of air traffic. With hundreds of planes taking off and landing every hour, an air traffic controller must have the mental agility to process multiple variables—such as equipment, weather patterns, traffic volume, precise communication with pilots, and quick calculations. In times of emergency, they must be able to make split-second decisions while effectively moderating the stress of knowing that the lives of pilots and passengers are in their hands.

In a similar manner, your working memory helps you managing the   10
deluge of information that comprises your life: the ringing cell phone,
the Twitter update, the presentation that must be rapidly assembled for a
client, and the constantly changing schedule.

Scientists at the cutting-edge are beginning to realize the importance
of working memory in daily life. In the last decade there has been an
explosion of research showing how a strong working memory is beneficial for a diversity of human experience:

STAY FOCUSED ON A TASK: Researchers at University of North Carolina
found that those with a higher working
memory were less likely than those with a
lower working memory to let their thoughts
wander from an appointed task.

SUPERTASK: Researchers from the University of Utah have
discovered that working memory gives some of
us an amazing ability to multitask. Most of us
can do one thing well, but two things poorly.
However, researchers found that those with a
high working memory are "supertaskers" that
can do two things at the same time just as well
as if they are only doing one.

SPORTS: Swedish researchers found that the better the
athlete was at a sport, the higher their scores
on working-memory-type tasks. A higher
working memory may help them process the
information on the field to help them predict,
adapt, and innovate in response to a dynamic
situation.

HAPPINESS: Our research of almost 4,000 adults shows that
working memory determines how optimistic
you are, which, in turn, can protect you from
experiencing the symptoms of depression.

ACADEMIC SUCCESS: Working memory even beats IQ at its own
game. Our research has found that working
memory is 3 to 4 times more accurate than IQ
in predicting grades in spelling, reading, and
math.

In studies with thousands of children, from gifted children to those
with learning needs, working memory plays a key role in learning. It
helps children work with information—with numbers for math, with

words for reading and writing, with things they already know so they can answer things they don't. In fact, this skill is so important that if you know a kindergartener's working memory, you will know their grades years later.

If you have a high IQ, you shouldn't feel threatened by working memory, because your working memory is your greatest cognitive asset, and in the information age how well you work with information, any information, can make the difference between success and failure.

Understanding the Text

1. Review the essay to find the Alloways' definition of working memory and their example of a career in which having good working memory is important. Put this definition into your own words, offering your own example of a job or career that might require good working memory.

2. According to the Alloways, what are the problems with traditional notions of IQ? Use passages from the text to support your answer.

Reflection and Response

3. How have digital technologies changed what it means to be intelligent? Locate quotations from the text where the Alloways discuss this issue and then present your response using a digital technology through, for example, a blog or vlog posting or a PowerPoint presentation.

4. The Alloways suggest that working memory is important for happiness. Respond to this assertion by making your own argument about what it takes to be happy and connecting to their discussion of working memory.

Making Connections

5. Part of the problem with IQ tests, according to the Alloways, is that they are culturally loaded. Select one other reading from this chapter and describe how it is culturally loaded as well. Is there a universal aspect to intelligence, or does what it means to be smart always depend on a local cultural context?

6. Although they suggest that working memory offers a better understanding of intelligence than traditional approaches measured through IQ tests, the Alloways still rely on a concept of intelligence centered around information. Apply Daniel Goleman's ("When Smart Is Dumb," p. 133) arguments to working memory. Does it represent a better concept of intelligence than the Alloways', or are there other aspects we must consider?

"Wisdom of the Crowd": The Myths and Realities

Philip Ball

British science writer Philip Ball spent two decades as editor at the prestigious journal *Nature*, where he continues to contribute his writing. That writing has also appeared in *New Scientist*, *New York Times*, *The Guardian*, *Financial Times*, *New Statesman*, and BBC Future, from which this selection is taken. He is also the author of nearly two dozen books, including *Patterns in Nature: Why the Natural World Looks the Way It Does* (2016), *Beyond Weird: Why Everything You Thought You Knew about Quantum Physics Is Different* (2018), and *How to Grow a Human: Adventures in How We Are Made and Who We Are* (2019). In this selection, Ball delves into a different approach to intelligence—group intelligence, or the "wisdom of crowds"—to figure out how it works, how it fails, and what we can do to make it even smarter.

Is *The Lord of the Rings* the greatest work of literature of the 20th Century? Is *The Shawshank Redemption* the best movie ever made? Both have been awarded these titles by public votes. You don't have to be a literary or film snob to wonder about the wisdom of so-called "wisdom of the crowd."

In an age routinely denounced as selfishly individualistic, it's curious that a great deal of faith still seems to lie with the judgment of the crowd, especially when it can apparently be far off the mark. Yet there is some truth underpinning the idea that the masses can make more accurate collective judgments than expert individuals. So why is a crowd sometimes right and sometimes disastrously wrong?

The notion that a group's judgment can be surprisingly good was most compellingly justified in James Surowiecki's 2005 book *The Wisdom of Crowds*, and is generally traced back to an observation by Charles Darwin's cousin Francis Galton in 1907. Galton pointed out that the average of all the entries in a "guess the weight of the ox" competition at a country fair was amazingly accurate—beating not only most of the individual guesses but also those of alleged cattle experts. This is the essence of the wisdom of crowds: their average judgment converges on the right solution.

Flawed Thinking

Still, Surowiecki also pointed out that the crowd is far from infallible. He explained that one requirement for a good crowd judgment is that people's decisions are independent of one another. If everyone let themselves be influenced by each other's guesses, there's more chance that the guesses will drift towards a misplaced bias. This undermining effect of social influence was demonstrated in 2011 by a team at the Swiss Federal Institute of Technology (ETH) in Zurich. They asked groups of participants to estimate certain quantities in geography or crime, about which none of them could be expected to have perfect knowledge but all could hazard a guess—the length of the Swiss-Italian border, for example, or the annual number of murders in Switzerland. The participants were offered modest financial rewards for good group guesses, to make sure they took the challenge seriously.

The researchers found that, as the amount of information participants were given about each other's guesses increased, the range of their guesses got narrower, and the center of this range could drift further from the true value. In other words, the groups were tending towards a consensus, to the detriment of accuracy.

This finding challenges a common view in management and politics that it is best to seek consensus in group decision making. What you can end up with instead is herding towards a relatively arbitrary position. Just how arbitrary depends on what kind of pool of opinions you start off with, according to subsequent work by one of the ETH team, Frank Schweitzer, and his colleagues. They say that if the group generally has good initial judgment, social influence can refine rather than degrade their collective decision.

Financial Meltdown

No one should need warning about the dangers of herding among poorly informed decision-makers: copycat behavior has been widely regarded as one of the major contributing factors to the financial crisis, and indeed to all financial crises of the past. The Swiss team commented that this detrimental herding effect is likely to be even greater for deciding problems for which no objectively correct answer exists, which perhaps explains how democratic countries occasionally elect such astonishingly inept leaders.

There's another key factor that makes the crowd accurate, or not. It has long been argued that the wisest crowds are the most diverse. That's a conclusion supported in a 2004 study by Scott Page of the University of Michigan and Lu Hong of Loyola University in Chicago. They showed that, in a theoretical model of group decision-making, a diverse group of problem-solvers made a better collective guess than that produced by the group of best-performing solvers. In other words, diverse minds do better, when their decisions are averaged, than expert minds.

In fact, here's a situation where a little knowledge can be a dangerous thing. A study in 2011 by a team led by Joseph Simmons of the Yale

School of Management in New Haven, Connecticut, found that group predictions about American football results were skewed away from the real outcomes by the over-confidence of the fans' decisions, which biased them towards alleged "favorites" in the outcomes of games.

All of these findings suggest that knowing who is in the crowd, and how diverse they are, is vital before you attribute to them any real wisdom. 10

> "These findings suggest that knowing who is in the crowd, and how diverse they are, is vital before you attribute to them any real wisdom."

Intelligence Upgrade

Could there also be ways to make an existing crowd wiser? Last month, Clintin Davis-Stober of the University of Missouri and his co-workers presented calculations at a conference on Collective Intelligence that provide a few answers.

They first refined the statistical definition of what it means for a crowd to be wise—when, exactly, some aggregate of crowd judgments can be considered better than those of selected individuals. This definition allowed the researchers to develop guidelines for improving the wisdom of a group. Previous work might imply that you should add random individuals whose decisions are unrelated to those of existing group members. That would be good, but it's better still to add individuals who aren't simply independent thinkers but whose views are "negatively correlated"—as different as possible—from the existing members. In other words, diversity trumps independence.

If you want accuracy, then, add those who might disagree strongly with your group. What do you reckon of the chances that managers and politicians will select such contrarian candidates to join them? All the same, armed with this information I intend to apply for a position in the Cabinet of the British government. They'd be wise not to refuse.

Understanding the Text

1. Define the "wisdom of the crowd" using Ball's text. What factors impact the wisdom of the crowd for better and worse?

2. Often the "wisdom of crowds" is reached, as in Ball's opening example from Francis Galton, by taking the average of all answers. How does that challenge our understanding of what "average" means? Explore the multiple meanings of this word in relation to Ball's argument.

3. What is a negative correlation? Define this term through Ball's text and then discuss what role it can play in harnessing the wisdom of crowds.

Reflection and Response

4. Is the wisdom of crowds actually a kind of intelligence? Evaluate Ball's argument by first offering your own definition of intelligence and then applying it to his essay.

5. "So why is a crowd sometimes right and sometimes disastrously wrong?," Ball asks (p. 162). Answer his question, drawing from the insights in his essay, and consider offering an example of your own that shows sometimes right, sometimes wrong nature of crowds.

Making Connections

6. Part of the goal of Ball's essay is to zero in on the factors that make the wisdom of crowds *successful*. Apply Robert J. Sternberg's ("What Is 'Successful' Intelligence?," p. 153) discussion of successful intelligence to Ball's essay. Are they successful in the same way? How might the rest of Sternberg's argument about the elements of successful intelligence apply to groups?

7. Is it possible to extend Howard Gardner's ("The Idea of Multiple Intelligences," p. 124) ideas of localizers and holists in conceptions of intelligence to Ball? To what extent do groups represent another level of holism in relation to intelligence? Similarly, how might Ball's insights about group intelligence contribute to Gardner's critique of traditional understandings of what it means to be smart?

We Need More Tests, Not Fewer

John D. Mayer

John D. Mayer is a professor of psychology at the University of New Hampshire, where his research focuses on personality psychology and intelligence. He is the author of nine books, including *Personal Intelligence: The Power of Personality and How It Shapes Our Lives* (2014), *The Elements of Mental Tests* (2016), and *Personality: A Systems Approach* (2018), and has served on the editorial boards of *Psychological Bulletin*, the *Journal of Personality*, and the *Journal of Personality and Social Psychology*. With Peter Salovey, the current president of Yale University, Mayer developed the concept of emotional intelligence discussed in other readings in this chapter.

Last week, the College Board announced that it was revising the SAT in an effort to make it more acceptable to test-takers, teachers, college admissions officers and the public more generally. That's a tough objective. The SAT tells us something about how smart we (or our children or students) are. Test-takers who receive lower scores than they had hoped for are likely to be dismayed at the news—and concerned about their academic future. It's no wonder that it's hard to discuss the test dispassionately.

Even before the announcement of the SAT's redesign, commentators were discussing the test's limitations. Writing in the *New Yorker*, Elizabeth Kolbert described its questions as superficial: "Critical thinking was never called for, let alone curiosity or imagination."

The SAT isn't perfect. Like any test, it can be misused, can misevaluate a person, and may reflect unequal educational opportunities. But what interview or grading process is free from such concerns? The SAT provides a valid measure of a person's ability to reason through verbal and mathematical materials, a skill required in college and in our increasingly information-oriented workplaces. Although there are conflicting reports on the issue, a study published in the journal *Educational and Psychological Measurement* in 2011 found that the SAT can meaningfully add to the prediction of a student's first-year college G.P.A., above his grades in high school alone. The fact that the SAT can, during a morning's testing, help predict this is, to me, an astonishing achievement that cannot be ignored.

Research indicates that mental tests do predict people's patterns of behavior in consequential ways. For instance, graduate students' GRE scores are correlated with the ratings faculty members later give them, their likelihood of remaining in a program, and the impact of their

Standardized tests are a fixture of public and private education.
Paul Bradbury/Caiaimage/Diomedia

publications (as measured by citations). And tests like the NEO-PI-R that measure social and emotional traits like conscientiousness and agreeableness can predict a person's longevity and likelihood of staying married.

In addition, tests are our only way to study and attempt to understand 5 ineffable° mental qualities like intelligence, openness to experience, and creativity. They help make the mysteries of mental life tangible. Neuroscientists use them to discover who excels in particular mental abilities, and to try to identify the parts of the brain responsible.

We cannot afford to ignore tests because they fall short of perfection or make us uncomfortable.

Some colleges, in response to the pushback against the SAT, have de-emphasized

> "We cannot afford to ignore tests because they fall short of perfection."

it, along with the ACT, and are allowing students to opt out. But there's a better way to make the SAT more acceptable in the long run: We should expand the types of tests we use so as to more fully reflect what students can do.

What if, in addition to the SAT, students were offered new tests that measured more diverse abilities? For future artists or musicians, there are tests that measure divergent thinking—a cornerstone of creativity largely ignored by the SAT. For future engineers, there are tests that measure spatial reasoning. And new measures of "personal intelligence"—the ability to reason about a person's motives, emotions and patterns

ineffable: beyond words; indescribable.

of activities—may also tell us something important about students' self-knowledge and understanding of others.

Colleges and universities could create a list of tests that have been proved to fairly and reasonably accurately measure ability, and students could pick ones in which they hoped to excel.

We can't expect these tests to predict first-year college G.P.A. as well as the SAT does. But they may predict other outcomes of importance, and help colleges to recognize the diversity of abilities in future students. 10

By allowing students to opt out of testing, we deprive colleges and universities of an important tool to compare applicants, and suggest to young people that self-knowledge isn't important. By adding tests, we send a different message: that information about ourselves is helpful to know, and that people are multifaceted and multitalented.

Understanding the Text

1. What are some of the points Mayer uses to defend intelligence testing? Use passages from his text in making your response.

2. Why, according to Mayer, should schools and universities expand testing for student applicants?

Reflection and Response

3. Respond to Mayer's text based on your own experience as a college student. Do you think the testing you went through was sufficient? Fair? Do you think your experience entering college would have been different with more tests that recognized other aspects of who you are? Be sure to engage specific passages from Mayer's text in making your response.

4. Mayer claims that "tests are our only way to study and attempt to understand ineffable mental qualities like intelligence, openness to experience, and creativity" (p. 167). Do you agree? How else might we measure those qualities? How might schools determine admissions without the use of tests?

Making Connections

5. According to Philip Ball ("'Wisdom of the Crowd': The Myths and Realities," p. 162), the wisdom of crowds can be particularly good at accurately judging situations and making decisions. How might it be possible to use the wisdom of crowds to address the problem of testing that Mayer explores? Use Ball's ideas to propose strategies to solve the challenges of admissions testing. Could group intelligence locate the best alternative to the SAT? Could it be used to determine college admissions? How would the inclusion of diversity in the decision-making process perhaps also benefit the larger admissions processes at some schools?

6. Robert J. Sternberg ("What Is 'Successful' Intelligence?," p. 153) illuminates the limits of IQ and other tests, particularly in relation to success in school and in life. Make a poster presentation that applies his critique to Mayer's argument in favor of more testing. A poster presentation is an academic genre used in many disciplines in which researchers summarize their findings on a poster board, using key data and images. As you craft your poster, be aware of the impact of spacing and visual arrangement.

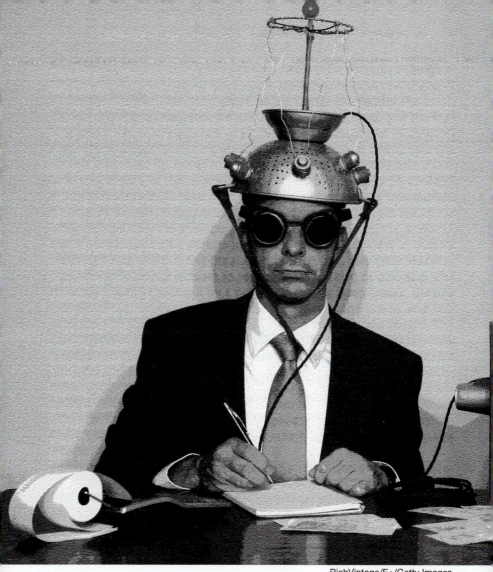

4 | Does Identity Determine Intelligence?

E
ven though we know they're problematic, even though we know they're usually inaccurate, stereotypes continue to circulate in our world. Perhaps the most common (and most damaging) stereotype about any group relates to that group's intelligence, or lack thereof. Whether positive ("Asians are smart") or negative ("Women aren't as intelligent as men"), these stereotypes foster prejudice and discrimination, blind us to the unique abilities of individuals, and substitute generalization for critical thinking. Stereotypes aren't very smart at all.

All too often, someone will try to use science to prove these stereotypes true, coating them in a thin veneer of objectivity. Just as often, the science in these studies turns out to be wrong or simply more complicated than once thought. The question of how identity — racial, ethnic, sexual, class, gender — relates to intelligence simply doesn't inspire any easy answers. That's where you come in. You've already spent some time thinking about different kinds of intelligence in different contexts, and this chapter is an opportunity to untangle the issues around intelligence and identity. These issues may be close to your own sense of self, making them particularly delicate, tricky to navigate — and important.

The essays in this chapter will give you tools to explore the relationship between intelligence and various categories of identity. Malcolm Gladwell opens this exploration by examining the Flynn effect, a phenomenon discovered by social scientist James Flynn, who made the remarkable observation that IQs around the world seem to be rising every year. Gladwell uses the Flynn effect to complicate persistent notions related to race, ethnicity, and intelligence. Jennifer Lee continues that conversation, tackling the "model minority" stereotype of Asian Americans and their remarkable academic success and tracing that success not to Asian culture or genetics, but to immigration laws. William Saletan initially bought into the troubling links between race and genetics that both Gladwell and Lee debunk, but in his essay, he explains why he was wrong and offers a first-hand experience of someone working through these issues, looking at the evidence, and reaching a now conclusion. Moving Into questions of sex and gender, Diane F. Halpern looks at the evidence about differences in intelligence between women and men for a review of scientific studies that reveals differences — which she cautions us not to think of as deficiencies. Too many people have done so for too long, which leads into Lily Rothman's history of the term "mansplaining," showing the real-world, long-standing consequences of stereotypes formulated around those differences. Mark Joseph Stern extends the conversation to the question of sexuality, looking at the sociological factors around the intelligence and success of LGBTQ+ people. Finally, Mike Rose closes our investigation by revealing the varied forms of intelligence exhibited by blue-collar and service workers.

The common thread uniting these essays is that aspects of our identity do not predetermine our intelligence, despite the stereotypes that continue to persist. But there are other lessons here as well. Science is less the source of a single truth and more an ongoing, revised, revisited search for truth. Speaking out against stereotypes and confronting them with hard critical thinking begins a process of change — and people can change their minds on these issues.

None of the Above

Malcolm Gladwell

Journalist Malcolm Gladwell, a staff writer for the *New Yorker*, has authored six books, including *The Tipping Point: How Little Things Can Make a Big Difference* (2000), *Blink: The Power of Thinking without Thinking* (2005), and *Talking to Strangers: What We Should Know about the People We Don't Know* (2019). Through his podcast company Pushkin Industries, he hosts two podcasts: *Revisionist History*, in which he revisits and reinterprets misunderstood and overlooked bits of history, and *Broken Record*, in which he interviews musicians with Bruce Headlam. Gladwell has also made *Time*'s list of the 100 Most Influential People and *Foreign Policy*'s Top Global Thinkers. The selection included here is from his work for the *New Yorker*.

One Saturday in November of 1984, James Flynn, a social scientist at the University of Otago, in New Zealand, received a large package in the mail. It was from a colleague in Utrecht, and it contained the results of I.Q. tests given to two generations of Dutch eighteen-year-olds. When Flynn looked through the data, he found something puzzling. The Dutch eighteen-year-olds from the nineteen-eighties scored better than those who took the same tests in the nineteen-fifties — and not just slightly better, *much* better.

Curious, Flynn sent out some letters. He collected intelligence-test results from Europe, from North America, from Asia, and from the developing world, until he had data for almost thirty countries. In every case, the story was pretty much the same. I.Q.s around the world appeared to be rising by 0.3 points per year, or three points per decade, for as far back as the tests had been administered. For some reason, human beings seemed to be getting smarter.

Flynn has been writing about the implications of his findings — now known as the Flynn effect — for almost twenty-five years. His books consist of a series of plainly stated statistical observations, in support of deceptively modest conclusions, and the evidence in support of his original observation is now so overwhelming that the Flynn effect has moved from theory to fact. What remains uncertain is how to make sense of the Flynn effect. If an American born in the nineteen-thirties has an I.Q. of 100, the Flynn effect says that his children will have I.Q.s of 108, and his grandchildren I.Q.s of close to 120 — more than a standard deviation higher. If we work in the opposite direction, the typical teenager of today, with an I.Q. of 100, would have had grandparents with average I.Q.s of 82 — seemingly below the threshold necessary to graduate from high school. And, if we go back even farther, the Flynn effect puts the average I.Q.s of the schoolchildren of 1900 at around 70, which is to suggest, bizarrely, that a century ago the United States was populated largely by people who today would be considered mentally retarded.

For almost as long as there have been I.Q. tests, there have been I.Q. fundamentalists. H. H. Goddard, in the early years of the past century, established the idea that intelligence could be measured along a single, linear scale. One of his partic-ular contributions was to coin the word "moron." "The people who are doing the drudgery are, as a rule, in their proper places," he wrote. Goddard was followed by Lewis Terman, in the nineteen-twenties, who rounded up the California children with the highest I.Q.s, and confidently predicted that they would sit at the top of every profession. In 1969, the psychometrician Arthur Jensen argued that programs like Head Start, which tried to boost the academic perfor-mance of minority children, were doomed to failure, because I.Q. was so heavily genetic; and in 1994 Richard Herrnstein and Charles Murray, in *The Bell Curve*, notoriously proposed that Americans with the lowest I.Q.s be sequestered in a "high-tech" version of an Indian reservation, "while the rest of America tries to go about its business." To the I.Q. fundamen-talist, two things are beyond dispute: first, that I.Q. tests measure some hard and identifiable trait that predicts the quality of our thinking; and, second, that this trait is stable—that is, it is determined by our genes and largely impervious to environmental influences.

> "For almost as long as there have been I.Q. tests, there have been I.Q. fundamentalists."

This is what James Watson, the co-discoverer of DNA, meant when 5 he told an English newspaper recently that he was "inherently gloomy" about the prospects for Africa. From the perspective of an I.Q. funda-mentalist, the fact that Africans score lower than Europeans on I.Q. tests suggests an ineradicable cognitive disability. In the controversy that followed, Watson was defended by the journalist William Saletan, in a three-part series for the online magazine *Slate*. Drawing heavily on the work of J. Philippe Rushton—a psychologist who specializes in compar-ing the circumference of what he calls the Negroid brain with the length of the Negroid penis—Saletan took the fundamentalist position to its logical conclusion. To erase the difference between blacks and whites, Saletan wrote, would probably require vigorous interbreeding between the races, or some kind of corrective genetic engineering aimed at upgrading African stock. "Economic and cultural theories have failed to explain most of the pattern," Saletan declared, claiming to have been "soaking [his] head in each side's computations and arguments." One argument that Saletan never soaked his head in, however, was Flynn's, because what Flynn discovered in his mailbox upsets the certainties upon which I.Q. fundamentalism rests. If whatever the thing is that I.Q. tests measure can jump so much in a generation, it can't be all that immutable and it doesn't look all that innate.

The very fact that average I.Q.s shift over time ought to create a "crisis of confidence," Flynn writes in "What Is Intelligence?," his latest attempt to puzzle through the implications of his discovery. "How could such huge gains be intelligence gains? Either the children of today were far brighter than their parents or, at least in some circumstances, I.Q. tests were not good measures of intelligence."

The best way to understand why I.Q.s rise, Flynn argues, is to look at one of the most widely used I.Q. tests, the so-called WISC (for Wechsler Intelligence Scale for Children). The WISC is composed of ten subtests, each of which measures a different aspect of I.Q. Flynn points out that scores in some of the categories—those measuring general knowledge, say, or vocabulary or the ability to do basic arithmetic—have risen only modestly over time. The big gains on the WISC are largely in the category known as "similarities," where you get questions such as "In what way are 'dogs' and 'rabbits' alike?" Today, we tend to give what, for the purposes of I.Q. tests, is the right answer: dogs and rabbits are both mammals. A nineteenth-century American would have said that "you use dogs to hunt rabbits."

"If the everyday world is your cognitive home, it is not natural to detach abstractions and logic and the hypothetical from their concrete referents," Flynn writes. Our great-grandparents may have been perfectly intelligent. But they would have done poorly on I.Q. tests because they did not participate in the twentieth century's great cognitive revolution, in which we learned to sort experience according to a new set of abstract categories. In Flynn's phrase, we have now had to put on "scientific spectacles," which enable us to make sense of the WISC questions about similarities. To say that Dutch I.Q. scores rose substantially between 1952 and 1982 was another way of saying that the Netherlands in 1982 was, in at least certain respects, much more cognitively demanding than the Netherlands in 1952. An I.Q., in other words, measures not so much how smart we are as how *modern* we are.

This is a critical distinction. When the children of Southern Italian immigrants were given I.Q. tests in the early part of the past century, for example, they recorded median scores in the high seventies and low eighties, a full standard deviation below their American and Western European counterparts. Southern Italians did as poorly on I.Q. tests as Hispanics and blacks did. As you can imagine, there was much concerned talk at the time about the genetic inferiority of Italian stock, of the inadvisability of letting so many second-class immigrants into the United

States, and of the squalor that seemed endemic to Italian urban neighborhoods. Sound familiar? These days, when talk turns to the supposed
genetic differences in the intelligence of certain races, Southern Italians
have disappeared from the discussion. "Did their genes begin to mutate
somewhere in the 1930s?" the psychologists Seymour Sarason and John
Doris ask, in their account of the Italian experience. "Or is it possible
that somewhere in the 1920s, if not earlier, the sociocultural history of
Italo-Americans took a turn from the blacks and the Spanish Americans
which permitted their assimilation into the general undifferentiated
mass of Americans?"

The psychologist Michael Cole and some colleagues once gave members of the Kpelle tribe, in Liberia, a version of the WISC similarities test:
they took a basket of food, tools, containers, and clothing and asked the
tribesmen to sort them into appropriate categories. To the frustration of
the researchers, the Kpelle chose functional pairings. They put a potato
and a knife together because a knife is used to cut a potato. "A wise man
could only do such-and-such," they explained. Finally, the researchers
asked, "How would a fool do it?" The tribesmen immediately re-sorted
the items into the "right" categories. It can be argued that taxonomical
categories are a developmental improvement—that is, that the Kpelle
would be more likely to advance, technologically and scientifically, if
they started to see the world that way. But to label them less intelligent
than Westerners, on the basis of their performance on that test, is merely
to state that they have different cognitive preferences and habits. And if
I.Q. varies with habits of mind, which can be adopted or discarded in a
generation, what, exactly, is all the fuss about?

When I was growing up, my family would sometimes play Twenty
Questions on long car trips. My father was one of those people who
insist that the standard categories of animal, vegetable, and mineral be
supplemented with a fourth category: "abstract." Abstract could mean
something like "whatever it was that was going through my mind when
we drove past the water tower fifty miles back." That abstract category
sounds absurdly difficult, but it wasn't: it merely required that we ask
a slightly different set of questions and grasp a slightly different set of
conventions, and, after two or three rounds of practice, guessing the
contents of someone's mind fifty miles ago becomes as easy as guessing
Winston Churchill. (There is one exception. That was the trip on which
my old roommate Tom Connell chose, as an abstraction, "the Unknown
Soldier"—which allowed him legitimately and gleefully to answer
"I have no idea" to almost every question. There were four of us playing.
We gave up after an hour.) Flynn would say that my father was teaching
his three sons how to put on scientific spectacles, and that extra practice

probably bumped up all of our I.Q.s a few notches. But let's be clear about what this means. There's a world of difference between an I.Q. advantage that's genetic and one that depends on extended car time with Graham Gladwell.

Flynn is a cautious and careful writer. Unlike many others in the I.Q. debates, he resists grand philosophizing. He comes back again and again to the fact that I.Q. scores are generated by paper-and-pencil tests—and making sense of those scores, he tells us, is a messy and complicated business that requires something closer to the skills of an accountant than to those of a philosopher.

For instance, Flynn shows what happens when we recognize that I.Q. is not a freestanding number but a value attached to a specific time and a specific test. When an I.Q. test is created, he reminds us, it is calibrated or "normed" so that the test-takers in the fiftieth percentile—those exactly at the median—are assigned a score of 100. But since I.Q.s are always rising, the only way to keep that hundred-point benchmark is periodically to make the tests more difficult—to "renorm" them. The original WISC was normed in the late nineteen-forties. It was then renormed in the early nineteen-seventies, as the WISC-R; renormed a third time in the late eighties, as the WISC III; and renormed again a few years ago, as the WISC IV—with each version just a little harder than its predecessor. The notion that anyone "has" an I.Q. of a certain number, then, is meaningless unless you know which WISC he took, and when he took it, since there's a substantial difference between getting a 130 on the WISC IV and getting a 130 on the much easier WISC.

This is not a trivial issue. I.Q. tests are used to diagnose people as mentally retarded, with a score of 70 generally taken to be the cutoff. You can imagine how the Flynn effect plays havoc with that system. In the nineteen-seventies and eighties, most states used the WISC-R to make their mental-retardation diagnoses. But since kids—even kids with disabilities—score a little higher every year, the number of children whose scores fell below 70 declined steadily through the end of the eighties. Then, in 1991, the WISC III was introduced, and suddenly the percentage of kids labelled retarded went up. The psychologists Tomoe Kanaya, Matthew Scullin, and Stephen Ceci estimated that, if every state had switched to the WISC III right away, the number of Americans labelled mentally retarded should have doubled.

That is an extraordinary number. The diagnosis of mental disability is one of the most stigmatizing of all educational and occupational classifications—and yet, apparently, the chances of being burdened with that label are in no small degree a function of the point, in the life cycle of the WISC, at which a child happens to sit for his evaluation. "As far 15 as I can determine, no clinical or school psychologists using the WISC over the relevant 25 years noticed that its criterion of mental retardation became more lenient over time," Flynn wrote, in a 2000 paper. "Yet no one drew the obvious moral about psychologists in the field: They simply were not making any systematic assessment of the I.Q. criterion for mental retardation."

Flynn brings a similar precision to the question of whether Asians have a genetic advantage in I.Q., a possibility that has led to great excitement among I.Q. fundamentalists in recent years. Data showing that the Japanese had higher I.Q.s than people of European descent, for example, prompted the British psychometrician and eugenicist Richard Lynn to concoct an elaborate evolutionary explanation involving the Himalayas, really cold weather, premodern hunting practices, brain size, and specialized vowel sounds. The fact that the I.Q.s of Chinese-Americans also seemed to be elevated has led I.Q. fundamentalists to posit the existence of an international I.Q. pyramid, with Asians at the top, European whites next, and Hispanics and blacks at the bottom.

Here was a question tailor-made for James Flynn's accounting skills. He looked first at Lynn's data, and realized that the comparison was skewed. Lynn was comparing American I.Q. estimates based on a representative sample of schoolchildren with Japanese estimates based on an upper-income, heavily urban sample. Recalculated, the Japanese average came in not at 106.6 but at 99.2. Then Flynn turned his attention to the Chinese-American estimates. They turned out to be based on a 1975 study in San Francisco's Chinatown using something called the Lorge-Thorndike Intelligence Test. But the Lorge-Thorndike test was normed in the nineteen-fifties. For children in the nineteen-seventies, it would have been a piece of cake. When the Chinese-American scores were reassessed using up-to-date intelligence metrics, Flynn found, they came in at 97 verbal and 100 nonverbal. Chinese-Americans had slightly lower I.Q.s than white Americans.

The Asian-American success story had suddenly been turned on its head. The numbers now suggested, Flynn said, that they had succeeded not because of their *higher* I.Q.s but despite their *lower* I.Q.s. Asians were overachievers. In a nifty piece of statistical analysis, Flynn then worked out just how great that overachievement was. Among whites, virtually everyone who joins the ranks of the managerial, professional, and technical occupations has an I.Q. of 97 or above. Among Chinese-Americans, that threshold is 90. A Chinese-American with an I.Q. of 90, it would appear, does as much with it as a white American with an I.Q. of 97.

There should be no great mystery about Asian achievement. It has to do with hard work and dedication to higher education, and belonging to a culture that stresses professional success. But Flynn makes one more observation. The children of that first successful wave of Asian-Americans really did have I.Q.s that were higher than everyone else's — coming in somewhere around 103. Having worked their way into the upper reaches of the occupational scale, and taken note of how much the professions value abstract thinking, Asian-American parents have evidently made sure that their own children wore scientific spectacles. "Chinese Americans are an ethnic group for whom high achievement preceded high I.Q. rather than the reverse," Flynn concludes, reminding us that in our discussions of the relationship between I.Q. and success we often confuse causes and effects. "It is not easy to view the history of their achievements without emotion," he writes. That is exactly right. To ascribe Asian success to some abstract number is to trivialize it.

Two weeks ago, Flynn came to Manhattan to debate Charles Murray   20
at a forum sponsored by the Manhattan Institute. Their subject was the black-white I.Q. gap in America. During the twenty-five years after the Second World War, that gap closed considerably. The I.Q.s of white Americans rose, as part of the general worldwide Flynn effect, but the I.Q.s of black Americans rose faster. Then, for about a period of twenty-five years, that trend stalled — and the question was why.

Murray showed a series of PowerPoint slides, each representing different statistical formulations of the I.Q. gap. He appeared to be pessimistic that the racial difference would narrow in the future. "By the nineteen-seventies, you had gotten most of the juice out of the environment that you were going to get," he said. That gap, he seemed to think, reflected some inherent difference between the races. "Starting in the nineteen-seventies, to put it very crudely, you had a higher proportion of black kids being born to really dumb mothers," he said. When the debate's moderator, Jane Waldfogel, informed him that the most recent data showed that the race gap had begun to close again, Murray seemed unimpressed, as if the possibility that blacks could ever make further progress was inconceivable.

Flynn took a different approach. The black-white gap, he pointed out, differs dramatically by age. He noted that the tests we have for measuring the cognitive functioning of infants, though admittedly crude, show the races to be almost the same. By age four, the average black I.Q. is 95.4 — only four and a half points behind the average white I.Q. Then the real gap emerges: from age four through twenty-four, blacks lose six-tenths of a point a year, until their scores settle at 83.4.

That steady decline, Flynn said, did not resemble the usual pattern of genetic influence. Instead, it was exactly what you would expect, given the disparate cognitive environments that whites and blacks encounter as they grow older. Black children are more likely to be raised in single-parent homes than are white children—and single-parent homes are less cognitively complex than two-parent homes. The average I.Q. of first-grade students in schools that blacks attend is 95, which means that "kids who want to be above average don't have to aim as high." There were possibly adverse differences between black teenage culture and white teenage culture, and an enormous number of young black men are in jail—which is hardly the kind of environment in which someone would learn to put on scientific spectacles.

Flynn then talked about what we've learned from studies of adoption and mixed-race children—and that evidence didn't fit a genetic model, either. If I.Q. is innate, it shouldn't make a difference whether it's a mixed-race child's mother or father who is black. But it does: children with a white mother and a black father have an eight-point I.Q. advantage over those with a black mother and a white father. And it shouldn't make much of a difference where a mixed-race child is born. But, again, it does: the children fathered by black American G.I.s in postwar Germany and brought up by their German mothers have the same I.Q.s as the children of white American G.I.s and German mothers. The difference, in that case, was not the fact of the children's blackness, as a fundamentalist would say. It was the fact of their *Germanness*—of their being brought up in a different culture, under different circumstances. "The mind is much more like a muscle than we've ever realized," Flynn said. "It needs to get cognitive exercise. It's not some piece of clay on which you put an indelible mark." The lesson to be drawn from black and white differences was the same as the lesson from the Netherlands years ago: I.Q. measures not just the quality of a person's mind but the quality of the world that person lives in.

Correction: In his December 17th piece, "None of the Above," 25 Malcolm Gladwell states that Richard Herrnstein and Charles Murray, in their 1994 book *The Bell Curve*, proposed that Americans with low I.Q.s be "sequestered in a 'high-tech' version of an Indian reservation." In fact, Herrnstein and Murray deplored the prospect of such "custodialism" and recommended that steps be taken to avert it. We regret the error.

Understanding the Text

1. Using Gladwell's text, define the Flynn effect and suggest how we might explain this phenomenon.

2. According to Gladwell, what do IQ fundamentalists believe? What makes these beliefs problematic?

3. What are "scientific spectacles"? Define this term and explain how it relates to Gladwell's larger argument.

Reflection and Response

4. In addition to being an author, Gladwell also hosts podcasts. Using a smartphone or other recording device, make your own podcast, addressing the social consequences of IQ tests and considering how might we mitigate them. You may want to interview others in your podcast, and you will definitely want to engage Gladwell's text closely. Be sure to consider all elements of your podcast, including background audio, ambient noise, and sound effects.

5. Why do fundamentalist notions of IQ persist despite seemingly abundant evidence that they're incorrect? Working from Gladwell's text, explore these ideas more deeply, considering why people might adopt them and what we might do to change them.

Making Connections

6. Gladwell references William Saletan's defense of James Watson. Use Saletan's essay ("Stop Talking about Race and IQ," p. 186) to extend Gladwell's arguments. How does Saletan's account of his actions, and his subsequent shift in thinking, reflect the points that Gladwell is trying to make?

7. One group Flynn examines in his research are Asians. Synthesize Gladwell's argument in this section with the points made by Jennifer Lee ("The Truth about Asian Americans' Success," p. 181). What factors actually account for the seemingly high IQ of Asians and Asian Americans?

The Truth about Asian Americans' Success

Jennifer Lee

Jennifer I ee, profocoor of suuiulugy at Columbia University, works on issues around immigration, education, and race. She has authored and coauthored several books, including *Civility in the City: Blacks, Jews, and Koreans in Urban America* (2002), *The Diversity Paradox: Immigration and the Color Line in Twenty-First Century America* (2010, with Frank D. Bean), and *The Asian American Achievement Paradox* (2015, with Min Zhou). Her work has also appeared in the *New York Times*, the *San Francisco Chronicle*, *CNN*, and *The Guardian*, and her research has been featured in the *Washington Post*, *The Economist*, *Slate*, and *BuzzFeed*.

Asian Americans are the highest-income, best-educated and fastest-growing racial group in the country. But not for the reasons you think.

For too long, conservative pundits and the news media have pointed to Asian Americans as the "model minority." They cite the Ivy League admissions and educational success of many children of blue-collar Asian immigrant workers as evidence of a superior culture—one of hard work and strong families—that puts Asian Americans on a sure path to success.

But it isn't Asian "culture" or any other attribute of ethnicity that is responsible for this success. Instead, it's a unique form of privilege that is grounded in the socioeconomic origins of some—not all—Asian immigrant groups.

Understanding this privilege offers insights into how we can help children from all backgrounds succeed.

In our new book, *The Asian American Achievement Paradox*—based on 5 a survey and 140 in-depth interviews of the adult children of Chinese, Vietnamese and Mexican immigrants in Los Angeles—fellow sociologist Min Zhou and I explain what actually fuels the achievements of some Asian American groups: U.S. immigration law, which favors highly educated, highly skilled immigrant applicants from Asian countries.

Based on the most recent available data, we found that these elite groups of immigrants are among the most highly educated people in their countries of origin and are often also more highly educated than the general U.S. population.

Take Chinese immigrants to the United States, for example: In 2010, 51 percent were college graduates, compared with only 4 percent of adults in China and only 28 percent of adults in the United States. The educational backgrounds of immigrant groups such as the Chinese in America—and other highly educated immigrant groups such as Korean and Indian—is where the concept of "Asian privilege" comes in.

When highly educated immigrant groups settle in the United States, they build what economist George Borjas calls "ethnic capital."

This capital includes ethnic institutions—such as after-school tutoring programs and after-school academies—which highly educated immigrants have the resources and know-how to recreate for their children. These programs proliferate in Asian neighborhoods in Los Angeles such as Koreatown, Chinatown and Little Saigon. The benefits of these programs also reach working-class immigrants from the same group.

> **"When highly educated immigrant groups settle in the United States, they build 'ethnic capital.'"**

Ethnic capital also translates into knowledge.   10

In churches, temples or community centers, immigrant parents circulate invaluable information about which neighborhoods have the best public schools, the importance of advance-placement classes and how to navigate the college admissions process. This information also circulates through ethnic-language newspapers, television and radio, allowing working-class immigrant parents to benefit from the ethnic capital that their middle-class peers create.

Our Chinese interviewees described how their non-English speaking parents turned to the Chinese Yellow Pages for information about affordable after-school programs and free college admissions seminars. This, in turn, helps the children whose immigrant parents toil in factories and restaurants attain educational outcomes that defy expectations.

The story of Jason, a young Chinese American man we interviewed, is emblematic of how these resources and knowledge can benefit working-class Chinese immigrants. Jason's parents are immigrants who do not speak English and did not graduate from high school. Yet, they were able to use the Chinese Yellow Pages to identify the resources that put Jason on the college track.

There, they learned about the best public schools in the Los Angeles area and affordable after-school education programs that would help Jason get good grades and ace the SAT. Jason's supplemental education—the hidden curriculum behind academic achievement—paid off when he graduated at the top of his class and was admitted to a top University of California campus.

This advantage is not available to other working-class immigrants.   15

Mexican immigrants, for example, are largely less-educated, low-wage workers because they arrived to the United States as a result of different immigration policies and histories. Theirs is a largely low-wage labor migration stream that began en masse with the 1942 Bracero program and continues today.

Based on the most recent census data, about 17 percent of Mexico's population are college graduates compared with 5 percent of Mexican immigrants in the United States. As a less-educated immigrant group, they lack the resources to generate the ethnic capital available to Chinese immigrants, and they rely almost exclusively on the public school system to educate their children.

Yet, despite their lack of ethnic capital, the children of Mexican immigrants make extraordinary educational gains and leap far beyond their parents. They double the high school graduation rates of their immigrant parents, double the college graduation rates of their immigrant fathers and triple that of their immigrant mothers.

The legal status of parents is key to success.

On average, the children of Mexican immigrant parents who are 20 undocumented attain 11 years of education. By contrast, those whose parents migrated here legally or entered the country as undocumented migrants but later legalized their status, attain 13 years of education on average, and this difference remains even after controlling for demographic variables.

The two-year difference is critical in the U.S. education system: It divides high school graduates from high school dropouts, making undocumented status alone a significant impediment to educational attainment and social mobility.

Undocumented status affects other immigrant groups, including Asians. There are currently more than 1.5 million undocumented Asians in the United States, accounting for 13.9 percent of the total undocumented population in the United States. This comes as a surprise to many Americans, who equate undocumented status with Mexicans.

The children of Mexican immigrants who surmount the disadvantage of their class origins and legal status and graduate from college pointed to an influential teacher, guidance counselor, coach or "college bound" program that helped them make it to college.

Camilla, a second-generation Mexican woman we interviewed, is a case in point.

No one in Camilla's family had attended a four-year university, but a 25 guidance counselor at her community college encouraged her to transfer to a four-year university and helped her with her application. As a result, Camilla ultimately went on to attend a top private university and later pursued a master's degree in social work.

Her educational mobility shows what is possible when schools provide adequate resources to support children's ambitions and potential. It is worth asking how much more Camilla and other children of Mexican immigrants might have attained had they had access to something like the "Asian privilege" of the children of Chinese immigrants.

How do we extend this privilege to students of all races and ethnicities?

Our research has made it clear to us that pundits should stop talking about Asian culture and start making supplemental education available to students of all racial and ethnic backgrounds, including Asian ethnic groups that lack ethnic capital and don't get a boost from this privilege, such as Hmong, Laotians and Cambodians.

Increasing funding for guidance counselors, coaches and college-bound classes is a start, but creating affordable after-school academies and tutoring programs in neighborhoods, for example, Los Angeles' Koreatown—which is home to Angelenos from diverse backgrounds—could give children of immigrants across racial, ethnic and class lines the resources they need to succeed.

This will help prepare them for the diverse college environments and workplaces that many will enter. Making supplementary education available to other working-class children will do more than level the playing field to make it to college; it will also help today's students succeed once they are there. 30

Understanding the Text

1. What is "Asian privilege," and how does it relate to "ethnic capital"? Use Lee's text to define these terms, explaining how they relate to her argument.

2. Using Lee's essay, explain the role immigration law plays in the perceived intelligence and academic achievement of ethnic groups in the United States.

Reflection and Response

3. What barriers exist for immigrants seeking the so-called American dream? Extrapolating from Lee's essay, write a paper in which you explore the most important factors required for immigrants to achieve this dream.

4. How are positive stereotypes as damaging as negative ones? Work with Lee's analysis to consider how stereotypes of Asian Americans as the "model minority" have harmed members of this group.

Making Connections

5. In looking at the success of Asian Americans, Lee also considers issues of socioeconomic class and the ways in which working-class immigrants benefited from the ethnic capital of more affluent groups. Mike Rose ("Blue-Collar Brilliance," p. 211) considers the particular intelligence of working-class individuals. Synthesize these two essays to formulate a broad concept of intelligence that accounts for success within and across socioeconomic classes. Does blue-collar intelligence play a role in upward class mobility? How important is it for different classes to work together to allow that to happen?

6. Mark Joseph Stern ("Are Gay People Smarter Than Straight People?," p. 207) also examines how legal factors play a larger role than stereotyped expectations when it comes to economic success, in this case for LGBTQ+ people. Work with both of these essays to define the relationship between justice and success. How do unjust laws impede success? What makes a law unjust? What are the social benefits of making sure all people are equally treated by law, whether immigration law or marital law?

Stop Talking about Race and IQ

William Saletan

William Saletan writes for *Slate* on topics that include politics, science, and technology. He is the author of two books, *Bearing Right: How Conservatives Won the Abortion War* (2003) and *Slate's Field Guide to the Candidates 2004* (2003). In this selection, Saletan shares the lessons he learned after infamously supporting genetic arguments about race and intelligence in a previous essay for *Slate* in 2007.

The race-and-IQ debate is back. The latest round started a few weeks ago when Harvard geneticist David Reich wrote a *New York Times* op-ed in defense of race as a biological fact. The piece resurfaced Sam Harris' year-old *Waking Up* podcast interview with Charles Murray, co-author of *The Bell Curve,* and launched a Twitter debate between Harris and Vox's Ezra Klein. Klein then responded to Harris and Reich in *Vox,* Harris fired back, and Andrew Sullivan went after Klein. Two weeks ago, Klein and Harris released a two-hour podcast in which they fruitlessly continued their dispute.

I've watched this debate for more than a decade. It's the same wreck, over and over. A person with a taste for puncturing taboos learns about racial gaps in IQ scores and the idea that they might be genetic. He writes or speaks about it, credulously or unreflectively. Every part of his argument is attacked: the validity of IQ, the claim that it's substantially heritable, and the idea that races can be biologically distinguished. The offender is denounced as racist when he thinks he's just defending science against political correctness.

I know what it's like to be this person because, 11 years ago, I was that person. I saw a comment from Nobel laureate James Watson about the black-white IQ gap, read some journal articles about it, and bought in. That was a mistake. Having made that mistake, I'm in no position to throw stones at Sullivan, Harris, or anyone else. But I am in a position to speak to these people as someone who understands where they're coming from. I believe I can change their thinking, because I've changed mine, and I'm here to make that case to them. And I hope those of you who find this whole subject vile will bear with me as I do.

Here's my advice: You can talk about the genetics of race. You can talk about the genetics of intelligence. But stop implying they're the same thing. Connecting intelligence to race adds nothing useful. It overextends the science you're defending, and it engulfs the whole debate in moral flames.

I'm not asking anyone to deny science. What I'm asking for is clarity. 5
The genetics of race and the genetics of intelligence are two different fields
of research. In his piece in the *Times*, Reich
wrote about prostate cancer risk, a context
in which there's clear evidence of a genetic
pattern related to ancestry. (Black men
with African ancestry in a specific DNA
region have a higher prostate cancer risk
than do black men with European ances-
try in that region.) Reich steered around intelligence where, despite racial
and ethnic gaps in test scores, no such pattern has been established.

> "The genetics of race and the genetics of intelligence are two different fields of research."

It's also fine to discuss the genetics of IQ—there's a serious line of
scientific inquiry around that subject—and whether intelligence, in any
population, is an inherited social advantage. We tend to worry that talk
of heritability will lead to eugenics. But it's also worth noting that, to the
extent that IQ, like wealth, is inherited and concentrated through assortative mating°, it can stratify society and undermine cohesion. That's
what much of *The Bell Curve* was about.

The trouble starts when people who write or talk about the heritability
of intelligence extend this idea to comparisons between racial and ethnic groups. Some people do this maliciously; others don't. You can call
the latter group naïve, credulous, or obtuse to prejudice. But they might
be open to persuasion, and that's my aim here. For them, the chain of
thought might go something like this: Intelligence is partly genetic, and
race is partly genetic. So maybe racial differences on intelligence tests can
be explained, in part, by genetics.

There are two scientific problems with making this kind of inference.
The first is that bringing race into the genetic conversation obscures the
causal analysis. Genes might play no role in racial gaps on IQ tests. But
suppose they did: To that extent, what would be the point of talking
about race? Some white kids, some black kids, and some Asian kids would
have certain genes that marginally favor intelligence. Others wouldn't.
It's still the genes, not race, that would matter.

This is a rare point of consensus in the IQ debate. In his interview
with Harris, Murray notes that in *The Bell Curve*, race was a crude proxy
for genetics. Since the book's publication in 1994, our ability to assess
genetic differences has come a long way. Today, scientists are evaluating thousands of genes that correlate with small increments in IQ. "The
blurriness of race is noise in the signal," Murray tells Harris. "It's going to
obscure . . . genetic differences in IQ."

assortative mating: pattern where individuals with similar characteristics mate with
one another more frequently than would be expected under a random mating pattern.

"Race science," the old idea that race is a biologically causal trait, may 10
live on as an ideology of hate. But as an academic matter, it's been discredited. We now know that genes flow between populations as they
do between families, blurring racial categories and reshuffling human
diversity. Genetic patterns can be found within groups, as in the case of
prostate cancer. But even then, as Ian Holmes notes in *The Atlantic*, the
patterns correlate with ancestry or population, not race.

The second problem with extending genetic theories of IQ to race
is that it confounds the science of heritability. Sullivan and Harris cite
research that indicates IQ is, loosely speaking, 40 percent to 80 percent
heritable. It can seem natural to extend these estimates to comparisons
between racial groups. That's what I did a decade ago. But it's a mistake
because these studies are done within, not between, populations. They
measure, for example, the degree to which being someone's twin or biological sibling, rather than simply growing up in the same household,
correlates with similarity of IQ. They don't account for many other differences that come into play when comparing whole populations. So if you
bring race into the calculation, you're stretching those studies beyond
their explanatory power. And you're introducing complicating factors:
not just education, income, and family structure, but neighborhood, net
worth—and discrimination, which is the variable most likely to correlate
directly with race.

Murray and others have answers to these objections. They argue that
education programs have failed to close racial gaps, that studies haven't
proved that getting adopted has much lasting effect on kids' IQ scores,
and that collective increases in IQ scores are based on factors other than
"general" intelligence. These are complex disputes full of nuances about
replicating studies, interpreting test questions, and extrapolating from
trend lines. But notice how far we've drifted from biology. The science
here is oblique, abstract, and tenuous. Are you still comfortable specu-
lating about genetics? Are you confident, for instance, that studies that
compare black children to white children properly account for family
assets and neighborhood, which differ sharply by race even within the
same income bracket?

It's one thing to theorize about race and genes to assist in disease pre-
vention, diagnosis, or treatment, as Reich has done. But before you seize
on his essay to explain racial gaps in employment, ask yourself: Given
the dubiousness of linking racial genetics to IQ, what would my words
accomplish? Would they contribute to prejudice? Would they be used
to blame communities for their own poverty? Would I be provoking
thought, or would I be offering whites an excuse not to think about the
social and economic causes of inequality?

Murray, Sullivan, and Harris try to soften their speculations by stipu-
lating, as I once did, that even if racial differences in IQ are genetic, you
shouldn't make assumptions about any individual. They're correct that
it's both wrong and irrational to make such inferences from aggregate
data. But it's also easier to treat people as individuals when you don't
start with racial generalizations.

If you're libertarian or conservative, you might think I'm calling for   15
censorship. I'm not. I'm just asking for precision. Genes are the mechanism under discussion. So talking about the genetics of race and the
genetics of IQ is more scientific, not less, than pulling race and IQ
together.

Many progressives, on the other hand, regard the whole topic of IQ
and genetics as sinister. That, too, is a mistake. There's a lot of hard science here. It can't be wished away, and it can be put to good use. The
challenge is to excavate that science from the muck of speculation about
racial hierarchies.

What's the path forward? It starts with letting go of race talk. No more
podcasts hyping gratuitous racial comparisons as "forbidden knowledge."
No more essays speaking of grim ethnic truths for which, supposedly,
we must prepare. Don't imagine that if you posit an association between
race and some trait, you can add enough caveats to erase the impression
that people can be judged by their color. The association, not the caveats,
is what people will remember.

If you're interested in race and IQ, you might bristle at these admo-
nitions. Perhaps you think you're just telling the truth about test scores,
IQ heritability, and the biological reality of race. It's not your fault, you
might argue, that you're smeared and misunderstood. Harris says all of
these things in his debate with Klein. And I cringe as I hear them, because
I know these lines. I've played this role. Harris warns Klein that even if
we "make certain facts taboo" and refuse "to ever look at population differences, we will be continually ambushed by these data." He concludes:
"Scientific data can't be racist."

No, data aren't racist. But using racial data to make genetic
arguments isn't scientific. The world isn't better off if you run ahead
of science, waving the flag of innate group differences. And if everyone
is misunderstanding your attempts to simultaneously link and distinguish race and IQ, perhaps you should take the hint. The problem isn't
that people are too dumb to understand you. It's that you're not understanding the social consequences of your words. When you drag race
into the IQ conversation, you bring heat, not light. Your arguments
for scientific candor will be more sound and more persuasive in a race-
neutral discussion.

The biology of intelligence is full of important questions. To what 20 extent is it one faculty or many? How do we get it, grow it, maintain it, and use it? If it's heritable, should we think of it less as merit and more as luck, like inheriting money? To what extent does a class structure based on intelligence duplicate or conceal a class structure based on family wealth? Is intelligence truly supplanting other kinds of inheritance as a competitive advantage? Is it unleashing social mobility? Or is it, through assortative mating, entrenching inequality? These are much better conversations than the one we've been stuck in. Let's get on with them.

Understanding the Text

1. Science is at the heart of Saletan's essay. Create a visual map of the science around race, genetics, and evolution using Saletan's arguments. You may want to create your map using a digital graphics program, but you may also consider graphing programs, picture collages, or your own sketch.

2. How does race obscure causal analysis when it comes to genetics and intelligence? To support your response, locate selections from Saletan where he explains this issue.

Reflection and Response

3. How can we best decouple genetics, race, and intelligence? Work from Saletan's analysis to identify what actions might clarify the boundaries of these terms more effectively.

4. Near the end of his essay, Saletan warns us of the "social consequences of [our] words" (p. 189). Expand on his point by writing an essay on this topic, using Saletan's argument as a starting point for a larger discussion of the ways in which words affect others and the society around us.

Making Connections

5. Diane F. Halpern ("Sex Differences in Intelligence," p. 191) also writes about the complex intersection of politics and science. Synthesize Halpern's and Saletan's essays to propose strategies we can use to negotiate the boundaries between politics and science. Can science be apolitical? Are there ways of insulating scientific inquiry from political agendas?

6. In many ways, this essay is about the consequences of bad science. Mark Joseph Stern ("Are Gay People Smarter Than Straight People?," p. 207) also writes about this issue. In both cases, the issue under discussion ends up being more complicated than the science involved. Work with both of these essays to explore what makes "good science" — thinking not only about methodology and rigor but also about understanding explanatory limitations or the influence of bias.

Sex Differences in Intelligence

Diane F. Halpern

Diane F. Halpern, dean emerita of social sciences at Minerva Schools at Keck Graduate Institute and emerita professor of psychology at Claremont McKenna College, is a widely recognized expert in psychology, with an emphasis on critical thinking, gender studies, and learning. She has served as the president of the American Psychological Association, the Western Psychological Association, and the Society for Teaching of Psychology. She is also the author of more than a dozen books, including *Women at the Top: Powerful Leaders Tell Us How to Combine Work and Family* (2008), *Sex Differences in Cognitive Abilities* (4th ed., 2011), and *Thought and Knowledge: An Introduction to Critical Thinking* (5th ed., 2013).

Research into the many questions about sex differences and similarities in intelligence is fraught with political minefields and emotional rhetoric from both ends of the political spectrum.[1] Many psychologists are opposed to any comparisons of women and men, especially when differences are found, fearing that the data will be interpreted and misused in ways that support a misogynist agenda. Such fears are understandable given the many social inequalities such as "mommy tracks" and "glass ceilings" that work against women in Western countries and the disproportionate rates of abortion and infanticide of females in many other regions of the world (Guttman, 1994; Kitzinger, 1994). Prejudice and discrimination flourish through cognitive and social processes in which members of one group think of those in other groups as being relatively homogenous, especially when compared with the variability in their group, and highly dissimilar and inferior to themselves (Reid & Holland, 1997). Those opposed to research on sex differences fear that it will increase prejudice and discrimination by legitimizing false stereotypes, obscuring similarities, and providing fuel for those who are determined to convince the world of the inferiority of females. Others have argued that the biological and social variables that vary as a function of one's sex are a critically important area of psychological inquiry, and, for this reason, comparisons between females and males should become a routine part of scientific reports (Eagly, 1990, 1994). Regardless of the position

---

[1]Some authors prefer to differentiate between the terms *sex* and *gender*, using sex to refer to biologically mediated differences and gender to refer to socially mediated differences. In accord with the psychobiosocial model presented, I believe that biological and social influences often are not separable; therefore, I use the more generic term *sex* to refer to differences between women and men regardless of their origin.

taken on the many questions that pertain to sex-related similarities and differences, most psychologists would agree that sex is a fundamental component of identity; it is the primary way of classifying humans into groups, a fact that can be seen in all of the artifacts of popular culture, such as best-selling books claiming that males and females are like alien beings (Gray, 1992) who speak separate languages (Tannen, 1990).

"Stereotypes do not result from research on the ways in which females and males differ."

Stereotypes do not result from research on the ways in which females and males differ; they arise inductively through experience (e.g., secretaries are usually female), they are "carefully taught," they are explicitly and implicitly learned, and they play pivotal roles in how people think about what is "natural" for each sex. Research is the only way in which psychologists can distinguish between those stereotypes that have a basis in fact (i.e., are statistically associated with one group more than another) and those that do not. Of course, research always takes place in a sociopolitical context that guides the research questions that are asked, the data that are collected, and most important, the way the data are interpreted, but it is the best tool available for reaching valid conclusions, especially when the topic is politically sensitive. Social constructivists emphasize the role of values and expectancies in the way a society "makes meaning" from data; empiricists counter that it is only through data that change over time and place can be tracked and similarities and differences can be identified. Amid the many controversies, one fact emerges clearly from a review of the voluminous literature: The many questions about cognitive sex differences and similarities are a major area of interest.

Differences Are Not Deficiencies

The research reviewed below clearly shows that there are many cognitive areas in which the sexes, on average, differ, and many in which there are no differences. Conclusions about differences do not mean that there is a better or smarter sex. If society routinely values those traits associated with one sex more than those associated with the other sex, then the problem lies in the value hierarchies of the society, not in the fact that there are differences. Some of the differences favor females and some favor males. It is about as meaningful to ask "Which is the smarter sex?" or "Which has the better brain?" as it is to ask "Which has the better genitals?" Bigotry does not stem from the fact that there are group differences; it arises in the evaluation of the differences, when group members decide that the traits and abilities associated with other groups are inferior to the ones found in their own group.

Changing Data, Changing Minds

Data regarding sex differences in cognition have been accumulating at a remarkably rapid rate in recent years, yet few people have revised or even questioned their personal beliefs about this controversial topic in light of all of the new information and new types of information (such as brain imaging techniques using normal humans engaging in different intellectual tasks) that are now available (Posner & Raichle, 1994). People make sense out of their experiences by filtering them through their mental models or belief systems. The strong tendency to maintain consistent belief systems means that people interpret information in ways that support their existing beliefs. Thus, advocates of different points of view (e.g., those who believe that sex differences in intelligence are created by social roles vs. those who believe they are caused by prenatal hormones) can each interpret the same data as supporting their diametrically opposed beliefs. An abundance of data has shown that when individuals are faced with information that contradicts their beliefs, they alter the information rather than change their models of the world (Lord, Ross, & Lepper, 1979). A mind (male or female) is a difficult thing to change.

A Psychobiosocial Model

Research and debate about the origins of sex differences are grounded in 5
the belief that the nonreproductive differences between males and females originate from sex-differentiated biological mechanisms (nature; e.g., "sex" hormones), socialization practices (nurture; e.g., girls are expected to perform poorly on tests of advanced mathematics), and their interaction. A psychobiosocial model offers an alternative conceptualization: It is based on the idea that some variables are both biological and social and therefore cannot be classified into one of these two categories. Consider, for example, the role of learning in creating and maintaining a (average) difference between females and males. Learning is both a socially mediated event and a biological one. Individuals are predisposed to learn some topics more readily than others. A predisposition to learn some behaviors or concepts more easily than others is determined by prior learning experiences, the neurochemical processes that allow learning to occur (release of neurotransmitters), and change in response to learning (e.g., long-term potentiation and changes in areas of the brain that are active during performance of a task; Posner & Raichle, 1994). Thus, learning depends on what is already known and on the neural structures and processes that undergird learning. Of course, psychological variables such as interest and expectancy are also important in determining how readily information is learned, but interest and expectancy are also affected by prior learning.

The model that is being advocated is predicated on an integral conceptual-ization of nature and nurture that cannot be broken into nature or nurture subcomponents. Neural structures change in response to environmental events; environmental events are selected from the environment on the basis of, in part, predilections and expectancies; and the biological and socially mediated underpinnings of learning help to create the predilec-tions and expectancies that guide future learning.

The What, Where, When, and Size of Cognitive Sex Differences

Because of restrictions on the length of this article, I have summarized the answers to many of the "journalist's questions" regarding sex differ-ences in the Appendix to this article. Each conclusion in the Appendix is supported by numerous separate studies. The many cognitive areas where differences are small, fragile, or nonexistent are not listed. Perusal of the Appendix shows that cognitive tests and tasks are grouped under broad headings—one for those at which females obtain higher scores and one for those at which males obtain higher scores. The overrepresentation of males at the low end of many distributions and the corresponding finding that males tend to be more variable than females are also shown in the Appendix (Feingold, 1995). I have rejected the older taxonomy that sorted experimental results into verbal, visual–spatial, and quantita-tive rubrics because there are too many discrepant findings for this tripar-tite organization (e.g., females excel at some spatial tasks, such as mirror tracing and memory for location, and some quantitative tasks, such as mathematical calculations, and males excel at some verbal tasks, such as analogies). The taxonomy is based on underlying cognitive processes and offers a more fine-grained analysis of how information is retrieved from memory and what participants are doing when they are working on a cognitive task (Halpern, 1992; Halpern & Crothers, 1997; Halpern & Wright, 1996). The idea that working memory can be separated into different functions is also consistent with recent work in cognitive psy-chology (e.g., Shah & Miyake, 1996), and the separation of cognitive tasks into component processing subsystems such as phonological and meaning subsystems is in accord with recent findings with brain imaging techniques (e.g., Posner & Raichle, 1994).

The size of the sex difference cannot be summarized in a single num-ber because it depends on moderating and context variables that include the specific nature of the task, the portion of the abilities continuum from which participants are selected, and the age of the participants. For example, sex differences in mental rotation have been studied for over 20 years and have been summarized in several meta-analytic reviews. The difference, favoring males, is very large ($d = 0.9$; Masters & Sanders, 1993) and has remained unchanged for almost two decades. The female advantage in fluency has a much smaller research literature, although it seems that it, too, may be quite large ($d = 1.2$; Hines, 1990). The size of the other differences is probably smaller than these extreme values. Males and females are also quite similar with regard to many intellectual abilities, especially preadolescents of average ability — a fact that cannot be appreciated from a list of differences (e.g., there is virtually no difference in mathematical problem solving prior to adolescence; Hyde, Fennema, & Lamon, 1990). Differences are most pronounced in the extreme ends of the abilities distributions and are much smaller over the average range of abilities, an important finding that needs to be balanced with the recognition that even a small difference can have a substantial real-world effect on the proportion of males and females scoring above any cutoff point that might correspond to a level needed for entry into a training program or a job (Rosenthal & Rubin, 1982).

It is well documented that males, on average, obtain higher scores on standardized tests that are designed to predict grades in college or graduate school, yet females, on average, get higher grades (Stricker, Rock, & Burton, 1993). The underprediction of female performance with these tests raises questions about how to interpret the test data. Analyses of cognitive abilities rarely include course grades, which measure achievement over time in multiple settings with different sorts of measures. Because females tend to perform better on written exams, the reliance on multiple-choice tests may be putting them at a disadvantage, although it could also be true that grades reflect other sorts of behaviors (neatness, studiousness) that are unrelated to cognition (Bridgeman & Moran, 1996). Additional support for this possibility comes from a report (U.S. Department of Education, 1997) on writing proficiency for children in Grades 4, 8, and 11 in 1984, 1988, and 1990, which showed that girls are better writers in each of the nine comparisons and that the size of the female advantage in writing is comparable with the much-debated average differences in English-language usage between Blacks and Whites.

Many of these differences appear early in life. The male advantage in transforming information in visual–spatial short-term memory is seen as early as it can be tested — perhaps at Age 3 — and in mathematical giftedness as early as preschool (Robinson, Abbott, Berninger, & Busse, 1996). The perceptual advantages seen in females appear early in infancy, with fluency differences in the toddler years (Reinisch & Sanders, 1992). Girls mature earlier than boys, so they frequently achieve cognitive milestones at a younger age. Boys are more likely to be miscategorized as learning disabled in early grades because they mature at a slower rate throughout childhood (Shaywitz et al., 1991).

There has been much interest in the possibility that sex differences in cognitive abilities are decreasing, a fact that might reflect the diminished effect of sex role stereotypes and other sex-differentiated environmental norms. Feingold (1988) and Hyde et al. (1990), for example, concluded that sex differences in cognition are diminishing, but numerous other researchers in more recent reviews have come to opposite conclusions, at least for a majority of the findings. It seems that evidence for a decreasing trend comes from those tests that had the smallest effect sizes, with little evidence of converging means from those tests with large effect sizes. In Voyer, Voyer, and Bryden's (1995) meta-analytic review of sex differences in spatial ability, they concluded that "a number of tests . . . show highly significant sex differences that are stable across age, at least after puberty, and have not decreased in recent years" (p. 264). They found that effect sizes on the mental rotations test have increased over time, whereas the effect sizes of some other spatial tests have decreased. However, when effect sizes for spatial tests, overall, were examined for change over time, the results were not statistically significant.

In an extensive meta-analytic review of tests of reading, writing, math, and science, Hedges and Nowell (1995) concluded, "Contrary to the findings of small scale studies, these average differences do not appear to be decreasing, but are relatively stable across the 32-year period investigated" (p. 45). The conclusion that many cognitive sex differences have not been decreasing is bolstered by a meta-analysis of parents' sex role socialization practices. Lytton and Romney (1991) found that parenting has not become less sex differentiated over the past two decades. Numerous others researchers share this conclusion, although some reviewers note that there may be some exceptions (e.g., Masters & Sanders, 1993; Stumpf & Stanley, 1996).

The question of whether intellectual sex differences are diminishing is complicated by numerous extraneous factors that have changed over time. It is now routine for testing companies to eliminate questions that yield large differences in response to public concern over sex differences in high-stakes examinations, such as those used in college admissions and in scholarship awards. In addition, a larger proportion of the population is taking these examinations than in the past. The simultaneous change in the nature of the tests and the population taking these tests would reduce the average between-sex difference in test scores even if there were no changes in the population (Halpern, 1989). The strongest evidence for convergence on cognitive tests occurs in the average-ability range; there is little evidence for convergence among the most gifted portions of the population (Feingold, 1996).

Finally, cross-cultural comparisons allow the possibility of determining if the sex-typical findings reported with samples from the United States are pan-cultural. Comparable cross-cultural data are always difficult to collect and interpret, especially if they concern verbal performance across countries with different languages. Representational sampling is also a problem both within and across cultures. Despite all of the difficulties, a large variety of data suggests that the sex differences reported with U.S. samples are also found in other countries (e.g., Beller & Gafni, 1996, in 20 countries that participated in the International Assessment of Educational Progress). Recently released results from the Third International Mathematics and Science Study (U.S. Department of Education, 1996), in which half a million students at five grade levels in 41 countries were assessed, add converging evidence to the conclusions about sex differences in science and math achievement. On the basis of data from eighth graders only (data from other grades have not been released at this time), Vogel (1996) provided this summary, "Boys in about 75% of the countries did significantly better than girls in science; in math they led in about 15% of the nations tested. In no country did girls significantly outperform boys" (p. 1296).

Practical Applications and Implications

For those concerned with the applications of research on cognitive sex differences, especially their implications for education, I offer these practical suggestions that are based on research findings:

1. Separate the fact that there are average differences in some cognitive abilities between males and females from the tendency to evaluate these differences as "better" or "worse." This is an important distinction regardless of the nature of the group. Do not permit the misuse of data for the advancement of biological politics, political correctness, or any other ideology. The truth about sex differences in intelligence depends on the nature of the cognitive task, the range of ability that was tested, the age and education of the participants, and numerous other modifying and context variables. There are intellectual areas in which females excel and others in which males excel; these data do not support the notion of a smarter sex, nor does it mean that the differences are immutable.
2. The research summarized here is based on group averages, and no one is average. These results cannot be applied to any individual because there is a great deal of overlap in all of the distributions of abilities. For example, even though boys outnumber girls among those who are in the most gifted abilities range on standardized

tests of mathematical achievement, there are many girls in this elite group. Similarly, boys excel in some tests of language usage, even though there are many more verbal tasks that show an average advantage for girls. We cannot afford to write off anyone or allow group membership to limit talent development.

3. Recent research has shown that beliefs about group differences exert powerful effects on thoughts and behaviors that occur without conscious awareness. These results highlight the importance of understanding stereotypes and offer a pessimistic outlook for the ease with which prejudice can be attenuated. For this reason, all of the stakeholders in education need to examine school texts for possible bias and speak to teachers and counselors about the nature of their group-based messages. We cannot pretend that children will select options that are best suited for their individual abilities and interests, if we do not give them real choices.

4. The hormone-like chemicals that are polluting our environment are having negative effects on the animals that live in and near the polluted areas. Alterations to the hormone-sensitive reproductive organs of these animals provide reasons to believe that these chemicals can affect the hormone-sensitive regions in the brain that support human intellectual functioning. No one can predict the long-term consequences of dumping chemicals into the environment, particularly pesticides that mimic the actions of sex hormones. It is likely that they will alter intelligence in humans who are exposed to them, a hypothesis that remains untested.

5. Support research on human cognition. Researchers may be close to genuine breakthroughs in cognitive aging. New reports show that estrogen therapy can delay or reduce the occurrence of Alzheimer's disease in elderly women. Although research on the effects of testosterone replacement therapy is decades behind that of estrogen replacement, both offer the possibility of great hope to an aging society.

6. Boys mature later than girls. Teachers should make sure that flexible criteria are used when making assignments to low-ability groups in the primary grades, especially in reading. Some of the boys will catch up with their peers, if they are not allowed to fall too far behind.

7. We have remedial instruction for reading and mathematics, but spatial reasoning, a skill that might benefit girls more than boys, is virtually never taught in school. There is ample evidence that training with spatial tasks will lead to improved achievement on spatial tests (Vasta, Knott, & Gaze, 1996). Researchers need to provide all children with opportunities to develop spatial reasoning skills.

8. Most of the standardized tests that are used for admissions to college, graduate, and professional schools; programs for gifted youth; and scholarships underpredict female performance and overpredict male performance. Multiple measures of ability and achievement must be used in these decisions, especially course grades and tests of writing, which tend to favor females.

9. There are no cognitive reasons to support sex-segregated education. But, given the primary importance of education in the development of intellectual skills and the finding that girls and boys often have different experiences in school (Kleinfeld & Yerian, 1995), there may be social reasons for sex-segregated learning environments. The fact that girls get better grades in every subject in school shows that they are learning at least as well as boys. For those concerned with increasing the number of females in science and math, the problem lies in convincing more females that "math counts" and to make academic and career choices that are "math-wise."

10. Interpret research findings with an amiable skepticism and examine conclusions to determine if they are data-based (Halpern, 1994). Conclusions about a topic as complex as cognitive sex differences will rest on the cumulative results of many studies. Although each person has social—political preferences for particular types of explanations, it is also necessary to strive to maintain an open-minded fairness when assessing a variety of theories and empirical findings, including the conclusions presented in this article. Explain the many pitfalls and pratfalls of this sort of research whenever simple statements like "It's all in the hormones" or "It's all in the mother's attitude" are made.

Perhaps the most important conclusion is that the brain remains plastic throughout life, which means that it is altered in response to experiences even into very old age. Somewhere, soon, (perhaps it has already happened) someone will be born who will be the oldest person to live into the 22nd century. A fitting gift from our generation to the next is the expectation that learning is a lifelong activity that depends on individual abilities and interests. The fact that females and males differ, on average, on some abilities must not be used to restrict individual choices. The conclusions that people make today about sex differences in intelligence may change radically in the future. There have been incredible changes in the composition of the workforce in the United States throughout the past 50 years, with increasing participation of women, in general, and mothers in particular. The workforce of the future will need to be better educated than any past generation. Our best hope for the future is a well-educated citizenry where individuals can develop their intellectual potential to its fullest.

References

Beller, M., & Gafni, N. (1996). The 1991 international assessment of educational progress in mathematics and sciences: The gender differences perspective. *Journal of Educational Psychology, 88,* 365–377.

Bridgeman, B., & Moran, R. (1996). Success in college for students with discrepancies between performance on multiple-choice and essay tests. *Journal of Educational Psychology, 88,* 333–340.

Eagly, A. H. (1990). On the advantages of reporting sex differences. *American Psychologist, 45,* 560–562.

Eagly, A. H. (1994). On comparing women and men [Special issue]. *Feminism and Psychology, 4,* 523–530.

Feingold, A. (1988). Cognitive gender differences are disappearing. *American Psychologist, 43,* 95–103.

Feingold, A. (1995). The additive effects of differences in central tendency and variability are important in comparisons between groups. *American Psychologist, 50,* 5–13.

Feingold, A. (1996). Cognitive gender differences: Where are they and why are they there? [Special issue]. *Learning and Individual Differences, 8,* 25–32.

Gray, J. (1992). *Men are from Mars, women are from Venus.* New York: HarperCollins.

Guttman, M. (1994, March 28) The war against women. *U.S. News & World Report,* pp. 42–45, 48–50.

Halpern, D. F. (1989). The disappearance of cognitive gender differences: What you see depends on where you look. *American Psychologist, 44,* 1156–1158.

Halpern. D. F. (1992). *Sex differences in cognitive abilities* (2nd ed.). Hillsdale, NJ: Erlbaum.

Halpern, D. F. (1994). Stereotypes, science, censorship, and the study of sex differences [Special issue]. *Feminism and Psychology, 4,* 523–530.

Halpern, D. F. & Crothers, M. (1997). The sex of cognition. In L. Ellis (Ed.), *Sexual orientation: Toward biological understanding* (pp. 181–197). Westport, CT: Praeger.

Halpern, D. F. & Wright, T. (1996). A process-oriented model of cognitive sex differences [Special issue]. *Learning and Individual Differences, 8,* 3–24.

Hedges, L. V., & Nowell, A. (1995, July 7). Sex differences in mental test scores, variability, and numbers of high-scoring individuals. *Science, 269,* 41–45.

Hines, M. (1990). Gonadal hormones and human cognitive development. In J. Balthazart (Ed.), *Brain and behaviour in vertebrates 1: Sexual differentiation, neuroanatomical aspects, neurotransmitters and neuropeptides* (pp. 51–63). Basel, Switzerland: Karger.

Hyde, J. S., Fennema, E., & Lamon, S. J. (1990). Gender differences in mathematics performance: A meta-analysis. *Psychological Bulletin, 107,* 139–153.

Kitzinger, C. (1994). Should psychologists study sex differences? *Feminism & Psychology, 4,* 501–506.

Kleinfeld, J. S., & Yerian, S. (Eds.). (1995). *Gender tales: Tensions in the schools.* New York: St. Martin's Press.

Lord, C., Ross, L., & Lepper, M. (1979). Biased assimilation and attitude polarization: The effects of prior theories on subsequently considered evidence. *Journal of Personality and Social Psychology, 37,* 2098–2109.

Lytton, H., & Romney, D. M. (1991). Parents' differential socialization of boys and girls: A meta-analysis. *Psychological Bulletin, 109,* 267–296.

Masters, M. S., & Sanders, B. (1993). Is the gender difference in mental rotation disappearing? *Behavior Genetics, 23,* 337–341.

Posner, M. I., & Raichle, M. E. (1994). *Images of mind.* New York: Freeman.

Reid, P., & Holland, N. E. (1997). Prejudice and discrimination: Old paradigms in new models for psychology. In D. F. Halpern & A. E. Voiskounsky (Eds.), *States of mind: American and post-Soviet perspectives on contemporary issues in psychology* (pp. 325–341). New York: Oxford University Press.

Reinisch, J. M., & Sanders, S. A. (1992). Prenatal hormonal contributions to sex differences in human cognitive and personality development. In A. A. Gerall, H. Moltz, & I. I. Ward (Eds.), *Sexual differentiation: Vol. 11. Handbook of behavioral neurobiology* (pp. 221–243). New York: Plenum.

Robinson, N. M., Abbott, R. D., Berninger, V. W., & Busse, J. (1996). The structure of abilities in math-precocious young children: Gender similarities and differences. *Journal of Educational Psychology, 88,* 341–352.

Rosenthal, R., & Rubin, D. B. (1982). Further meta-analytic procedures for assessing cognitive gender differences. *Journal of Educational Psychology, 74,* 708–712.

Shah, P., & Miyake, A. (1996). The separability of working memory resources for spatial thinking and language processing: An individual differences approach. *Journal of Experimental Psychology: General, 125,* 4–27.

Shaywitz, B. A., Bennet, A., Shaywitz, S. E., Liberman, I. Y., Fletcher, J. M., Shankweiler, D. P., Duncan, J. S., Katz, L., Liberman, A. M., Francis, D. J., et al. (1991). Neurolinguistic and biologic mechanisms in reading. In D. D. Drake & D. B. Gray (Eds.), *The reading brain: The biological basis of dyslexia* (pp. 27–52). Parkton, MD: York Press.

Stricker, L. J., Rock, D. A., & Burton, N. W. (1993). Sex differences in predictions of college grades from Scholastic Aptitude scores. *Journal of Educational Psychology, 85,* 710–718.

Stumpf, H., & Stanley, J. C. (1996). Gender-related differences on the College Board's advanced placement and achievement tests, 1982–1992. *Journal of Educational Psychology, 88,* 353–364.

Tannen, D. (1990). *You just don't understand: Men and women in conversation.* New York: Morrow.

U.S. Department of Education. (1996). *The third international mathematics and science study.* Washington, DC: Author. Retrieved from World Wide Web: http://www.ed.gov/nces

U.S. Department of Education. (1997). *National assessment of educational progress* (Indicator 32: Writing Proficiency; prepared by the Educational Testing Service). Washington, DC: Author. Retrieved from World Wide Web: http://www.ed.gov/nces

Vasta, R., Knott, J. A., & Gaze, C. E. (1996). Can spatial training erase the gender differences on the water-level task? *Psychology of Women Quarterly, 20,* 549–568.

Vogel, G. (1996, November 22). School achievement: Asia and Europe top in world, but reasons are hard to find. *Science, 274,* 1296.

Voyer, D., Voyer, S., & Bryden, M. P. (1995). Magnitude of sex differences in spatial abilities: A meta-analysis and consideration of critical variables. *Psychological Bulletin, 117,* 250–270.

Understanding the Text

1. Where do stereotypes come from? Review Halpern's essay for sections where she discusses the origins and persistence of social biases and stereotypes.

2. What is the psychobiosocial model of sex differences? Define it using Halpern's text and then explain it in your own words.

Reflection and Response

3. "A mind," Halpern writes, "is a difficult thing to change" (p. 193). Working from her essay overall, suggest what we can do to change when it comes to sex differences in intelligence. What role can science play? What other institutions or mechanisms would be needed to make this change?

4. How should schools change to minimize or erase sex differences in intelligence? Develop Halpern's suggestions to propose a plan for a more equitable system of education.

Making Connections

5. While Halpern looks at sex differences in intelligence, Malcom Gladwell ("None of the Above," p. 172) examines the evidence around ethnic differences in intelligence. Synthesize their arguments to explore how social factors impact perceptions of intelligence and to determine what role science can play in changing these perceptions.

6. Lily Rothman ("A Cultural History of Mansplaining," p. 203) documents the long historical consequences of sex differences in intelligence. Use her essay to complicate Halpern's argument. Given the deeply ingrained behavior of men in relation to women, can we erase stereotypes about sex differences in intelligence? How might empowering women's voices be used to reach that goal?

7. John D. Mayer ("We Need More Tests, Not Fewer," p. 166) argues for expanded intelligence testing for college and university admissions, yet Halpern, near the end of her essay, suggests that these tests inherently reflect gender biases. Evaluate the arguments of these authors and then create a poster presentation about college admissions testing. A poster presentation is an academic genre used in many disciplines in which researchers summarize their findings on a poster board, using key data and images. As you craft your poster, be aware of the impact of spacing and visual arrangement.

A Cultural History of Mansplaining

Lily Rothman

Lily Rothman is a New York–based journalist who currently serves as a senior editor at *TIME* magazine, where she focuses on the magazine's historical coverage and its online archive called The Vault. Her work has also appeared in *Slate*, the *Boston Herald*, the *Washington Post*, *Money*, and *The Atlantic*, from which this selection is taken.

Not all that long ago, an American statesman of considerable influence wrote an opinion piece for this very publication, about a political issue that directly affects women. It was perhaps the finest example of mansplaining ever published.

This election season, the idea of "mansplaining"—explaining without regard to the fact that the explainee knows more than the explainer, often done by a man to a woman—has exploded into mainstream political commentary. Hugo Schwyzer over at Jezebel noted its growth in September, writing that it has "moved beyond the feminist blogosphere." And, sure enough, these days pretty much every time a male politician opens his mouth about so-called women's issues he is dubbed, like so or like so, a mansplainer.

But the article in question wasn't written this year. Its author was Lyman Abbott, a prominent New England theologian, and it appeared in the Sept.1903 issue of *The Atlantic*. The article was called "Why Women Do Not Wish the Suffrage." Abbott writes:

> I believe it is because woman feels, if she does not clearly see, that the question of woman suffrage is more than merely political; that it concerns the nature and structure of society,—the home, the church, the industrial organism, the state, the social fabric. And to a change which involves a revolution in all of these she interposes an inflexible though generally a silent opposition. It is for these silent women—whose voices are not heard in conventions, who write no leaders, deliver no lectures, and visit no legislative assemblies—that I speak.

See, even though the women in question haven't said anything about it, Lyman Abbott *totally* knows what they want better than they do. Any woman in favor of suffrage just doesn't get the true female experience as well as he does.

Turns out 2012 isn't really the year of the mansplainer. The only reason we think it so is that the word itself didn't exist until recently. 5

The commonly cited birthday of the idea is 2008. That year, a portion of an essay by Rebecca Solnit, called "Men Explain Things To Me," appeared in the *Los Angeles Times*. Solnit didn't use the word "mansplain"; she merely, well, explained it, describing the time a man explained a book to her without acknowledging that she herself wrote it. (This August, she wrote that the men-explaining-things essay has been one of the most reposted pieces she's ever done.) According to Know Your Meme, the word first showed up online about a month after the *LA Times* piece, in the comments section on a LiveJournal community. Awareness increased slowly but steadily, mostly on feminist blogs, until it was suddenly all over the place: a Google trends graph of searches for the word is mostly a straight line until this past summer, when in August it appeared in a *GQ* political blog titled "The Mittsplainer" as well as an *xoJane.com* post critical of the word. There's another even larger jump in October, perhaps linked to the birth of Mansplaining Paul Ryan.

The idea wasn't political in origin, and mansplaining happens in academia and offices and dining rooms. But it makes sense that politics brought it to the general public's attention. When it comes to politics, it seems men have been talking about the female experience since basically forever.

John Adams, whose relationship with Abigail Adams is supposed to be a shining example of spousedom, mansplained the need to make husbands the legal masters of wives. In a March 1776 letter, Abigail told him

"Flora: 'Let's talk as man to man'," by Frederic Dorr Steele, 1910.
Library of Congress, Prints and Photographs Division [LC-DIG-ds-10035].

that men who have absolute control over their wives are bound to use them cruelly, and warns that women might not feel obligated to obey laws made by a body in which they have no representation. He responds:

> *Depend upon it, we know better than to repeal our masculine systems. Although they are in full force, you know they are little more than theory . . . We are obliged to go fair and softly, and, in practice, you know we are the subjects. We have only the name of masters, and rather than give up this, which would completely subject us to the despotism of the petticoat, I hope General Washington and all our brave heroes would fight.*

In other words, he tells his wife, who has expressed worry over the way men treat their wives, that he knows better than she does about the experience of being a wife.

And in a 1980 presidential debate, President Carter brought up the 10 fact that, after four decades of support for the Equal Rights Amendment, the Republican party had removed that language from their platform. Reagan mansplains:

> *I would like to call the attention of the people to the fact that that so-called simple amendment would be used by mischievous men to destroy discriminations that properly belong, by law, to women respecting the physical differences between the two sexes, labor laws that protect them against things that would be physically harmful to them.*

In other words, Ronald Reagan knows best what women can and can't do.

But just because it's been around so long doesn't mean mansplaining is a necessary condition of male politicians speaking about issues that women experience first-hand. Politicians on both sides of the aisle have avoided it, and eloquently. President Ford, a Republican, spoke in favor of the Equal Rights Amendment, making the point in 1976 that even instances of discrimination that may seem "petty and even ridiculous" to others hurt the people against whom the discrimination occurs. More recently, in his debate with Paul Ryan, Vice President Biden said that he can't know how a pregnant woman feels about her body. While both men were capable of a thought experiment about what they might do in a woman's place, they were also apparently capable of retaining the awareness that they could not know for sure.

It's a fine line, but seeing mansplaining everywhere — especially once you know it's been around so long — is perhaps as dangerous

> "Even an inveterate mansplainer can have a moment of clarity."

as allowing it to go unnoticed. It's a bad idea to discourage the valuable exercise of putting oneself in another's shoes, regardless of gender. And even an inveterate mansplainer can have a moment of clarity. It turns out that, even in his trophy-worthy mansplanation of suffrage, Lyman Abbott captured the mindset required to acknowledge that—while no one can know what someone somewhere else on the gender spectrum feels about being there—humans are still capable of empathy: "Man is not an inferior woman. Woman is not an inferior man."

Understanding the Text

1. What exactly is "mansplaining"? Define this term using Rothman's text, offer an example from the essay that illustrates that meaning, and then extend that definition through an example from your own life or from popular culture.

2. What is suffrage? How does it relate to the larger issues of mansplaining specifically or women and intelligence more generally?

Reflection and Response

3. Much of Rothman's essay focuses on mansplaining in politics. Write an essay in which you work from this base to consider the linkages between power and intelligence. Does intelligence determine success in politics? Does success in politics offer a platform for determining intelligence? How does mansplaining work to reinforce existing power structures?

4. Rothman ends her essay with the idea of empathy. Expand on this conclusion to consider the ways in which empathy can be used as a tool to confront mansplaining or, more generally, linkages between sex and intelligence. How might empathy help alter these practices? What strategies might we use to promote it? Is empathy itself gendered, and, if so, how might that complicate empathy as a solution? What other solutions might we pursue to counter mansplaining?

Making Connections

5. Mike Rose ("Blue-Collar Brilliance," p. 211) examines a similar set of assumptions about intelligence — based not on gender, but on class. Working from both Rose's and Halpern's essays, write a paper in which you consider the ways we stereotype people based on aspects of their identity. Consider as well the consequences of those stereotypes. Does either essay offer a mechanism for change?

6. Jennifer Lee ("The Truth about Asian Americans' Success," p. 181) considers connections between economic power and perceived intelligence, whereas Rothman focuses on political power. Working with both texts, write an essay about the complex intersections between intelligence, stereotypes, economics, and politics.

Are Gay People Smarter Than Straight People?

Mark Joseph Stern

After receiving his law degree from Georgetown University, Mark Joseph Stern became a staff writer for *Slate*, where he writes essays on science, legal, and LGBTQ+ issues. He is also the author of *American Justice 2019: The Roberts Court Arrives* (2019), which examines shifts in the Supreme Court following the retirement of Justice Anthony Kennedy.

Last week, the MacArthur Foundation revealed the recipients of its so-called "genius" awards, a $625,000 grant dispensed over five years to innovators, visionaries, and trailblazers. Of the 24 winners this year, at least three are openly gay, meaning gay people are significantly over-represented among the genius pool. The news has led some to speculate that gay geniuses outnumber straight ones, proportionally, in the population at large. Are gay people really smarter than straight people?

It's a tricky question, but at least one researcher thinks he has the answer—and the data to prove it. Last year, Satoshi Kanazawa argued in the *Journal of Biosocial Science* that gay people are typically born with more intelligence than the average heterosexual. Kanazawa explained his findings through the Savanna-IQ Interaction Hypothesis, which holds that smart people are better able to override their evolutionary impulses, adapting to new stimuli and desires more effectively than average or dumb people can. Just as smart people are ostensibly more likely to be vegetarians—a choice that requires shutting off the evolutionary impulse toward meat—so, too, are smart people more willing to engage with same-sex desires.

But there's a major problem with this premise. Kanazawa asserts that homosexuality is an evolutionary handicap because it prevents reproduction. This notion, though widely accepted in pop culture, is debatable at best. Some scientists speculate that the same genetic factors that cause homosexuality in one gender also induce hyperfertility in the other, a theory called sexually antagonistic selection. A gay man might be at an evolutionary dead end, in other words, but his sisters will be blessed with extreme fecundity, more than making up the balance. Homosexuality, according to this theory, isn't some evolutionary defect: It's a biological boon.

Even more obvious, however, is the common sense objection: What if smarter people simply feel more comfortable coming out? Assume, for the sake of argument, that intelligent people are, for whatever reason, more open-minded than dumb people. This would lead more intelligent gay people to come out while leaving dumber gay people in the closet, thereby completely skewing the data. Sexual orientation surveys are, after all, self-reported, leaving ample room for fibs and falsehoods. This eminently plausible alternative explanation, combined with Kanazawa's alarmingly spotty record of scientific integrity, probably reduces his hypothesis to just another dingbat theory.

Where scientific arguments falter, however, sociological arguments 5 pick up steam. Gay couples are more likely to have higher household incomes and college degrees than straight couples—two possible proxies for intelligence. Gay men in college, moreover, have higher-than-average GPAs and are significantly more likely to participate in extracurricular activities. Gays are wealthier and better educated than most Americans; shouldn't that indicate that they're also smarter?

If you're prone to gay exceptionalism, you might believe so. But there's good cause for skepticism. Here, again, an alternative explanation seems highly persuasive: Gay people might just work harder than their heterosexual counterparts. Starting in childhood, most gay people are acutely aware of the challenges they'll face, the roadblocks they'll encounter, the discrimination they'll battle. Gays born into small towns—which tend toward homophobia—understand early on that they must escape in order to find acceptance. For LGBT youths, escape usually hinges on two all-important factors: good grades and money. When excelling in school and making money are the only escape hatch to happiness, hitting the books and working overtime have a lot more appeal.

> "Gay people might just work harder than their heterosexual counterparts."

For many gay people, that lurking fear of instability never goes away—and why should it? The government still discriminates against gay couples in both obvious and insidious ways. In most states, gay people can still be fired for being gay. Many states ban gay adoption; others keep gay people out of their partners' hospital rooms. With this constant threat of bigotry in the background, is it any wonder that gay people strive for good grades and great jobs? Gay couples plan well for their financial futures not because they're brilliant money managers, but because they have little to no social safety net. Before the fall of DOMA°,

DOMA: Defense of Marriage Act, a federal law that went into effect in 1996, defining marriage for federal purposes as the union of one man and one woman. It was ruled unconstitutional by the U.S. Supreme Court in 2013 and 2015.

many gay couples couldn't share health insurance, and none could share Social Security benefits. Even today, many still can't formally adopt a child with their partner. Financial security can't solve all of these problems. But it helps to provide LGBT Americans a safety net denied to them by their own government.

The next time some study claims to show a link between sexuality and intelligence, then, it's probably best to ignore it. Gays might be overrepresented in the "genius" pool—and the Ivy League, and the Fortune 500—but there are more than enough dumb gays to even out the numbers. Homosexuality isn't a magical spark that ignites the fire of brilliance. It's just a biological quirk. If we're going to insist that gay love is no different from straight love, we'll have to accept that gay brains are no better, or worse, than straight ones.

Understanding the Text

1. What is Savanna-IQ Interaction Hypothesis? What makes it problematic?
2. What is "gay exceptionalism"? Explain this concept through Stern's essay and consider what role it plays in his larger argument.
3. Stern writes, "Where scientific arguments falter, however, sociological arguments pick up steam" (p. 208). What makes scientific arguments different from sociological ones, particularly since sociology is considered a social science? Working from Stern's descriptions of these arguments, and perhaps investigating the issue through an internet search, draw out the relationships, connections, and disconnections between these domains of knowledge.

Reflection and Response

4. How does the relationship between intelligence and sexuality illustrate the problem of causality? Use Stern's analysis to discuss the more general problem of locating causality through science or other forms of research.
5. How does equality impact perceptions of intelligence? Locate passages from Stern's text where he talks about how LGBTQ+ people have had to respond to discrimination and what effect that has had on their success and perceived intelligence.

Making Connections

6. William Saletan ("Stop Talking about Race and IQ," p. 186) also looks at the difficulties involved when seeking scientific explanations for the intelligence of groups. Using both Saletan's and Stern's texts, write an essay about the

limits of science. Your work on causality in question 4 might be a useful starting point. What problems with causality does Saletan encounter? How might his critique of the science of race and intelligence be extended to LGBTQ+ people?

7. Stern's description of the kinds of discrimination LGBTQ+ people face is reminiscent of the problems women face as described by Lily Rothman ("A Cultural History of Mansplaining," p. 203). Apply Rothman's essay to Stern's discussion. How might empathy help address these problems? What sort of political actions might be effective? What other solutions might be possible?

Blue-Collar Brilliance

Mike Rose

Currently a research professor in the Graduate School of Education and Information Studies at UCLA, Mike Rose has a long and distinguished history of studying language and literacy. He is the author of nearly a dozen books, including *Lives on the Boundary: The Struggles and Achievements of America's Underprepared* (1989), *Possible Lives: The Promise of Public Education in America* (1995), and *The Mind at Work: Valuing the Intelligence of the American Worker* (2004). He has received a number of awards, including a Guggenheim Fellowship, and his work has been recognized by the McDonnell Foundation Program in Cognitive Studies for Educational Practice, the National Council of Teachers of English, and the Modern Language Association.

My mother, Rose Meraglio Rose (Rosie), shaped her adult identity as a waitress in coffee shops and family restaurants. When I was growing up in Los Angeles during the 1950s, my father and I would occasionally hang out at the restaurant until her shift ended, and then we'd ride the bus home with her. Sometimes she worked the register and the counter, and we sat there; when she waited booths and tables, we found a booth in the back where the waitresses took their breaks.

There wasn't much for a child to do at the restaurants, and so as the hours stretched out, I watched the cooks and waitresses and listened to what they said. At mealtimes, the pace of the kitchen staff and the din from customers picked up. Weaving in and out around the room, waitresses warned *behind you* in impassive but urgent voices. Standing at the service window facing the kitchen, they called out abbreviated orders. *Fry four on two*, my mother would say as she clipped a check onto the metal wheel. Her tables were *deuces*, *four-tops*, or *six-tops* according to their size; seating areas also were nicknamed. The *racetrack*, for instance, was the fast-turnover front section. Lingo conferred authority and signaled know-how.

Rosie took customers' orders, pencil poised over pad, while fielding questions about the food. She walked full tilt through the room with plates stretching up her left arm and two cups of coffee somehow cradled in her right hand. She stood at a table or booth and removed a plate for this person, another for that person, then another, remembering who had the hamburger, who had the fried shrimp, almost always getting it right. She would haggle with the cook about a returned order and rush by us, saying, *He gave me lip, but I got him.* She'd take a minute to flop down in the booth next to my father. *I'm all in*, she'd say, and whisper something about a customer. Gripping the outer edge of the table with one hand, she'd watch the room and note, in the flow of our conversation, who needed a refill, whose order was taking longer to prepare than it should, who was finishing up.

I couldn't have put it in words when I was growing up, but what I observed in my mother's restaurant defined the world of adults, a place where competence was synonymous with physical work. I've since studied the working habits of blue-collar workers and have come to understand how much my mother's kind of work demands of both body and brain. A waitress acquires knowledge and intuition about the ways and the rhythms of the restaurant business. Waiting on seven to nine tables, each with two to six customers, Rosie devised memory strategies so that she could remember who ordered what. And because she knew the average time it took to prepare different dishes, she could monitor an order that was taking too long at the service station.

Like anyone who is effective at physical work, my mother learned *to* *work smart*, as she put it, *to make every move count*. She'd sequence and 5 group tasks: What could she do first, then second, then third as she circled through her station? What tasks could be clustered? She did everything on the fly, and when problems arose—technical or human—she solved them within the flow of work, while taking into account the emotional state of her co-workers. Was the manager in a good mood? Did the cook wake up on the wrong side of the bed? If so, how could she make an extra request or effectively return an order?

And then, of course, there were the customers who entered the restaurant with all sorts of needs, from physiological ones, including the emotions that accompany hunger, to a sometimes complicated desire for human contact. Her tip depended on how well she responded to these needs, and so she became adept at reading social cues and managing feelings, both the customers' and her own. No wonder, then, that Rosie was intrigued by psychology. The restaurant became the place where she studied human behavior, puzzling over the problems of her regular customers and refining her ability to deal with people in a difficult world. She took pride in *being among the public*, she'd say. *There isn't a day that goes by in the restaurant that you don't learn something.*

My mother quit school in the seventh grade to help raise her brothers and sisters. Some of those siblings made it through high school, and some dropped out to find work in railroad yards, factories, or restaurants. My father finished a grade or two in primary school in Italy and never darkened the schoolhouse door again. I didn't do well in school either. By high school I had accumulated a spotty academic record and many hours of hazy disaffection. I spent a few years on the vocational track, but in my senior year I was inspired by my English teacher and managed to squeak into a small college on probation.

My freshman year was academically bumpy, but gradually I began to see formal education as a means of fulfillment and as a road toward making a living. I studied the humanities and later the social and psychological sciences and taught for 10 years in a range of situations—elementary school, adult education courses, tutoring centers, a program for Vietnam veterans who wanted to go to college. Those students had socioeconomic and educational backgrounds similar to mine. Then I went back to graduate school to study education and cognitive psychology and eventually became a faculty member in a school of education.

Intelligence is closely associated with formal education—the type of schooling a person has, how much and how long—and most people seem to move comfortably from that notion to a belief that work requiring less schooling requires less intelligence. These assumptions run through our cultural history, from the post–Revolutionary War period, when mechanics were characterized by political rivals as illiterate and therefore incapable of participating in government, until today. More than once I've heard a manager label his workers as "a bunch of dummies." Generalizations about intelligence, work, and social class deeply affect our assumptions about ourselves and each other, guiding the ways we use our minds to learn, build knowledge, solve problems, and make our way through the world.

> "Generalizations about intelligence, work, and social class deeply affect our assumptions about ourselves and each other."

Although writers and scholars have often looked at the working class, they have generally focused on the values such workers exhibit rather than on the thought their work requires—a subtle but pervasive omission. Our cultural iconography promotes the muscled arm, sleeve rolled tight against biceps, but no brightness behind the eye, no image that links hand and brain. 10

One of my mother's brothers, Joe Meraglio, left school in the ninth grade to work for the Pennsylvania Railroad. From there he joined the Navy, returned to the railroad, which was already in decline, and eventually joined his older brother at General Motors where, over a 33-year career, he moved from working on the assembly line to supervising the paint-and-body department. When I was a young man, Joe took me on a tour of the factory. The floor was loud—in some places deafening—and when I turned a corner or opened a door, the smell of chemicals knocked my head back. The work was repetitive and taxing, and the pace was inhumane.

Still, for Joe the shop floor provided what school did not; it was *like schooling*, he said, a place where *you're constantly learning*. Joe learned the most efficient way to use his body by acquiring a set of routines that were quick and preserved energy. Otherwise he would never have survived on the line.

As a foreman, Joe constantly faced new problems and became a consummate multi-tasker, evaluating a flurry of demands quickly, parceling out physical and mental resources, keeping a number of ongoing events in his mind, returning to whatever task had been interrupted, and maintaining a cool head under the pressure of grueling production schedules. In the midst of all this, Joe learned more and more about the auto industry, the technological and social dynamics of the shop floor, the machinery and production processes, and the basics of paint chemistry and of plating and baking. With further promotions, he not only solved problems but also began to find problems to solve: Joe initiated the redesign of the nozzle on a paint sprayer, thereby eliminating costly and unhealthy overspray. And he found a way to reduce energy costs on the baking ovens without affecting the quality of the paint. He lacked formal knowledge of how the machines under his supervision worked, but he had direct experience with them, hands-on knowledge, and was savvy about their quirks and operational capabilities. He could experiment with them.

In addition, Joe learned about budgets and management. Coming off the line as he did, he had a perspective of workers' needs and management's demands, and this led him to think of ways to improve efficiency on the line while relieving some of the stress on the assemblers. He had each worker in a unit learn his or her co-workers' jobs so they could rotate across stations to relieve some of the monotony. He believed that rotation would allow assemblers to get longer and more frequent breaks. It was an easy sell to the people on the line. The union, however, had to approve any modification in job duties, and the managers were wary of the change. Joe had to argue his case on a number of fronts, providing him a kind of rhetorical education.

Eight years ago I began a study of the thought processes involved 15 in work like that of my mother and uncle. I catalogued the cognitive demands of a range of blue-collar and service jobs, from waitressing and hair styling to plumbing and welding. To gain a sense of how knowledge and skill develop, I observed experts as well as novices. From the details of this close examination, I tried to fashion what I called "cognitive biographies" of blue-collar workers. Biographical accounts of the lives of scientists, lawyers, entrepreneurs, and other professionals are rich with detail about the intellectual dimension of their work. But the life stories of working-class people are few and are typically accounts of hardship and courage or the achievements wrought by hard work.

Our culture — in Cartesian fashion — separates the body from the mind, so that, for example, we assume that the use of a tool does not involve abstraction. We reinforce this notion by defining intelligence solely on grades in school and numbers on IQ tests. And we employ social biases pertaining to a person's place on the occupational ladder. The distinctions among blue, pink, and white collars carry with them attributions of character, motivation, and intelligence. Although we rightly acknowledge and amply compensate the play of mind in white-collar and professional work, we diminish or erase it in considerations about other endeavors — physical and service work particularly. We also often ignore the experience of everyday work in administrative deliberations and policymaking.

But here's what we find when we get in close. The plumber seeking leverage in order to work in tight quarters and the hair stylist adroitly handling scissors and comb manage their bodies strategically. Though work-related actions become routine with experience, they were learned at some point through observation, trial and error, and, often, physical or verbal assistance from a co-worker or trainer. I've frequently observed novices talking to themselves as they take on a task, or shaking their head or hand as if to erase an attempt before trying again. In fact, our traditional notions of routine performance could keep us from appreciating the many instances within routine where quick decisions and adjustments are made. I'm struck by the thinking-in-motion that some work requires, by all the mental activity that can be involved in simply getting from one place to another: the waitress rushing back through her station to the kitchen or the foreman walking the line.

The use of tools requires the studied refinement of stance, grip, balance, and fine-motor skills. But manipulating tools is intimately tied to knowledge of what a particular instrument can do in a particular situation and do better than other similar tools. A worker must also know the characteristics of the material one is engaging — how it reacts to various cutting or compressing devices, to degrees of heat, or to lines of force. Some of these things demand judgment, the weighing of options, the consideration of multiple variables, and, occasionally, the creative use of a tool in an unexpected way.

In manipulating material, the worker becomes attuned to aspects of the environment, a training or disciplining of perception that both enhances knowledge and informs perception. Carpenters have an eye for length, line, and angle; mechanics troubleshoot by listening; hair stylists are attuned to shape, texture, and motion. Sensory data merge with concept, as when an auto mechanic relies on sound, vibration, and even smell to understand what cannot be observed.

Planning and problem solving have been studied since the earliest 20 days of modern cognitive psychology and are considered core elements in Western definitions of intelligence. To work is to solve problems. The big difference between the psychologist's laboratory and the workplace is that in the former the problems are isolated and in the latter they are embedded in the real-time flow of work with all its messiness and social complexity.

Much of physical work is social and interactive. Movers determining how to get an electric range down a flight of stairs require coordination, negotiation, planning, and the establishing of incremental goals. Words, gestures, and sometimes a quick pencil sketch are involved, if only to get the rhythm right. How important it is, then, to consider the social and communicative dimension of physical work, for it provides the medium for so much of work's intelligence.

Given the ridicule heaped on blue-collar speech, it might seem odd to value its cognitive content. Yet, the flow of talk at work provides the channel for organizing and distributing tasks, for troubleshooting and problem solving, for learning new information and revising old. A significant amount of teaching, often informal and indirect, takes place at work. Joe Meraglio saw that much of his job as a supervisor involved instruction. In some service occupations, language and communication are central: observing and interpreting behavior and expression, inferring mood and motive, taking on the perspective of others, responding appropriately to social cues, and knowing when you're understood. A good hair stylist, for instance, has the ability to convert vague requests (*I want something light and summery*) into an appropriate cut through questions, pictures, and hand gestures.

Verbal and mathematical skills drive measures of intelligence in the Western Hemisphere, and many of the kinds of work I studied are thought to require relatively little proficiency in either. Compared to certain kinds of white-collar occupations, that's true. But written symbols flow through physical work.

Numbers are rife in most workplaces: on tools and gauges, as measurements, as indicators of pressure or concentration or temperature, as guides to sequence, on ingredient labels, on lists and spreadsheets, as markers of quantity and price. Certain jobs require workers to make, check, and verify calculations, and to collect and interpret data. Basic math can be involved, and some workers develop a good sense of numbers and patterns. Consider, as well, what might be called material mathematics: mathematical functions embodied in materials and actions, as when a carpenter builds a cabinet or a flight of stairs. A simple mathematical act can extend quickly beyond itself. Measuring, for example, can involve more than recording the dimensions of an object. As I watched a cabinetmaker measure a long strip of wood, he read a number off the tape out loud, looked back over his shoulder to the kitchen wall, turned back to his task, took another measurement, and paused for a moment in thought. He was solving a problem involving the molding, and the measurement was important to his deliberation about structure and appearance.

In the blue-collar workplace, directions, plans, and reference books rely   25 on illustrations, some representational and others, like blueprints, that require training to interpret. Esoteric symbols—visual jargon—depict switches and receptacles, pipe fittings, or types of welds. Workers themselves often make sketches on the job. I frequently observed them grab a pencil to sketch something on a scrap of paper or on a piece of the material they were installing.

Though many kinds of physical work don't require a high literacy level, more reading occurs in the blue-collar workplace than is generally thought, from manuals and catalogues to work orders and invoices, to lists, labels, and forms. With routine tasks, for example, reading is integral to understanding production quotas, learning how to use an instrument, or applying a product. Written notes can initiate action, as in restaurant orders or reports of machine malfunction, or they can serve as memory aids.

True, many uses of writing are abbreviated, routine, and repetitive, and they infrequently require interpretation or analysis. But analytic moments can be part of routine activities, and seemingly basic reading and writing can be cognitively rich. Because workplace language is used in the flow of other activities, we can overlook the remarkable coordination of words, numbers, and drawings required to initiate and direct action.

If we believe everyday work to be mindless, then that will affect the work we create in the future. When we devalue the full range of everyday cognition, we offer limited educational opportunities and fail to make fresh and meaningful instructional connections among disparate kinds of skill and knowledge. If we think that whole categories of people—identified by class or occupation—are not that bright, then we reinforce social separations and cripple our ability to talk across cultural divides.

Affirmation of diverse intelligence is not a retreat to a softhearted definition of the mind. To acknowledge a broader range of intellectual capacity is to take seriously the concept of cognitive variability, to appreciate in all the Rosies and Joes the thought that drives their accomplishments and defines who they are. This is a model of the mind that is worthy of a democratic society.

Understanding the Text

1. What forms of intelligence are at play in blue-collar and service work? Review Rose's essay to list all the kinds of educational experiences and resulting smarts he observed by looking at his family and other workers.

2. Why have we historically devalued the intelligence of workers? How is it connected to class biases? To our definition of intelligence?

Reflection and Response

3. Part of the problem, Rose suggests, is that our definition of intelligence is tied to formal schooling. Craft a definition of intelligence that would account for all kinds of workers, regardless of their amount of schooling or the kind of work they do.

4. Rose ends his essay by claiming that expanding our notions of intelligence reflects "a model of the mind that is worthy of a democratic society" (p. 217). What do you think he means by that?

Making Connections

5. Diane F. Halpern ("Sex Differences in Intelligence," p. 191) makes a number of recommendations to address sex differences in education. Apply her solutions to the issue of class and intelligence. Based on Rose's observations, which of Halpern's recommendations might be effective at changing the way we think about the intelligence of workers? Is class bias more pervasive in education than gender bias? Can formal schooling account for worker intelligence at all?

6. How does blue-collar and service worker intelligence further trouble the beliefs of IQ fundamentalists? Apply Rose's insights to Malcolm Gladwell's analysis ("None of the Above," p. 172).

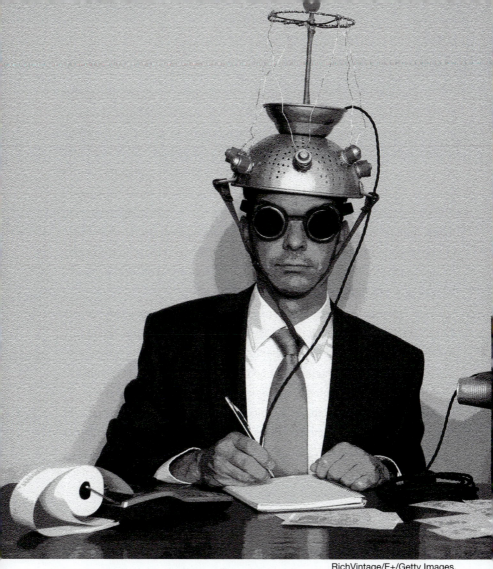

5

What Is Extreme Intelligence?

Ｆor many of the chapters of this book, we've been thinking about how to solve a central problem when it comes to intelligence: the process of thinking about intelligence is really just intelligence thinking about itself. To locate some objectivity about this subject, we've examined intelligence that sits a little distant from us (in animals or computers) or that extends a little beyond our usual understandings (like multiple intelligences). Studying extreme intelligence accomplishes a similar goal. When we look at things at their extreme, we see aspects of them supersized for examination, or stretched to the point of breaking, or magnified so that we can see fine details. All these close examinations help us understand not just extreme intelligence, but intelligence more generally as well.

What constitutes extreme intelligence? Well, think of terms like "genius," "prodigy," "gifted"—individuals whose intelligence (and talents) so far exceeds the norm that they represent something else entirely, sometimes beyond feeling entirely human. But no matter how superhuman geniuses might seem from a distance, a closer look inevitably reveals the same humanity we all share, with all its faults and failings. Exploring the extreme intelligence of geniuses and prodigies gives us a deeper understanding of intelligence, of what it can and can't do, of what it means to be human.

Claudia Kalb opens this exploration with a thorough examination of what makes a genius, examining the phenomenon from perspectives ranging from neuroscience to creativity. Daniel Pink continues this conversation around genius by looking at two different and divergent models of what a genius can be, drawing from detailed economic analysis of some of the most famous artists in the world. Matthew Francis hones in on one very familiar genius—Albert Einstein. But rather than focusing on the image of Einstein as genius, Francis looks at the function of his celebrity status in forging a particular image of what genius looks like while also revealing some of Einstein's personal shortcomings. Francis suggests that geniuses are far from perfect, a point reinforced by Irina Aristarkhova, who looks at the troubling behavior of some "genius" artists who sexually harass and

photo: RichVintage/E+/Getty Images.

abuse others, focusing on the moral mapping of genius to "good" that allows some men to get away with evil behavior. Emily Atkin continues the discussion of genius and gender dynamics by noting that genius is a term more often applied to men than to women. This disparity is reflected, too, in the number of women interested in certain fields, such as science and engineering. Sam Riches takes the conversation in a new direction with a discussion about athletes and what makes one a sports genius. Even in that arena, there is room for critique, as Riches also examines the racial dimensions of genius and sports. Finally, David Z. Hambrick synthesizes many of these discussions by looking at the related term "prodigy," exploring the genetic, environmental, and personal factors that propel some children to extraordinary success at an early age.

Across all this material, the human dimension of intelligence, even at its extreme, becomes clear again and again. That human dimension brings us back to the central question of this text: what is intelligence? It's a question that thinking through these readings will help you answer for yourself.

What Makes a Genius?

Claudia Kalb

Journalist Claudia Kalb writes primarily about medicine, mental health, and science for publications such as *National Geographic*, *Smithsonian*, *Scientific American*, and *Newsweek*. She has received a number of awards, including a Casey Fellowship at the Journalism Center on Children and Families at the University of Maryland, a Boot Camp Fellowship at the Knight Science Journalism Program at MIT, and a John S. Knight Journalism Fellowship at Stanford University. She is also the author of *Andy Warhol Was a Hoarder: Inside the Minds of History's Great Personalities* (2016), a *New York Times* bestseller.

The Mütter Museum in Philadelphia houses an array of singular medical specimens. On the lower level the fused livers of nineteenth-century conjoined twins Chang and Eng float in a glass vessel. Nearby, visitors can gawk at hands swollen with gout, the bladder stones of Chief Justice John Marshall, the cancerous tumor extracted from President Grover Cleveland's jaw, and a thighbone from a Civil War soldier with the wounding bullet still in place. But there's one exhibit near the entrance that elicits unmatchable awe. Look closely at the display, and you can see smudge marks left by museumgoers pressing their foreheads against the glass.

The object that fascinates them is a small wooden box containing 46 microscope slides, each displaying a slice of Albert Einstein's brain. A magnifying glass positioned over one of the slides reveals a piece of tissue about the size of a stamp, its graceful branches and curves resembling an aerial view of an estuary. These remnants of brain tissue are mesmerizing even though—or perhaps because—they reveal little about the physicist's vaunted powers of cognition. Other displays in the museum show disease and disfigurement—the results of something gone wrong. Einstein's brain represents potential, the ability of one exceptional mind, one genius, to catapult ahead of everyone else. "He saw differently from the rest of us," says visitor Karen O'Hair as she peers at the tea-colored sample. "And he could extend beyond that to what he couldn't see, which is absolutely amazing."

Throughout history rare individuals have stood out for their meteoric contributions to a field. Lady Murasaki for her literary inventiveness. Michelangelo for his masterful touch. Marie Curie for her scientific acuity. "The genius," wrote German philosopher Arthur Schopenhauer, "lights on his age like a comet into the paths of the planets." Consider Einstein's impact on physics. With no tools at his disposal other than the force of his own thoughts, he predicted in his general theory of relativity that massive accelerating objects—like black holes orbiting each other—would create ripples in the fabric of space-time. It took one hundred years, enormous computational power, and massively sophisticated technology to definitively prove him right, with the physical detection of such gravitational waves less than two years ago.

Einstein revolutionized our understanding of the very laws of the universe. But our understanding of how a mind like his works remains stubbornly earthbound. What set his brainpower, his thought processes, apart from those of his merely brilliant peers? What makes a genius?

Philosophers have long been pondering the origins of genius. Early 5 Greek thinkers believed an overabundance of black bile—one of the four bodily humors proposed by Hippocrates—endowed poets, philosophers, and other eminent souls with "exalted powers," says historian Darrin McMahon, author of *Divine Fury: A History of Genius*. Phrenologists attempted to find genius in bumps on the head; craniometrists collected skulls—including philosopher Immanuel Kant's—which they probed, measured, and weighed.

The Kamioka Gravitational Wave Detector.
PAOLO WOODS/National Geographic Image Collection.

None of them discovered a single source of genius, and such a thing is unlikely to be found. Genius is too elusive, too subjective, too wedded to the verdict of history to be easily identi-

"Genius is too elusive, too subjective, too wedded to the verdict of history to be easily identified."

fied. And it requires the ultimate expression of too many traits to be simplified into the highest point on one human scale. Instead we can try to understand it by unraveling the complex and tangled qualities—intelligence, creativity, perseverance, and simple good fortune, to name a few—that entwine to create a person capable of changing the world.

Intelligence has often been considered the default yardstick of genius—a measurable quality generating tremendous accomplishment. Lewis Terman, the Stanford University psychologist who helped pioneer the IQ test, believed a test that captured intelligence would also reveal genius. In the 1920s he began tracking more than 1,500 Californian schoolkids with IQs generally above 140—a threshold he labeled as "near genius or genius"—to see how they fared in life and how they compared with other children. Terman and his collaborators followed the participants, nicknamed "Termites," for their lifetimes and mapped their successes in a series of reports, *Genetic Studies of Genius*. The group included members of the National Academy of Sciences, politicians, doctors, professors, and musicians. Forty years after the study began, the researchers documented the thousands of academic reports and books they published, as well as the number of patents granted (350) and short stories written (about 400).

But monumental intelligence on its own is no guarantee of monumental achievement, as Terman and his collaborators would discover. A number of the study's participants struggled to thrive, despite their towering IQ scores. Several dozen flunked out of college at first. Others, tested for the study but with IQs that weren't high enough to make the cut, grew up to become renowned in their fields, most famously Luis Alvarez and William Shockley, both of whom won Nobel Prizes in physics. There's precedent for such underestimation: Charles Darwin recalled being considered "a very ordinary boy, rather below the common standard in intellect." As an adult he solved the mystery of how the splendid diversity of life came into being.

Scientific breakthroughs like Darwin's theory of evolution by natural selection would be impossible without creativity, a strand of genius that Terman couldn't measure. But creativity and its processes can be explained, to a certain extent, by creative people themselves. Scott Barry Kaufman, scientific director of the Imagination Institute in Philadelphia, has been bringing together individuals who stand out as trailblazers in their fields—people like psychologist Steven Pinker and comedian Anne Libera of the Second City—to talk about how their ideas and insights are kindled. Kaufman's goal is not to elucidate genius—he considers the word to be a societal judgment that elevates a chosen few while over-looking others—but to nurture imagination in everyone.

These discussions have revealed that the aha moment, the flash of clarity that arises at unexpected times—in a dream, in the shower, on a walk—often emerges after a period of contemplation. Information comes in consciously, but the problem is processed unconsciously, the resulting solution leaping out when the mind least expects it. "Great ideas don't tend to come when you're narrowly focusing on them," says Kaufman.

Studies of the brain offer hints at how these aha moments might happen. The creative process, says Rex Jung, a neuroscientist at the University of New Mexico, relies on the dynamic interplay of neural networks operating in concert and drawing from different parts of the brain at once—both the right and left hemispheres and especially regions in the prefrontal cortex. One of these networks fosters our ability to meet external demands—activities we must act on, like going to work and paying our taxes—and resides largely in outer areas of the brain. The other cultivates internal thought processes, including daydreaming and imagining, and stretches mainly across the brain's middle region.

Jazz improvisation provides a compelling example of how neural networks interact during the creative process. Charles Limb, a hearing specialist and auditory surgeon at UC San Francisco, designed an iron-free keyboard small enough to be played inside the confines of an MRI scanner. Six jazz pianists were asked to play a scale and a piece of mem-orized music and then to improvise solos as they listened to the sounds of a jazz quartet. Their scans demonstrate that brain activity was "fun-damentally different" while the musicians were improvising, says Limb. The internal network, associated with self-expression, showed increased activity, while the outer network, linked to focused attention and also self-censoring, quieted down. "It's almost as if the brain turned off its own ability to criticize itself," he says.

This may help explain the astounding performances of jazz pianist Keith Jarrett. Jarrett, who improvises concerts that last for as long as two hours, finds it difficult—impossible, actually—to explain how his music takes shape. But when he sits down in front of audiences, he purposefully pushes notes out of his mind, moving his hands to keys he had no inten-tion of playing. "I'm bypassing the brain completely," he tells me. "I am being pulled by a force that I can only be thankful for." Jarrett specifically remembers one concert in Munich, where he felt as if he had disappeared

10

into the high notes of the keyboard. His creative artistry, nurtured by decades of listening, learning, and practicing melodies, emerges when he is least in control. "It's a vast space in which I trust there will be music," he says.

One sign of creativity is being able to make connections between seemingly disparate concepts. Richer communication between areas of the brain may help make those intuitive leaps possible. Andrew Newberg, director of research at the Marcus Institute of Integrative Health at Thomas Jefferson University Hospitals, is using diffusion tensor imaging, an MRI contrast technique, to map neural pathways in the brains of creative people. His participants, who come from Kaufman's pool of big thinkers, are given standard creativity tests, which ask them to come up with novel uses for everyday objects like baseball bats and toothbrushes. Newberg aims to compare the connectivity in the brains of these high achievers against that of a group of controls to see if there is a difference in how effectively the various regions of their brains interact. His ultimate goal is to scan as many as 25 in each category and then pool the data so he can look for similarities within each group as well as differences that may appear across vocations. For instance, are certain areas more active in a comedian's brain compared with a psychologist's?

A preliminary comparison of one "genius"—Newberg uses the word 15 loosely to distinguish the two groups of participants—and one control reveals an intriguing contrast. On the subjects' brain scans, swaths of red, green, and blue illuminate tracts of white matter, which contain the wiring that allows neurons to transmit electrical messages. The red blotch on each image is the corpus callosum, a centrally located bundle of more than 200 million nerve fibers that joins the two hemispheres of the brain and facilitates connectivity between them. "The more red you see," Newberg says, "the more connecting fibers there are." The difference is notable: The red section of the "genius" brain appears to be about twice as wide as the red of the control brain.

"This implies that there's more communication going on between the left and the right hemispheres, which one might expect in people who are highly creative," says Newberg, stressing that this is an ongoing study. "There's more flexibility in their thought processes, more contributions from different parts of the brain." The green and blue swaths show other areas of connectivity, stretching from front to back—including dialogue among the frontal, parietal, and temporal lobes—and may reveal additional clues, says Newberg. "I don't know yet what else we might find out. This is just one piece."

Even as neuroscientists try to understand how the brain fosters the development of paradigm-shifting thought processes, other researchers are wrestling with the question of when and from what this capacity develops. Are geniuses born or made? Francis Galton, a cousin of Darwin, objected to what he called "pretensions of natural equality," believing that genius was passed down through family bloodlines. To prove it, he mapped the lineages of an array of European leaders in disparate fields—from Mozart and Haydn to Byron, Chaucer, Titus, and Napoleon. In 1869 Galton published his results in *Hereditary Genius,* a book that would launch the "nature versus nurture" debate and spur the misbegotten field of eugenics. Geniuses were rare, Galton concluded, numbering roughly one in a million. What was not unusual, he wrote, were the many instances "in which men who are more or less illustrious have eminent kinsfolk."

Advances in genetic research now make it possible to examine human traits at the molecular level. Over the past several decades, scientists have been searching for genes that contribute to intelligence, behavior, and even unique qualities like perfect pitch. In the case of intelligence, this research triggers ethical concerns about how it might be used; it is also exceedingly complex, as thousands of genes may be involved—each one with a very small effect. What about other kinds of abilities? Is there something innate in having an ear for music? Numerous accomplished musicians, including Mozart and Ella Fitzgerald, are believed to have had perfect pitch, which may have played a role in their extraordinary careers.

Genetic potential alone does not predict actual accomplishment. It also takes nurture to grow a genius. Social and cultural influences can provide that nourishment, creating clusters of genius at moments and places in history: Baghdad during Islam's Golden Age, Kolkata during the Bengal Renaissance, Silicon Valley today.

A hungry mind can also find the intellectual stimulation it needs at home—as in suburban Adelaide, Australia, in the case of Terence Tao, widely considered one of the greatest minds currently working in mathematics. Tao showed a remarkable grasp of language and numbers early in life, but his parents created the environment in which he could flourish. They provided him with books, toys, and games and encouraged him to play and learn on his own—a practice his father, Billy, believes stimulated his son's originality and problem-solving skills. Billy and his wife, Grace, also sought out advanced learning opportunities for their son as he began his formal education, and he was fortunate to meet educators who helped foster and stretch his mind. Tao enrolled in high school classes when he was seven years old, scored 760 on the math section of the SAT at age eight, went to university full-time when he was 13, and became a professor at UCLA at 21. "Talent is important," he once wrote on his blog, "but how one develops and nurtures it is even more so."

20

Natural gifts and a nurturing environment can still fall short of producing a genius, without motivation and tenacity propelling one forward. These personality traits, which pushed Darwin to spend two decades perfecting *Origin of Species* and Indian mathematician Srinivasa Ramanujan to produce thousands of formulas, inspire the work of psychologist Angela Duckworth. She believes that a combination of passion and perseverance—what she calls "grit"—drives people to achieve. Duckworth, herself a MacArthur Foundation "genius" and a professor of psychology at the University of Pennsylvania, says the concept of genius is too easily cloaked in layers of magic, as if great achievement erupts spontaneously with no hard work. She believes there are differences when it comes to individual talent, but no matter how brilliant a person, fortitude and discipline are critical to success. "When you really look at somebody who accomplishes something great," she says, "it is not effortless."

Nor does it happen on the first try. "The number one predictor of impact is productivity," says Dean Keith Simonton, professor emeritus of psychology at UC Davis and a longtime scholar of genius. Big hits emerge after many attempts. "Most articles published in the sciences are never cited by anybody," says Simonton. "Most compositions are not recorded. Most works of art aren't displayed." Thomas Edison invented the phonograph and the first commercially viable light bulb, but these were just two of the thousand-plus U.S. patents he was awarded.

Lack of support can stunt prospects for potential geniuses; they never get the chance to be productive. Throughout history women have been denied formal education, deterred from advancing professionally, and under-recognized for their achievements. Mozart's older sister, Maria Anna, a brilliant harpsichordist, had her career cut short by her father when she reached the marriageable age of 18. Half the women in the Terman study ended up as homemakers. People born into poverty or oppression don't get a shot at working toward anything other than staying alive. "If you do believe that genius is this thing that can be singled out and cultivated and nurtured," says historian Darrin McMahon, "what an incredible tragedy that thousands of geniuses or potential geniuses have withered and died."

Sometimes, by sheer good fortune, promise and opportunity collide. If there were ever an individual who personified the concept of genius in every aspect, from its ingredients to its far-reaching impact, it would be Leonardo da Vinci. Born in 1452 to unmarried parents, Leonardo began life in a stone farmhouse in Italy's Tuscan hills, where olive trees and dusky blue clouds blanket the Arno Valley. From these simple beginnings, Leonardo's intellect and artistry soared like Schopenhauer's comet.

The breadth of his abilities—his artistic insights, his expertise in human anatomy, his prescient engineering—is unparalleled.

Leonardo's pathway to genius began with an apprenticeship with 25 master artist Andrea del Verrocchio in Florence when he was a teen-ager. Leonardo's creativity was so robust that in his lifetime he filled thousands of pages in his notebooks, which brimmed with studies and designs, from the science of optics to his famed inventions, including a revolving bridge and a flying machine. He persisted no matter the chal-lenge. "Obstacles cannot crush me," he wrote. "He who is fixed to a star does not change his mind." Leonardo also lived in a place (Florence) and at a time (the Italian Renaissance) when the arts were cultivated by wealthy patrons and inventiveness coursed through the streets, where great minds, including Michelangelo and Raphael, jostled for acclaim.

Leonardo delighted in envisioning the impossible—hitting a target that, as Schopenhauer wrote, "others cannot even see." Today an inter-national group of scholars and scientists has taken on a similar mission, and its subject is just as elusive: Leonardo himself. The Leonardo Project is tracing the artist's genealogy and hunting down his DNA to learn more about his ancestry and physical characteristics, to verify paintings that have been attributed to him—and, most remarkably, to search for clues to his extraordinary talent.

Team member David Caramelli's high-tech molecular anthropology lab at the University of Florence sits in a sixteenth-century building with a glorious view of the Florentine skyline. Jutting out majestically is the dome of the city's prominent cathedral, Santa Maria del Fiore, whose original crowning copper-gilt ball was made by Verrocchio and raised to the top of the cupola with Leonardo's help in 1471. This juxaposi-tion of past and present is a fitting setting for Caramelli's expertise in ancient DNA. Two years ago he published preliminary genetic analyses of a Neanderthal skeleton. Now he is poised to apply similar techniques to Leonardo's DNA, which the team is hoping to extract from some form of biological relic—the artist's bones, a strand of hair, skin cells left behind on his paintings or notebooks, or perhaps even saliva, which Leonardo may have used to prepare canvases for his silverpoint drawings.

It is an ambitious plan, but team members are optimistically laying the groundwork. Genealogists are tracking down Leonardo's living rel-atives on his father's side for cheek swabs, which Caramelli will use to identify a genetic marker to confirm the authenticity of Leonardo's DNA if it is found. Physical anthropologists are seeking access to remains that are believed to be Leonardo's at Amboise castle in France's Loire Valley, where he was buried in 1519. Art historians and geneticists, including specialists at the institute of genomics pioneer J. Craig Venter, are experimenting with techniques to obtain DNA from fragile Renaissance-era paintings and paper. "The wheels are starting to turn," says Jesse Ausubel, vice chairman of the Richard Lounsbery Foundation and an environmental scientist at Rockefeller University in New York City, who is coordinating the project.

One of the group's early goals is to explore the possibility that Leonardo's genius stemmed not only from his intellect, creativity, and cultured environment but also from his exemplary powers of perception. "In the same way that Mozart may have had extraordinary hearing," says Ausubel, "Leonardo appears to have had extraordinary visual acuity." Some of the genetic components of vision are well identified, including the red and green color-vision pigment genes, located on the X chromosome. Thomas Sakmar, a specialist in sensory neuroscience at Rockefeller, says it's conceivable that scientists could explore those regions of the genome to see if Leonardo had any unique variations that changed his color palette, allowing him to see more hues of red or green than most people are able to perceive.

The Leonardo Project team doesn't yet know where to look for answers 30 to other questions, such as how to explain Leonardo's remarkable ability to visualize birds in flight. "It's as if he was creating stroboscopic photographs of stop-action," says Sakmar. "It's not far-fetched that there would be genes related to that ability." He and his colleagues view their work as the beginning of an expedition that will lead them down new pathways as DNA gives up its secrets.

The quest to unravel the origins of genius may never reach an end point. Like the universe, its mysteries will continue to challenge us, even as we reach for the stars. For some, that is as it should be. "I don't want to figure it out at all," says Keith Jarrett when I ask if he is comfortable not knowing how his music takes hold. "If someone offered me the answer, I'd say, Take it away." In the end it may be that the journey is illuminating enough and that the insights it reveals along the way—about the brain, about our genes, about the way we think—will nurture glimmers of genius in not just the rare individual but in us all.

Understanding the Text

1. Kalb explores a number of approaches to defining and investigating genius. Using PowerPoint or some other presentation software, make a series of slides that outline each of these avenues.

2. The title of Kalb's essay would seem to presuppose a more fundamental question: what *is* a genius? Working from her detailed analyses of the factors that go into making a genius, formulate a working definition of genius. Is there a stable definition we can apply broadly? What do geniuses do that mark them as geniuses?

Reflection and Response

3. Answer Kalb's titular question by writing an essay in which you synthesize and develop her points to determine the necessary factors required in making a genius. Your work in questions 1 and 2 may be useful in formulating your response.

4. In what ways is genius contingent? Working from Kalb's essay, write a paper in which you examine factors that can obscure or hinder genius. What social, economic, or environmental conditions are necessary for genius?

Making Connections

5. Half the women in Lewis Terman's study, Kalb notes, ended up as homemakers. Apply Emily Atkin's analysis ("The Sexism of 'Genius,'" p. 249) to Kalb's larger discussion. What role does gender play in making and recognizing a genius? How might we change that role to make genius a more equitable category?

6. In looking at David Galenson's work, Daniel Pink ("What Kind of Genius Are You?," p. 232) seems to offer still further elements that could make a genius. Synthesize Galenson's work with Kalb's ideas. Are Galenson's two different kinds of genius accounted for in Kalb's analysis? How does Galenson's work, especially his work on experimental innovators, complicate Kalb's approach to genius?

What Kind of Genius Are You?

Daniel Pink

Daniel Pink is a business thinker, best-selling author, and television host who focuses on work and behavior. He has written six books, including *Free Agent Nation: How America's New Independent Workers Are Transforming the Way We Live* (2001), *To Sell Is Human: The Surprising Truth about Moving Others* (2012), *Drive: The Surprising Truth about What Motivates Us* (2012), and *When: The Scientific Secrets of Perfect Timing* (2018). His writing has also appeared in *Wired*, the *New York Times*, *Slate*, and *Harvard Business Review*, and he was the host of *Crowd Control*, a series about human behavior on the National Geographic Channel.

In the fall of 1972, when David Galenson was a senior economics major at Harvard, he took what he describes as a "gut" course in 17th-century Dutch art. On the first day of class, the professor displayed a stunning image of a Renaissance Madonna and child. "Pablo Picasso did this copy of a Raphael drawing when he was 17 years old," the professor told the students. "What have you people done lately?" It's a question we all ask ourselves. What have we done lately? It rattles us each birthday. It surfaces whenever an upstart twenty something pens a game-changing novel or a 30-year-old tech entrepreneur becomes a billionaire. The question nagged at Galenson for years. In graduate school, he watched brash colleagues write dissertations that earned them quick acclaim and instant tenure, while he sat in the library meticulously tabulating 17th- and 18th-century indentured-servitude records. He eventually found a spot on the University of Chicago's Nobelist-studded economics faculty, but not as a big-name theorist. He was a colonial economic historian — a utility infielder on a team of Hall of Famers.

Now, however, Galenson might have done something at last, something that could provide hope for legions of late bloomers everywhere. Beavering away in his sunny second-floor office on campus, he has scoured the records of art auctions, counted entries in poetry anthologies, tallied images in art history textbooks — and then sliced and diced the numbers with his econometric ginsu knife. Applying the fiercely analytic, quantitative tools of modern economics, he has reverse engineered ingenuity to reveal the source code of the creative mind.

> "Genius comes in two very different forms, embodied by two very different types of people."

What he has found is that genius — whether in art or architecture or even business — is not the sole province of 17-year-old Picassos and

22-year-old Andreessens. Instead, it comes in two very different forms, embodied by two very different types of people. "Conceptual innovators," as Galenson calls them, make bold, dramatic leaps in their disciplines. They do their breakthrough work when they are young. Think Edvard Munch, Herman Melville, and Orson Welles. They make the rest of us feel like also-rans. Then there's a second character type, someone who's just as significant but trudging by comparison. Galenson calls this group "experimental innovators." Geniuses like Auguste Rodin, Mark Twain, and Alfred Hitchcock proceed by a lifetime of trial and error and thus do their important work much later in their careers. Galenson maintains that this duality — conceptualists are from Mars, experimentalists are from Venus — is the core of the creative process. And it applies to virtually every field of intellectual endeavor, from painters and poets to economists.

After a decade of number crunching, Galenson, at the not-so-tender age of 55, has fashioned something audacious and controversial: a unified field theory of creativity. Not bad for a middle-aged guy. What have you done lately?

Galenson's quest to unlock the secret of innovation began almost by 5 accident. In the spring of 1997, he decided to buy a painting, a small gouache° by the American artist Sol LeWitt. But before he put down his money, he called a friend in the art world, who told him that the price was too high. We're selling that size for less, she said.

"I thought, this is like carpet," Galenson tells me one afternoon in his office. Size determines price? His friend hadn't even seen the painting. What about when the piece was created, what stage it represented in the artist's career? His friend said that didn't matter. "I thought, it has to matter."

Galenson was right, of course. Art isn't carpet. And age does matter. The relationship between age and other economic variables was at the foundation of Galenson's academic work. His first book examined the relationship of age to productivity among indentured servants in colonial America. His second book looked at the relationship of age to the price of slaves. "It was the same regression," Galenson says, still amazed years after the discovery. "A hedonic° wage regression!"

So he bought the painting and set out to answer questions about art the way any LeWitt-loving economist would.

Galenson collected data, ran the numbers, and drew conclusions. He selected 42 contemporary American artists and researched the auction

gouache: a method of painting using opaque pigments ground in water and thickened with a gluelike substance.
hedonic: relating to terms of pleasant sensations.

prices for their works. Then, controlling for size, materials, and other variables, he plotted the relationship between each artist's age and the value of his or her paintings. On the vertical axis, he put the price each painting fetched at auction; on the horizontal axis, he noted the age at which the artist created the work. When he tacked all 42 charts to his office wall, he saw two distinct shapes.

For some artists, the curve hit an early peak followed by a grad- 10 ual decline. People in this group created their most valuable works in their youth—Andy Warhol at 33, Frank Stella at 24, Jasper Johns at 27. Nothing they made later ever reached those prices. For others, the curve was more of a steady rise with a peak near the end. Artists in this group produced their most valuable pieces later in their careers—Willem de Kooning at 43, Mark Rothko at 54, Robert Motherwell at 72. But their early work wasn't worth much.

Galenson decided to test the robustness of his conclusions about artists' life cycles by looking at variables other than price. Art history textbooks presumably reflect the consensus among scholars about which works are important. So he and his research assistants gathered up textbooks and began tabulating the illustrations as a way of inferring importance. (The methodology is analogous to Google's PageRank system: The more books that "linked" to a particular piece of art, the more important it was assumed to be.)

When Galenson's team correlated the frequency of an image with the age at which the artist created it, the same two contrasting graphs reappeared. Some artists were represented by dozens of pieces created in their twenties and thirties but relatively few thereafter. For other artists, the reverse was true.

Galenson, a classic library rat, began reading biographies of the artists and accounts by art critics to add some qualitative meat to these quantitative bones. And then the theory came alive. These two patterns represented two types of artists—indeed, two types of humans.

The insight was so powerful that Galenson soon turned his full attention to the subject. He elaborated his theory in 24 additional papers and set down his findings in a pair of books, *Painting Outside the Lines: Patterns of Creativity in Modern Art*, published in 2001, and *Old Masters and Young Geniuses: The Two Life Cycles of Artistic Creativity*, published earlier this year.

Pablo Picasso and Paul Cézanne are the archetypes of the Galensonian 15 universe. Picasso was a conceptual innovator. He broke with the past to invent a revolutionary style, Cubism, that jolted art in a new direction. His *Demoiselles d'Avignon*, regarded by critics as the most important painting of the past 100 years, appears in more art history textbooks than any other 20th-century piece. Picasso completed *Demoiselles* when he was 26.

He lived into his nineties and produced many other well-known works, of course, but Galenson's analysis shows that of all the Picassos that appear in textbooks, nearly 40 percent are those he completed before he turned 30.

Cézanne was an experimental innovator. He progressed in fits and starts. Working endlessly to perfect his technique, he moved slowly toward a goal that he never fully understood. As a result, he bloomed late. The highest-priced Cézannes are paintings he made in the year he died, at age 67. Cézanne is well represented in art history textbooks; he's the third-most-illustrated French artist of the 20th century. But of all his reproduced images, just 2 percent are from his twenties. Sixty percent were completed after he turned 50, and he painted more than one-third during his sixties.

Picasso and Cézanne represent radically different approaches to creation. Picasso thought through his works carefully before he put brush to paper. Like most conceptualists, he figured out in advance what he was trying to create. The underlying idea was what mattered; the rest was mere execution. The hallmark of conceptualists is certainty. They know what they want. And they know when they've created it. Cézanne was different. He rarely preconceived a work. He figured out what he was painting by actually painting it. "Picasso signed virtually everything he ever did immediately," Galenson says. "Cézanne signed less than 10 percent."

Experimentalists never know when their work is finished. As one critic wrote of Cézanne, the realization of his goal "was an asymptote° toward which he was forever approaching without ever quite reaching."

Galenson later applied his methodology to poetry. He counted the poems that appear in major anthologies and recorded the age at which the poet wrote each entry. Once again, conceptual poets like T. S. Eliot, Ezra Pound, and Sylvia Plath, each of whom made sudden breaks from convention and emphasized abstract ideas over visual observations, were early achievers. Eliot wrote "The Love Song of J. Alfred Prufrock" at 23 and "The Wasteland" at 34. Pound published five volumes of poetry before he turned 30. On the other hand, experimental poets like Wallace Stevens, Robert Frost, and William Carlos Williams, whose work is grounded in concrete images and everyday language, took years to mature. For example, both Pound and Frost lived into their eighties. But by the time Pound turned 40, he had essentially exhausted his creative output. Of his anthologized poems, 85 percent are from his twenties and thirties. By comparison, Frost got a late start. He has more poems in anthologies than any other American poet, but he wrote 92 percent of them after his 40th birthday.

asymptote: a line that continually approaches a given curve but does not meet it.

On and on it goes. Conceptualist F. Scott Fitzgerald wrote *The Great* 20 *Gatsby*—light on character development, heavy on symbolism—when he was 29. Experimentalist Mark Twain frobbed° around with different writing styles and formats and wrote *The Adventures of Huckleberry Finn* at 50. Conceptualist Maya Lin redefined our notion of national monuments while still a college student; experimentalist Frank Lloyd Wright created Fallingwater when he was 70.

The theory even applies to economists. Over lunch at the University of Chicago's faculty club, Galenson tells me the story of Paul Samuelson, one of the most renowned economists of the last century. No shrinking violet, Samuelson titled his dissertation "Foundations of Economic Analysis." As a 25-year-old, he sought to reinvent the entire field—and later won a Nobel Prize for ideas he came up with as a grad student. Swift, deductive, certain. That's a conceptual economist.

An experimental economist is someone like . . . Galenson. He progresses more quietly, more inductively, step-by-careful-step. And he often sails into the winds of indifference—from the art world, which believes that creativity is too elusive for econometric analysis, and from colleagues who can't comprehend why he's wasting his time with picture books. At one point, he leans over his chicken sandwich and tells me quietly and in mild horror, "I don't have a colleague who knows a Manet from a Monet."

Yet Galenson, whose parents were both economists, pushes on, ever approaching the asymptote. "Most people in economics do their best work before the age of 35. And I was constantly irritated that these guys were getting ahead of me," Galenson says. "But from very early in my career, I knew I could do really good work. I didn't know exactly how, and I didn't know when. I just had this vague feeling that my work was going to improve."

The most-reproduced 19th-century work in U.S. and European art history texts is Georges Seurat's *Sunday on La Grande Jatte*. The painting, completed in Paris in 1886, now hangs on the second floor of the Art Institute of Chicago. One morning in April, I visit the museum with Galenson to look at this and other masterpieces.

Walking the floors of a museum with David Galenson is a treat. He is 25 astonishingly well informed about art. For nearly every painting I point to, he accurately pinpoints the year it was made, tells me its backstory, and describes something my pedestrian eyes haven't noticed. He is an erudite, insightful guide who keeps things entertaining with salty asides. "Monet had a lot of balls," he explains in one gallery. "Renoir was a very

---

frobbed: tinkered or experimented.

peculiar guy," he says later. Several times during our four-hour journey through the museum, tourists and schoolteachers sidle up to eavesdrop on his commentary.

Galenson threads his small frame through the swarm of visitors gathered in front of *La Grande Jatte*, considers it for a moment, and then launches into an explanation of why this artist was the quintessential conceptual innovator. "Seurat starts off at the official academy," Galenson says. "He goes and finds the Impressionists, and he works with them. But he's a very nerdy guy. He's sort of a proto-scientist, and he wants to be systematic." Seurat knew about recent discoveries on optical perception—including that people perceive a hue more vividly when it's paired with its opposite on the color wheel. So he broke from the Impressionists to study the science. He made dozens of preparatory studies for the painting, then executed it with scientific precision.

As Galenson explains, "This guy comes along and says, 'Look, Impressionism has been all the rage. But these guys are unsystematic, they're casual. I'm going to make a scientific, progressive art. And this is going to be the prototype of the new art. In the future, everyone will paint scientifically.'" Seurat was 25. "This is his dissertation, basically. This is like 'Foundations of Economic Analysis,'" Galenson tells me. "It's like Samuelson saying, 'I'm going to unite all of economics.' Seurat is saying, 'We're discovering the underlying principles of representation.' One of them is the systematic use of color. And this is the masterpiece." *La Grande Jatte* changed the practice of nearly every painter of its time.

Alas, this is the only painting for which Seurat is remembered—in part, because he died five years after completing it. But that would be the case even had he lived far longer, Galenson maintains. "He did the most important work of his generation; he couldn't have done it again. There's no law you can't do it again. But once you've written *Gatsby*, it's very unlikely you're going to outdo it." (Indeed, Fitzgerald went on to write two more novels, one published posthumously, but neither approached the importance of *The Great Gatsby*.)

We meander through the museum and stop awhile in Gallery 238, which includes two paintings by Jackson Pollock. Galenson gestures toward the first, *The Key*, done in 1946, when Pollock was 34 years old. It looks like a child's drawing—thick lines, crayony colors, underwhelming. "Pollock was a really bad artist at this point," Galenson says.

Nearby is another Pollock, *Greyed Rainbow*, a large and explosive work 30 done in 1953. It's spectacular. Pollock was an experimental innovator who spent two decades tinkering, and this painting is a triumph of that process. To paint it, he laid the canvas on the floor, splattered it with paint, walked around it, tacked it to the wall, looked at it, put it back on the ground, splattered it with more paint, and so on. "This painting is full of innovations," Galenson says, "but Pollock arrived here by trial and error. He was a slow developer."

"Take a few steps back," Galenson directs me. "If you were to describe this to somebody and see the jagged edges, you might say this is a really agitated painting. If you had this in your house, would it make you nervous?"

No, I answer.

"No. It's perfectly resolved. This is a great visual artist making a great work," Galenson says. "He didn't start this way."

We walk back to *The Key*. "Look at this thing," Galenson says. "It's a piece of crap. If that weren't by a famous artist, it wouldn't be here."

"Seurat died at 31," Galenson reminds me. "If Pollock had died at 31, 35 you never would have heard of him."

Galenson's theory of artistic life cycles is hardly bulletproof. Picasso, the marquee youthful innovator, painted his incomparable condemnation of the Spanish Civil War, *Guernica*, at the creaky age of 56. Is that somehow an exception? Sylvia Plath, a prolific conceptualist poet, did extraordinary work in her twenties but committed suicide in her early thirties. Couldn't she have continued innovating if she'd lived? Philip Roth won a National Book Award for *Goodbye, Columbus* in his twenties and a Pulitzer Prize for *American Pastoral* in his sixties. Where does he belong?

Galenson recognizes the limits of dogmatic duality. In his later papers, as well as in the book he published this year, he has refined his theory to make it less binary. He now talks of a continuum—with extreme conceptual innovators at one end, extreme experimental innovators at the other, and moderates in the middle. He allows that people can change camps over the course of a career, but he thinks it's difficult. And he acknowledges that he's charting tendencies, not fixed laws.

Just because a theory isn't perfect, though, doesn't mean it's not valuable. What Galenson has done—and what might deliver the recognition that bypassed him in his youth—is to identify two significant gaps in our understanding of the world and of ourselves.

The first gap exists within his own field. Galenson mentions that his professional colleagues scratch their heads over his research. "It doesn't fit immediately into what economists do," he tells me. "The word *creativity* won't appear in the index of an economics textbook." Then, ever the empiricist, he rises from his chair, grabs a textbook off a shelf, and shows me the lacuna in the end pages.

That's a serious omission. Although Galenson has limited his analy- 40
sis mostly to artists, he believes the pattern he's uncovered also applies
to science, technology, and business. Economic activity is all about
creation—even more so today, as advanced economies shed routine
work and gain advantage through innovation and ingenuity.

If the link between age and creative capacity applies outside the
bounds of the arts, then every economic institution—universities, companies, governments—should take note. Galenson's ideas may yield
clues about how to foster fresh thinking in a wide range of organizations,
industries, and disciplines. If nurturing innovators is an economic imper-
ative, the real peculiarity isn't that Galenson is studying creativity; it's
that other economists aren't.

Which leads to the second gap. Consider the word *genius*. "Since the
Renaissance, genius has been associated with virtuosos who are young.
The idea is that you're born that way—it's innate and it manifests itself
very young," Galenson says. But that leaves the vocabulary of human
possibility incomplete. "Who's to say that Virginia Woolf or Cézanne
didn't have an innate quality that simply had to be nourished for 40
or 50 years before it bloomed?" The world exalts the young turks—the
Larrys and the Sergeys, the Picassos and the Samuelsons. And it should.
We need those brash, certain, paradigm-busting youthful conceptualists.
We should give them free rein to do bold work and avoid saddling them
with rules and bureaucracy.

But we should also leave room for those of us who have, er, avoided
peaking too early, whose most innovative days may lie ahead. Nobody
would have heard of Jackson Pollock had he died at 31. But the same
would be true had Pollock given up at 31. He didn't. He kept at it. We
need to look at that more halting, less certain fellow and perhaps not
write him off too early, give him a chance to ride the upward curve of
middle age.

Of course, not every unaccomplished 65-year-old is some undiscov-
ered experimental innovator. This is a universal theory of creativity, not
a Viagra for sagging baby boomer self-esteem. It's no justification for lazi-
ness or procrastination or indifference. But it might bolster the resolve of
the relentlessly curious, the constantly tinkering, the dedicated tortoises
undaunted by the blur of the hares. Just ask David Galenson.

Understanding the Text

1. What are the two kinds of genius, according to David Galenson? Refer to the specific passages of Pink's text where he offers these definitions.

2. "Galenson recognizes the limits of dogmatic duality," Pink writes (p. 238). Explain what Pink means by this statement. What are the problems with such a duality?

3. What are the two gaps that Galenson's work has identified? What makes them important?

Reflection and Response

4. What role does creativity play in the economy? Consider Galenson's insights and Pink's observations about Galenson's work in writing your response.

5. How does Galenson's work challenge our traditional notions of genius? Working from his ideas and Pink's discussion, develop a definition of genius that accounts for the range of approaches discussed in this essay. Your work in questions 1 through 3 might be useful in making your response.

Making Connections

6. Irina Aristarkhova ("Genius and Evil: #MeToo in the Art World," p. 245) also looks at genius in the art world, but she focuses on the moral values assigned to genius and the reprehensible behavior of some "genius" artists. Craft a visual essay that synthesizes her critique with Pink's essay to make a statement about the function of genius in art. You may want to create a series of images by hand, collage, or digital program, or you may simply want to incorporate visual elements into a written essay. In all cases, be thoughtful about the design, meaning, and relationship of visual elements to other elements.

7. Galenson extends his ideas from the world of art to other areas of creative production, such as literature. Do his ideas also apply to sports? Extend Pink's discussion to Sam Riches's essay ("The Genius Problem," p. 252). Are there both types of innovators in sport? How is creativity further impacted through physical expression?

Cognitive Celebrity

Matthew Francis

Matthew Francis is a science writer whose work has appeared online in *Slate*, *Ars Technica*, and the *Daily Beast*. His work has also been published in *Popular Science*, *Smithsonian Air and Space Magazine*, and *Physics World*. He is currently working on a book with comics artist Maki Naro titled *Who Owns an Asteroid?*

Before he died, Albert Einstein requested that his whole body be cremated as soon as possible after death, and his ashes scattered in an undisclosed location. He didn't want his mortal remains to be turned into a shrine, but his request was only partially heeded. Einstein's closest friend, the economist Otto Nathan, disposed of his ashes according to his wishes, but not before Thomas Harvey, the pathologist who performed the autopsy, removed his brain. Family and friends were aghast, but Harvey convinced Einstein's son Hans Albert to give his reluctant permission after the fact. The eccentric doctor kept the brain in a glass jar of formalin inside a cider box under a cooler, until 1998, when he returned it to Princeton Hospital, and from time to time, he would send little chunks of it to interested scientists.

Most of us will never be victims of brain-theft, but Einstein's status as the archetypical genius of modern times singled him out for special treatment. An ordinary person can live and die privately, but a genius — and his gray matter — belongs to the world. Even in his lifetime, which coincided with the first great flowering of mass media, Einstein was a celebrity, as famous for his wit and white shock of hair as he was for his science. Indeed, his life seems to have been timed perfectly to take advantage of the proliferations of newspapers and radio shows, whose reports often framed Einstein's theories as being incomprehensible to anyone but the genius himself.

There's no doubt that Einstein's contributions to science were revolutionary. Before he came along, cosmology was a part of philosophy but, thanks to him, it's become a branch of science, tasked with no less than a mathematical history and evolution of the Universe. Einstein's work also led to the discovery of exotic physical phenomena such as black holes, gravitational waves, quantum entanglement, the Big Bang, and the Higgs boson. But despite this formidable scientific legacy, Einstein's fame owes something more to our culture's obsession with celebrity. In many ways, Einstein was well-suited for celebrity. Apart from his distinctive coif, he had a way with words and, as a result, he is frequently quoted, occasionally with *bon mots* he didn't actually say.

More than anything, Einstein possessed the distinctive mystique of genius, a sense that he was larger than life, or different from the rest of us in some fundamental way, which is why so many people were desperate to get hold of his brain.

Many people have wondered whether genius is a physical attribute, 5 a special feature that could be isolated in the brain, and Einstein's gray matter is considered a fertile experimental ground for testing this claim. Unfortunately, as the psychologist Terence Hines has argued, the published studies that were carried out on Einstein's brain are flawed in important ways. In each case, researchers compared parts of Einstein's brain to people assumed to be "normal," but in most of these studies the scientists knew which brain sample was Einstein's. They set about looking for differences — *any* differences — between Einstein and the control brains and, when you approach science in this way, it's very easy to find differences.

> "Many people have wondered whether genius is a physical attribute, a special feature that could be isolated in the brain."

After all, there was only one Einstein, just as there's only one "you" and only one "me." The only way to be sure that Einstein's brilliance was due to his anatomy would be to analyze his brain alongside *many* other people like him, in contrast to people unlike him. Otherwise, it's impossible to tell the difference between the unique physiological characteristics of his genius and random variation between individuals. But that doesn't mean we can't investigate his genius. For while we might not have good studies of his brain, we do have the story of his life, and the contents of his mind, in the form of his research.

Einstein is often remembered as a harmless, other-worldly figure, detached from mundane problems. Certainly he had his eccentricities: he wore sweatshirts that grew rattier over the years, because wool sweaters made him itch. He didn't like socks, and sometimes wore women's shoes on vacation. But the conventional narrative of Einstein as tweedy eccentric ignores his radical politics and occasionally troubled personal life. After all, Einstein was a socialist and advocate for one-world government and, until Hitler rose to power, championed demilitarisation and pacifism. He was also passionately anti-racist, hosting the African-American contralto Marian Anderson at his house when Princeton hotels refused to serve her in 1937, and after.

But Einstein was no saint. He cheated on his first wife Mileva Marić with his cousin Elsa Einstein, whom he later married and cheated on in turn. He was known to write sexist doggerel in letters to his friends, and he had difficult relationships with his children — though he could be extremely kind to other people's children, and even helped youngsters in his neighborhood with their homework.

In other words, Einstein was—like all of us—a bundle of contradictions, someone who behaved well sometimes and badly at others. As a world-famous scientist, he had a louder amplifier than an ordinary person, but if we expect a genius to be somehow fundamentally different from the rest of humanity, studying Einstein's life and opinions will disappoint.

Which leaves us with what established Einstein's reputation: his science. Like Isaac Newton before him, Einstein sometimes had trouble recognizing the implications of his ideas, to the point where it's likely that he would have trouble recognizing the way general relativity is researched and taught today. In 1939, he published a paper intending to show that black holes didn't and couldn't exist. The term "black hole" wasn't around back then, but several physicists proposed that gravity might cause objects to collapse on themselves. Einstein's usually excellent intuition failed him in this case. His calculations were technically correct, but he hated the idea of black holes so much that he failed to see that, with enough density, gravity overwhelms all other forces, making collapse inevitable.

To be fair to Einstein, general relativity was still an esoteric theory in 1939. Very few researchers used it, and the observational methods required to show that black holes exist—radio and X-ray astronomy—were in their infancy. But black holes weren't Einstein's only weakness as a scientist. He was also justifiably modest about his mathematical ability. He relied on others, including his first wife Mileva and his good friend, the physicist Michele Besso, to help him work out thorny problems. Today they would receive co-author credits on Einstein's papers, but that wasn't the practice at the time.

And as is always the case with scientific geniuses, Einstein's theories would exist even if he had not. Special relativity, general relativity, and the photon model of light might not have been developed by the same individual, but *someone* would have sussed them out. Henri Poincaré, Hendrik Lorentz and others worked out much of relativity before 1905, just as Gottfried Leibniz independently worked out the calculus in parallel with Newton, and Alfred Russel Wallace developed natural selection in isolation from Charles Darwin. Historians of science once subscribed to a "Great Man" theory, but we now know that transformative ideas emerge from the work of many talented individuals, instead of emerging *ex nihilo°* from one brilliant mind.

Nor was Einstein the only physicist to make brilliant discoveries in the early 20th century. Marie Curie, Niels Bohr, Erwin Schrödinger and Werner Heisenberg all accomplished the same, and so did many others. Were they lesser geniuses than Einstein? Curie won two Nobel Prizes and contributed

ex nihilo: out of nothing.

directly to research that led to several others, yet she isn't considered the archetype of genius—despite having crazy hair to rival Einstein's. But of course there are two unfortunate biases against Curie: her gender and the fact that she was an experimentalist, not a theoretician.

This difference is instructive. Thanks to the diversity of human experience and human talents, we know that genius isn't a monolithic quality that appears in identical form everywhere we find it. Einstein's genius was different from Curie's, and scientific genius is different from musical genius. Celebrity, on the other hand, tends to follow more predictable patterns. Once a person becomes famous, they tend to stay that way. Had he lived in another era, Einstein might have been a decent physicist, but he wouldn't have been the Einstein we know. But because he lived in a special sliver of time, after the lights of fame had begun to shine bright, and before science came to be seen as a team sport, he has become our genius.

Understanding the Text

1. According to Francis, genius "belongs to the world" (p. 241). Explain what he means by that, using examples from his text and then offering an additional example of your own. What are the consequences of this fact for geniuses?

2. What made Einstein a genius according to Francis? Review Francis's text and locate passages where he discusses the factors that contributed not simply to Einstein's intelligence, but also to his cultural status as *the* genius.

Reflection and Response

3. What is the relationship between genius and celebrity? How does one inform or create the other?

4. Building from question 3, how might celebrity mitigate the social impact of genius today? Make a tabloid cover about Einstein, based on his shortcomings as discussed by Francis, with bold headlines and, if you wish, pictures and graphics. Does modern media complicate the relationship between genius and celebrity?

Making Connections

5. Irina Aristarkhova ("Genius and Evil: #MeToo in the Art World," p. 245) looks at the ways in which genius obscures the troubling behaviors of some artists. Extend her critique to Einstein, using Francis's discussion of Einstein's own troubling behaviors. Using both of these essays, consider how we can resolve the tension between morality and genius.

6. Claudia Kalb ("What Makes a Genius?," p. 222) also considers the lingering fascination with Einstein's brain. Apply her extended discussion of different aspects of genius to Francis's essay. Given both of their discussions, in what ways was Einstein a genius, and in what ways was he not?

Genius and Evil: #MeToo in the Art World

Irina Aristarkhova

Irina Aristarkhova is an associate professor of art and women's studies in the School of Art and Design at the University of Michigan, where her work focuses on the relation between technology and aesthetic, cultural, sexual, and political differences. She is the author of a number of articles as well as the book *Hospitality of the Matrix: Philosophy, Biomedicine, and Culture* (2012).

This May, the National Gallery of Art in Washington, D.C., was to showcase the work of two famous artists: one of painter Chuck Close and another of photographer Thomas Roma. Both exhibitions, however were cancelled due to allegations of sexual harassment.

The public debate sparked by the cancellations has centered around the question, is it possible to separate the value of art from the personal conduct of the artist?

As a scholar of aesthetics and gender studies, I believe, in the wake of #MeToo, this is a good time to revisit the argument of Russian poet Alexander Pushkin about the incompatibility of genius and evil.

Genius and Evil

In his short play from 1830, "Mozart and Salieri," Pushkin fictionalizes an encounter between the composer Antonio Salieri and his younger friend, Wolfgang Amadeus Mozart, in Vienna, Austria. Based on existing rumors at the time, Pushkin presents Salieri as envious of Mozart's genius to the point of poisoning him at the meeting.

Pushkin's claim in this play was that the human value of good defines 5 genius, and hence committing a crime disqualifies one from being a genius. Based on this presentation of Salieri as evil, his reputation as a composer was tarnished.

After new research suggested that Mozart died from natural causes, most probably a strep infection, views on Salieri's music also changed. With this new information, Pushkin's argument was revisited, and Salieri's reputation in the music community started to improve, demonstrated by recorded albums and staging of his operas.

> "Art makers and their audiences become emotionally attached to artists and composers as individuals."

This goes to show how art makers and their audiences become emotionally attached to artists and composers as individuals, and not just to their music or painting. Pushkin himself identified strongly with Mozart.

And the change in attitudes to Salieri also supports Pushkin's original argument that how genius is understood is strongly correlated with human values, where good and genius reinforce each other.

The Debate

In the current debate in the art world over this issue, several experts have said that the value of art should not be associated with the personal conduct of its maker. For example, Tom Eccles, executive director of the Center for Curatorial Studies at Bard College, suggested that "we can't not show artists because we don't agree with them morally; we'd have fairly bare walls." An example would be be that of the famous painter Caravaggio, who was accused of murder and whose works continue to be on display.

However, James Rondeau, the president and director of the Art Institute of Chicago, disagreed that museums could present their decisions about the value of the artwork as totally separate from today's ethics. Rondeau said:

> The typical "we don't judge, we don't endorse, we just put it up for people to experience and decide" falls very flat in this political and cultural moment.

The #MeToo Ethical Challenge

This public debate has gained significant traction in the art world because the #MeToo movement has redefined sexual harassment as evil. Started by Tarana Burke, an African-American civil rights activist in 2006 and spread by Alyssa Milano, an American actress and activist, as a Twitter campaign in 2017, the #MeToo movement has become a social media–driven collective voice. It has presented sexual harassment and sexual violence as harm serious enough to warrant recognition and social change.

Consequently, a number of artists have come out with their experience of sexual harassment. Five women came forward accusing Thomas Roma, a photographer and professor, of sexual misconduct. In the case of Chuck Close, artists Langdon Graves, Delia Brown and Julia Fox described in interviews and on social media platforms the anguish and self-doubt his actions had caused them as individuals and also as artists.

Delia Brown, for example, described how Chuck Close told her at a dinner that he was a fan of her work and asked her to pose for a portrait at his studio. She said she was "over the moon" and excited "because having your portrait done as an artist by Chuck Close is tantamount to being canonized."

However, she was shocked when he asked her to model topless, not a practice that he pursued with other famous artists. Brown refused. Explaining her anguish, she felt he saw her only as a body rather than an important artist and felt manipulated. She said "a sense of distrust and disgust" has stayed with her. Other artists made similar allegations of having been invited to Close's studio to pose for him and being shocked by his behavior.

Chuck Close chose to downplay the harm done to them as persons   15
and artists by dismissing their words. He said the "last time I looked, discomfort was not a major offense."

Genius Redefined

The point this reinforces is that if sexual harassment is wrong then the value of artwork being exhibited in a public museum is questionable.

Scholar Roxane Gay, the best-selling author of the essay collection *Bad Feminist*, sums up why it is so evil, when she explains the cost to women. She says:

> *I remember how many women's careers were ruined; I think of those who gave up their dreams because some 'genius' decided indulging his thirst for power and control mattered more than her ambition and dignity. I remember all the silence, decades and decades of enforced silence, intimidation, and manipulation, that enabled bad men to flourish. When I do that, it's quite easy for me to think nothing of the supposedly great art of bad men.*

This debate has also shown how the definitions of evil in Pushkin's "genius and evil" argument are also subjective and depend on human values at a particular time. #MeToo has changed the public view on sexual harassment. Indeed, the public debate surrounding the decision by the National Gallery of Art to cancel two exhibitions has been as much about the value of human beings as it has been about the value of art.

Understanding the Text

1. What is the relationship between genius and morality? Trace Aristarkhova's analysis of the linkages between genius, good, and evil, referring to specific passages in her text.

2. How are victims of sexual harassment harmed? Work from Aristarkhova's discussion and then extend it by considering the consequences of this behavior.

Reflection and Response

3. Is it possible to separate the value of art from the personal conduct of the artist? Write an essay in which you navigate the moral terrain around this issue, considering the role of art and the consequences of personal conduct. How can we best make these decisions?

4. Aristarkhova considers the morality of genius. Extrapolate from her discussion to create a definition of genius that accounts for morality. Your work in question 1 above might be useful.

Making Connections

5. Emily Atkin ("The Sexism of 'Genius,'" p. 249), in looking at the gender implications of the term "genius," touches on many of the same concerns as Aristarkhova. Write an essay in which you synthesize their positions to examine the consequences of gendered applications of genius.

6. Both Aristarkhova and David Z. Hambrick ("What Makes a Prodigy?," p. 257) discuss Mozart as a representative example of a prodigy or genius. For Hambrick, though, part of Mozart's success came from simple hard work. Use Hambrick's larger discussion about personal and environmental factors in prodigies and geniuses to complicate the linkages between morality and genius that Aristarkhova explores. Does focusing on personal conduct of artists or prodigies, either through their sexual misconduct or a rage to master, help sharpen the line between genius and the moral good? Does recognizing that genius is never purely "inborn" similarly create a space to separate issues of morality from issues of prodigy?

The Sexism of "Genius"

Emily Atkin

Emily Atkin is a contributing editor at the *New Republic*. Her work has also appeared in *Newsweek*, *Slate*, and *Mother Jones*. She has written extensively on climate, having served as deputy climate editor at ThinkProgress, and writes a daily newsletter about the climate crisis called HEATED.

Most people struggle to grasp Stephen Hawking's groundbreaking work on black hole dynamics or gravitational singularity, or the mechanics of how galaxies arise in the universe. I do, anyway. But there's one thing about the theoretical physicist, who died this week, that everyone understands: He was a genius.

That's reflected in the many tributes to Hawking's remarkable life, which ended on Wednesday after a long battle with Amyotrophic Lateral Sclerosis, also known as Lou Gehrig's disease. Hawking was a "rare genius," according to *The Guardian*; "a genius who could laugh at himself," according to The Daily Beast. The Agence France-Presse described Hawking as "a genius who dedicated his life to unlocking the secrets of the Universe." Amanda Gefter wrote in *The Atlantic*: "There's just something about a guy who speaks in a computer voice that automatically makes him sound like a genius."

Hawking deserves the title, if we're judging by the Oxford Dictionary: A genius possesses "exceptional intellectual or creative power or other natural ability." Hawking most certainly fits that definition, which, though quite broad, is overwhelmingly applied to male scientists. As a result, young women tend not to see themselves as geniuses—or being capable of becoming geniuses—and are therefore less motivated to pursue jobs in STEM fields. Many men deemed "geniuses" also tend to be excused for poor, even abusive, social and workplace behavior.

Hawking himself objected to the word "genius," at least to describe himself. When asked by a college student in 1993 how it felt to be labeled "the smartest person in the world," Hawking reportedly began typing rapidly. "It is very embarrassing," he reportedly said. "It is rubbish, just media hype. They just want a hero, and I fill the role model of a disabled genius. At least, I am disabled, but I am no genius." Hawking was also a self-described feminist, telling British journalist Piers Morgan last year that he was concerned about equal representation in the private sector. "Women are at least the equals of men, or better," he said.

Hawking would likely appreciate the scientific literature showing how 5
terms like "genius," coupled with the rise of celebrity scientists (who
happen to be mostly male), have harmed women in science.

Stockholm University gender studies professor Hillevi Ganetz examined
the rise of Nobel laureates—science's original celebrity geniuses—for a
2015 article published in the journal *Celebrity Studies*. The overwhelming
majority of laureates are men, she noted; and when women are honored,
interviewers ask questions about their clothes, their families, their domestic habits, while the male honorees are asked about hobbies and research.
Thus, male laureates are presented as serious scientists with innate brilliance, female laureates as anomalies who succeeded through hard work.
"The female genius must be hidden in favor of presenting a respectable
femininity and a focus on the domestic sphere," Ganetz wrote.

This unequal treatment has affected how women and young girls view
themselves. A 2016 study in the journal *Social Psychological and Personality
Science* found it difficult for many people to associate "woman" with "genius." "We commonly think of genius as male," study author and Cornell University researcher Kristen Elmore told *Fortune*. Another study published in the journal *Science* in 2015 found that women graduate students were more likely to avoid academic
disciplines associated with raw, inherent intelligence—fields like philos-
ophy, physics, and math. Sarah-Jane Leslie, the Princeton University philosophy professor who conducted the study, partially blamed pop culture,
where "genius men are often portrayed as being innately smart, never
having had to work hard to gain their insights," NBC News reported.

> "This unequal treatment has affected how women and young girls view themselves."

A 2017 study published in the journal *Nature* showed that girls as
young as six were more likely to characterize boys with brilliance than
themselves. "This study shows that girls are internalizing those cultural
messages early in development, believing that, yes they may work hard,
but they are not naturally really smart," Kentucky University psychology professor Christia Brown told *The Guardian*. "These beliefs can have
important implications for what types of academic paths children choose
to take, and shows why girls are opting out of majors like physics, despite
earning high grades in school."

Meanwhile, men deemed "geniuses" by their peers are often excused
for abusive behavior toward women. This has been well-explored in the
arts; men like Harvey Weinstein and Louis C.K. shaped their respective
fields despite years of sexual misconduct. But the phenomenon is revealing itself in science, too, as celebrity "genius" scientists like theoretical
physicist Lawrence Krauss and astronomer Geoffrey Marcy face allegations of serial sexual harassment.

Hawking represented the word "genius" well. To those who believe   10
in the idea of genius—and many people don't—he was objectively one.
But he was also a man who, despite his celebrity and power, was widely
considered to have treated people with respect. But too many "geniuses"
are neither geniuses nor gentlemen. One solution would be to rescue the
word, by applying it more selectively to men and more generously to
women. Another, simpler solution would be to retire it altogether.

Understanding the Text

1. How is the term "genius" gendered? Review Atkin's text and note all the ways this term affects genders differently. Then, using PowerPoint or some other presentation software, create a presentation about gender and genius.

2. What are some possible solutions to resolving the problems with gender and genius? Start with Atkin's observations, but then also extrapolate from the scientific studies she examines to propose solutions of your own.

Reflection and Response

3. Atkin quotes Amanda Gefter, who says of Stephen Hawking, "There's just something about a guy who speaks in a computer voice that automatically makes him sound like a genius" (p. 249). What role did Hawking's disability play in his being called a genius? More broadly, although Atkin focuses on gender, what other aspects of identity impact the category of genius? Are whites more likely to be considered geniuses than blacks? What role might class play? You might want to draw from some of your work in Chapter 4 in making your response.

4. Atkin suggests at the end of her essay that one solution to the gendered problems of genius is to retire the word altogether. What then? Write an essay in which you imagine a path beyond the word "genius." How might we account for extraordinary individuals without the word? How might we avoid gender disparity?

Making Connections

5. In response to being called a genius, Stephen Hawking claims that in part it's "just media hype" (p. 249). Matthew Francis ("Cognitive Celebrity," p. 241) also looks at the role that media plays in categorizing people as geniuses. Use Francis's discussion to deepen Atkin's analysis. Are geniuses born, or are they made through celebrity? How does media shape the way we perceive individuals? How might that be related to the genius gender gap that forms the center of Atkin's essay?

6. Atkin explains that "male laureates are presented as serious scientists with innate brilliance, female laureates as anomalies who succeeded through hard work" (p. 250). This dichotomy seems to echo Daniel Pink's ("What Kind of Genius Are You?", p. 232) of David Galenson's work. Place these essays in conversation to either reveal the gendered dimensions of Galenson's work or to argue for the different sort of genius that comes from hard work in people of any gender.

The Genius Problem

Sam Riches

Canadian writer and journalist Sam Riches has published widely, including online at the *New Yorker*, *Wired*, and Salon.com, as well as the *Globe and Mail*, *Best Canadian Sports Writing*, and *Pacific Standard*. His writing focuses on sports and, in the wake of legalization in Canada, cannabis. The essay presented here was published in *Pacific Standard*, which focuses on stories that promote a more just society.

For an oft-used term, there is no objective definition of genius. There are a slew of familiar names often associated with the idea of genius — Galileo, Newton, Archimedes — and there is a general understanding that genius is not dictated by intelligence alone, but rather by rare thought, those who look at a problem and identify a solution that only they are capable of seeing.

"Imagination is more important than knowledge," Einstein said. "Knowledge is limited. Imagination encircles the world." British physicist W. L. Bragg said that "the most important thing in science is not so much to obtain new facts as to discover new ways of thinking about them." Creativity and innovation certainly seem vital to the equation then and this could be what separates a genius from, say, a Mensa member, who might be an impressive, logical thinker but does not necessarily reveal new planes of thought.

Creativity expert Michael Michalko wrote that "regular" people think reproductively, that they revisit ideas that are proven. Geniuses, on the other hand, think productively, producing solutions that previously failed to exist. If an individual changes the way the world perceives something, Newton's Universal Law of Gravitation, for example, that, it would seem, would qualify as a work of genius.

In sports, genius is often ascribed to those who reinvent some facet of the game they play. LeBron James has helped usher in a new era of basketball, where traditional positions have been eroded by lavish athleticism and abstract versatility. James can win games on either side of the ball, from the wing, or in the post, with power or grace. It's a trope to say his game defies definition but essentially it does, he is unparalleled. Similarly, Lawrence Taylor's strength and athleticism altered the path of football. "He changed the way defense is played, the way pass-rushing is played, the way linebackers play and the way offenses block linebackers," said John Madden, his former coach. In hockey, Wayne Gretzky shredded previous notions of offense, and often credited his success to a simple rule — "I skate to where the puck is going to be, not where it has been." Despite being lithe in a physical game, he became hockey's greatest player by mastering an anticipatory style, rooted in spacial awareness.

These are just some examples. Innovation, of course, arrives in dif- 5 ferent forms, but beyond athleticism and intellect, or obsession and creativity, what other factors go into the equation? In sports, who gets appointed genius and why?

> "In sports, who gets appointed genius and why?"

In 2006, David Foster Wallace profiled Roger Federer for the *New York Times*, in a seminal piece of sportswriting that captured the tennis player at the peak of his form. Foster Wallace writes of the "beauty" and "genius" of Federer's game, the moments that are so exceptional they trigger a physical reaction from the viewer, "the jaw drops and eyes protrude and sounds are made that bring spouses in from other rooms to see if you're O.K."

Foster Wallace's interpretation of Federer's ability, and the genius label associated with it, was not about ways of thinking or seeing the game. For Foster Wallace there was a metaphysical explanation for Federer's domination. "Federer is one of those rare, preternatural athletes who appear to be exempt, at least in part, from certain physical laws," he wrote.

Federer is not physically imposing—not now at 34, and not earlier in his career—but he remains balletic on the court, and the speed that he has lost he's replaced with a cunning and unrelenting style of play—part fearlessness, part dissidence—that can leave both tennis fans and opponents scratching their heads. But it works.

John Vrooman, who teaches economics at Vanderbilt University, says adaptation is part of the genius equation. The genius arrives, he says, when they use their skill to counter the game as it adjusts to them. Vrooman cites LeBron James as an example, and how his game has evolved and responded to the adjustments made by every defense in the league tasked with trying to stop him.

"Geniuses see parallels that other flat-landed two-dimensional think- 10 ers cannot see," Vrooman says. "In effect they are virtually thinking in three dimensions and all other two-dimensional thought moves in slow motion. LeBron and Michael Jordan know what their opponent is going to do before their opponent does. They think and play in another quantum dimension at a quantum speed on a whole other level."

If this is true, and their thinking is unconventional, their perspective unique, it would align with the notion of genius as productive thinker. Einstein said that he thought musically: "I live my daydreams in music. I see my life in terms of music." Similarly, the theoretical physicist

Richard Feynman described formulas as having colors, viewing his work through a prism of synesthesia°. For him, mathematical concepts became intuitive manipulations, perhaps in the same way that James can manipulate a basketball game.

Michael Giardina, the editor of the *Sociology of Sport Journal* and an associate professor of sport management at Florida State University, says when discussing genius in sport it's important not to lose sight of the role sociocultural narratives and language plays in characterizing a particular athlete as a genius or not.

He cites Greg Maddux as an example. Maddux is one of baseball's greatest pitchers; *Baseball* magazine described him as "what baseball should be," *Sports Illustrated* called him the "greatest pitcher you'll ever see," and, throughout his career, he was regarded as cerebral and intelligent, traits that were reflected in his nickname, the Professor. Giardina questions, though, whether Maddux thought the game in a different way, or if his reputation for intelligence was based more on his style of play—precision, not power—and his appearance.

"He was an average-looking athlete, who wore glasses, threw in the low-90s, played lots of golf yet made batters look foolish with pinpoint location and control," Giardina writes via email. In contrast, Roger Clemens was arguably as dominant as Maddux but genius is not a term applied to his career. Clemens was physically imposing at 6'3" and 225 pounds, and threw the ball much harder, with a fastball capable of reaching the 100-mile-per-hour plateau. Maddux bore signifiers often associated with intelligence, he was frail compared to his peers, not exceptionally athletic—still, without a glaring physical advantage, he was wildly successful. Intelligence became the easy explanation. This was not the case for Clemens.

During last year's NFL Draft, Aaron Gordon of Vice Sports exposed himself to an unhealthy amount of verbiage to chart the buzzwords used by ESPN draft analysts when evaluating the incoming crop of rookies. Over three days, 256 players cycled through the draft, with various analysts offering up opinions at any given time. Here is some of what he found: 15

- "Only black players were described as: gifted, aggressive, explosive, raw, and freak."
- "Only white players were described as: intelligent, cerebral, fundamentally, overachiever, technician, workmanlike, desire, and brilliant."

synesthesia: A condition where one type of stimulation evokes the sensation of another, as when the hearing of a sound produces the visualization of a color.

A 2004 study, published in the *Sociology of Sport Journal*, analyzed the coverage of 304 athletes over five years. The results indicated that black athletes were more likely to be described in physical terms when compared to their white counterparts who played the same positions. The discourse surrounding Serena Williams, for example, is often centered on her body, rather than her ability, despite her genius in the sport.

A 2008 study in the *Journal of African American Studies* examined how NFL draft experts evaluate black college quarterbacks. It found that the experts "buy into and perpetuate" racial stereotypes about black athletes that limits their abilities and adversely impacts their chances of pro-success. "What the literature tends to show is that, from a young age athletes are routinely guided into certain positions by coaches based on the beliefs about 'natural ability' and 'intelligence' that the commentators on ESPN espoused at the draft," Giardina writes.

The role of quarterback remains one of the most heavily segregated positions in the NFL: it's overwhelmingly white, while other positions, like running back, cornerback, safety, wide receiver, and defensive tackle — high-impact, physical positions — are filled by black athletes. Harry Edwards, professor emeritus in sociology at the University of California–Berkeley coined the term "stacking" in 1967 to explain this phenomenon.

Stacking is prevalent across sports, not just football, and can be defined as placing athletes in certain roles based on racial stereotypes. In Edwards' words, it's the "disproportionate concentration . . . of ethnic minorities — particularly blacks — in specific team positions." In his book, *Taboo: Why Black Athletes Dominate Sports and Why We're Afraid to Talk About It*, author Jon Entine writes, "African-Americans are concentrated in sports and positions that demand speed and quickness, the 'reactive' positions. Whites, on the other hand, are over-represented at so-called strategic positions that presumably demand decision-making skills."

Stacking is not limited to the playing field. NFL head coaches, offensive coordinators, defensive coordinators, and special teams coordinators, among other positions, are predominantly white men. The only position where it swings the other way is running back coach. A study of 323 college football coaches found that, "relative to white coaches, black coaches' career prospects are harmed by their disproportionate placement into jobs that inhibit mobility." This stratification funnels black athletes and coaches into less desirable positions, often with lower pay and shorter shelf life. [20]

NFL coaches were interviewed for a 2007 study about stacking and racial prejudice in football. Black coaches said that race is an issue in the NFL, and across sports, while white coaches maintained that "race plays no part in which positions athletes play." All of this points toward the abilities of black athletes and coaches, distilled through a socio-cultural lens, as distorted—projected and interpreted by underlying social prejudices. Beyond sports, this is indicative of dominance and subordination structured along class, race, and gender lines.

So which athletes are genius? That depends on whom you ask.

Understanding the Text

1. Explain the different between reproductive and productive thinking, offering an example from one of the sports figures that Riches discusses.

2. What is "stacking"? Define this term using Riches's text. How does it relate to genius in sports?

Reflection and Response

3. How does race impact perceptions of genius in sports? Write an essay in which you analyze the racial dimensions of sports. How can we promote change in this area? Would a different definition of genius help?

4. Riches opens his essay by observing that there is no objective definition of genius. Working from the rest of his essay, develop a definition of genius that encompasses sport. What makes a sports genius? What factors beyond athletic ability play a role?

Making Connections

5. Claudia Kalb ("What Makes a Genius?," p. 222) discusses genius extensively. Apply her discussion to Riches's essay to explain genius in sports. Which elements of genius examined by Kalb help explain Riches's discussion of genius in sports?

6. David Z. Hambrick ("What Makes a Prodigy?," p. 257) discusses the complicated interrelationship between hard work and innate talent that produces a prodigy. Use his discussion to extend the notion of genius in sports. Are some athletes prodigies? How do we differentiate between genius and prodigy? Is that difference useful? Is the "rage to master" as essential in sports as in other areas of genius talent?

What Makes a Prodigy?

David Z. Hambrick

David (Zack) Hambrick is a psychology professor at Michigan State University, where his work focuses on expertise and the relationships between practice and proficiency in various skills. In particular, he has argued that working memory, a concept you may have encountered in Ross Alloway and Tracy Alloway's essay in Chapter 3 (p. 158), is as important as practice in attaining mastery across a range of fields.

This January, Wolfgang Amadeus Mozart, classical music's original *wunderkind*, turns 260. Before his untimely death, at age 35, Mozart composed 61 symphonies, 49 concertos, 23 operas, 17 masses, and scores of other works. He was said to be composing on his deathbed. But through a dozen or so major biographies and the 1984 movie *Amadeus,* what has most captivated the popular imagination are Mozart's childhood accomplishments. As the historian Paul Johnson recounts in *Mozart: A Life,* Mozart began playing the clavier at age 4 and was composing at 5. The following year, he played for the Holy Roman Empress of the Habsburg Dynasty and her musically inclined daughter, Marie Antoinette. At age 7, he toured Germany and played for Louis XV at a dinner party in Paris, and by age 14, he had composed an opera. Thus did Mozart accomplish more by the age that someone today would enter high school than one of his contemporaries would hope to accomplish in a long composing career.

What explains prodigies? How can a person accomplish so much so fast? Psychologists have long debated this question. According to one account, it is possible that most anyone could be a prodigy, with the right environment. As the late psychologist Michael Howe argued, "With sufficient energy and dedication on the parents' part, it is possible that it may not be all that difficult to produce a child prodigy." Extraordinary opportunity is indeed a theme that runs through the biographies of many prodigies. Mozart's father, Leopold, was a highly sought after music teacher, and gave up his own promising career as a musician to mange his son's career. More recently, Tiger Woods' father introduced him to golf at age 2. When Venus and Serena Williams were children, they moved with their family from California to Florida so they could train at an elite tennis academy.

However, recent research indicates that basic cognitive abilities known to be influenced by genetic factors also play a role in prodigious achievement. In the most extensive study of prodigies to date, the psychologist Joanne Ruthsatz and her colleagues administered a standardized test of intelligence to 18 prodigies—five in art, eight in music, and five in math. There was a wide range of IQs in the sample, from 100—the average for the general population—to 147—well above the usual cutoff for "intellectually gifted." However, with an average score of 140 (above the 99th percentile), nearly all of the prodigies did extraordinarily well on the tests of *working memory*. Analogous to the central processing unit of a computer, working memory is a cognitive system responsible for carrying out the mental operations involved in complex tasks such as problem solving and language comprehension. It is what you use when you compute a tip for a dinner check in your head, or when you hold in mind the steps of a complex skill you are trying to learn.

Working memory is measured with tests that involve both remembering information for a short period of time and manipulating that information in some way. For example, in backward digit span, the test-taker is read a sequence of random digits, such as 8 3 2 9 5 1 3 7 5 0. The goal is then to recall the digits back in the reverse order—0 5 7 3 1 5 9 2 3 8 for the preceding sequence. As measured by tests like these, people differ substantially in the capacity of their working memory system—some people have a "bigger" working memory than other people. Moreover, this variation is substantially influenced by genetic factors, with estimates of heritability typically around 50 percent.

With an average score of 148, the music prodigies in the Ruthsatz 5 study were especially high in working memory (the average for the math prodigies was 135 and for art prodigies was 132). In fact, all eight of the music prodigies were at or above the 99th percentile, and four were at or above the *99.9th* percentile. The odds of eight randomly selected people scoring this high on a test are essentially zero. Ruthsatz and colleagues concluded that a superior working memory is one characteristic that prodigies in art, music, and math have in common.

Prodigies also exhibit an unusual commitment to their domain, which the developmental psychologist Ellen Winner calls a "rage to master." Winner describes children who possess this quality in the following terms: "Often one cannot tear these children away from activities in their area of giftedness, whether they involve an instrument, a computer, a sketch pad, or a math book. These children have a powerful interest in the domain in which they have high ability, and they can focus so intently on work in this domain that they lose sense of the outside world." Winner argues that this single-mindedness is a *part* of innate talent rather than a cause of it—a convergence of genetically-influenced aptitude, interest, and drive that predisposes a person to obsessively engage in some activity. And "rage to master" is a good description of Mozart's personality. In her landmark biographical study of 301 geniuses, Catherine Cox noted that from "before his 6th year, Mozart's sole absorbing interest was in music, and even the games he played had some musical element."

Consistent with Winner's thesis, results of a recent study of more than 10,000 twins by Miriam Mosing, Fredrik Ullén, and their colleagues at Sweden's Karolinska Institute revealed that a common set of genes influence both music aptitude *and* the propensity to practice—an example of a phenomenon known as genetic pleiotropy, which occurs when one gene (or set of genes) influences multiple traits.

Taken together, these findings add to a growing body of evidence indicating that exceptional performance in music, the arts, sports, science, and other complex domains is, at its core, determined multiply — the product of both environmental factors and of genetically-influenced traits. More generally, psychologists who study expertise are moving beyond the question of whether experts are "born" or "made." As the psychologist Jonathan Wai put it, it is increasingly clear that "Experts are born, then made."

> "Psychologists who study expertise are moving beyond the question of whether experts are 'born' or 'made.'"

Understanding the Text

1. Make a list of the factors that, according to Hambrick, go into making a prodigy. How do these elements interact with one another?

2. What is working memory, and what role does it play in the development of prodigies? Support your response with Hambrick's text.

Reflection and Response

3. Hambrick ends his essay by quoting psychologist Jonathan Wai, who says, "Experts are born, then made" (p. 259). Write an essay in which you elaborate on this quotation, drawing from Hambrick's ideas about all the factors that go into making a prodigy.

4. Make a visual representation of how genetic and environmental (or nature and nurture, or biological and cultural) factors interact in the production of a prodigy. Consider how your visual elements represent *process*, whether by using a flowchart or timeline or by making the relationships between stages of inquiry clear. What comes first? Does one outweigh the other? Where does the development of a prodigy start? Can we identify a starting point?

Making Connections

5. What's the difference between a genius and a prodigy? Use Claudia Kalb's ("What Makes a Genius?," p. 222) discussion of genius, synthesizing with Hambrick's discussion of prodigies. What qualities do these categories share in common? Where do they diverge, and what are the implications of those differences?

6. Matthew Francis ("Cognitive Celebrity," p. 241) suggests that part of Einstein's reputation as a genius came from the intersection of media and celebrity. Using Francis's insights, write an essay in which you consider the role of these factors in recognizing child prodigies. How many prodigies, for example, had already achieved notoriety for their talents? Does media help create prodigies like Mozart or the Williams sisters, and if so, at what cost?

B eing a college student means being a college writer. No matter what field you are studying, your instructors will ask you to make sense of what you are learning through writing. When you work on writing assignments in college, you are, in most cases, being asked to write for an academic audience.

Writing academically means thinking academically — asking a lot of questions, digging into the ideas of others, and entering into scholarly debates and academic conversations. As a college writer, you will be asked to read different kinds of texts; understand and evaluate authors' ideas, arguments, and methods; and contribute your own ideas. In this way, you present yourself as a participant in an academic conversation.

What does it mean to be part of an *academic conversation*? Well, think of it this way: you and your friends may have an ongoing debate about the best film trilogy of all time. During your conversations with one another, you analyze the details of the films, introduce points you want your friends to consider, listen to their ideas, and perhaps cite what the critics have said about a particular trilogy. This kind of conversation is not unlike what happens among scholars in academic writing — except they could be debating the best public policy for a social problem or the most promising new theory in treating disease.

If you are uncertain about what academic writing *sounds like* or if you're not sure you're any good at it, this section offers guidance for you at the sentence level. It helps answer questions such as these:

How can I present the ideas of others in a way that demonstrates my understanding of the debate?

How can I agree with someone, but add a new idea?

How can I disagree with a scholar without seeming rude?

How can I make clear in my writing which ideas are mine and which ideas are someone else's?

The following sections offer sentence guides for you to use and adapt to your own writing situations. As in all writing that you do, you will have to think about your purpose (reason for writing) and your audience (readers) before knowing which guides will be most appropriate for a particular piece of writing or for a certain part of your essay.

The guides are organized to help you present background information, the views and claims of others, and your own views and claims — all in the context of your purpose and audience.

Academic Writers Present Information and Others' Views

When you write in academic situations, you may be asked to spend some time giving background information for or setting a context for your main idea or argument. This often requires you to present or summarize what is known or what has already been said in relation to the question you are asking in your writing.

SG1   Presenting What Is Known or Assumed

When you write, you will find that you occasionally need to present something that is known, such as a specific fact or a statistic. The following structures are useful when you are providing background information.

As we know from history, _____.

X has shown that _____.

Research by X and Y suggests that _____.

According to X, _____ percent of _____ are/favor _____.

In other situations, you may have the need to present information that is assumed or that is conventional wisdom.

People often believe that _____.

Conventional wisdom leads us to believe _____.

Many Americans share the idea that _____.

_____ is a widely held belief.

In order to challenge an assumption or a widely held belief, you have to acknowledge it first. Doing so lets your readers see that you are placing your ideas in an appropriate context.

Although many people are led to believe X, there is significant benefit to considering the merits of Y.

College students tend to believe that _____ when, in fact, the opposite is much more likely the case.

SG2   Presenting Others' Views

As a writer, you build your own *ethos*, or credibility, by being able to fairly and accurately represent the views of others. As an academic writer, you will be expected to demonstrate your understanding of a text by summarizing the views or arguments of its author(s). To do so, you will use language such as the following.

X argues that _____.

X emphasizes the need for _____.

In this important article, X and Y claim _____.

X endorses _____ because _____.

X and Y have recently criticized the idea that _____.

_____, according to X, is the most critical cause of _____.

Although you will create your own variations of these sentences as you draft and revise, the guides can be useful tools for thinking through how best to present another writer's claim or finding clearly and concisely.

SG3   Presenting Direct Quotations

When the exact words of a source are important for accuracy, authority, emphasis, or flavor, you will want to use a direct quotation. Ordinarily, you will present direct quotations with language of your own that suggests how you are using the source.

X characterizes the problem this way: ". . ."

According to X, _____ is defined as ". . ."

". . . ," explains X.

X argues strongly in favor of the policy, pointing out that ". . ."

Note: You will generally cite direct quotations according to the documentation style your readers expect. MLA style, often used in English and in other humanities courses, recommends using the author name paired with a page number, if there is one. APA style, used in most social sciences, requires the year of publication generally after the mention of the source, with page numbers after the quoted material. In *Chicago* style, used in history and in some humanities courses, writers use superscript numbers (like this[6]) to refer readers to footnotes or endnotes. In-text citations, like the ones shown below, refer readers to entries in the works cited or reference list.

MLA	Lazarín argues that our overreliance on testing in K-12 schools "does not put students first" (20).
APA	Lazarín (2014) argues that our overreliance on testing in K-12 schools "does not put students first" (p. 20).
Chicago	Lazarín argues that our overreliance on testing in K-12 schools "does not put students first."[6]

Many writers use direct quotations to advance an argument of their own:

> Standardized testing makes it easier for administrators to measure student performance, but it may not be the best way to measure it. Too much testing wears students out and communicates the idea that recall is the most important skill we want them to develop. Even education policy advisor Melissa Lazarín argues that our overreliance on testing in K-12 schools "does not put students first" (20).

Student writer's Idea

Source's Idea

SG4   Presenting Alternative Views

Most debates, whether they are scholarly or popular, are complex—often with more than two sides to an issue. Sometimes you will have to synthesize the views of multiple participants in the debate before you introduce your own ideas.

> On the one hand, X reports that _____, but on the other hand, Y insists that _____.

> Even though X endorses the policy, Y refers to it as " . . . "

> X, however, isn't convinced and instead argues _____.

> X and Y have supported the theory in the past, but new research by Z suggests that _____.

Academic Writers Present Their Own Views

When you write for an academic audience, you will indeed have to demonstrate that you are familiar with the views of others who are asking the same kinds of questions as you are. Much writing that is done for academic purposes asks you to put your arguments in the context of existing arguments—in a way asking you to connect the known to the new.

When you are asked to write a summary or an informative text, your own views and arguments are generally not called for. However, much of the writing you will be assigned to do in college asks you to take a persuasive stance and present a reasoned argument—at times in response to a single text, and at other times in response to multiple texts.

SG5 Presenting Your Own Views: Agreement and Extension

Sometimes you agree with the author of a source.

X's argument is convincing because _____.

Because X's approach is so _____, it is the best way to _____.

X makes an important point when she says _____.

Other times you find you agree with the author of a source, but you want to extend the point or go a bit deeper in your own investigation. In a way, you acknowledge the source for getting you so far in the conversation, but then you move the conversation along with a related comment or finding.

X's proposal for _____ is indeed worth considering. Going one step further, _____.

X makes the claim that _____. By extension, isn't it also true, then, that _____?

_____ has been adequately explained by X. Now, let's move beyond that idea and ask whether _____.

SG6 Presenting Your Own Views: Queries and Skepticism

You may be intimidated when you're asked to talk back to a source, especially if the source is a well-known scholar or expert or even just a frequent voice in a particular debate. College-level writing asks you to be skeptical, however, and approach academic questions with the mind of an investigator. It is OK to doubt, to question, to challenge—because the end result is often new knowledge or new understanding about a subject.

Couldn't it also be argued that _____?

But is everyone willing to agree that this is the case?

While X insists that _____ is so, he is perhaps asking the wrong question to begin with.

The claims that X and Y have made, while intelligent and well-meaning, leave many unconvinced because they have failed to consider _____.

A Note about Using First Person "I"

Some disciplines look favorably upon the use of the first person "I" in academic writing. Others do not and instead stick to using third person. If you are given a writing assignment for a class, you are better off asking your instructor what he or she prefers or reading through any samples given than guessing what might be expected.

First person (I, me, my, we, us, our)

I question Heddinger's methods and small sample size.

Harnessing children's technology obsession in the classroom is, I believe, the key to improving learning.

Lanza's interpretation focuses on circle imagery as symbolic of the family; my analysis leads me in a different direction entirely.

We would, in fact, benefit from looser laws about farming on our personal property.

Third person (names and other nouns)

Heddinger's methods and small sample size are questionable.

Harnessing children's technology obsession in the classroom is the key to improving learning.

Lanza's interpretation focuses on circle imagery as symbolic of the family; other readers' analyses may point in a different direction entirely.

Many Americans would, in fact, benefit from looser laws about farming on personal property.

You may feel as if not being able to use "I" in an essay in which you present your ideas about a topic is unfair or will lead to weaker statements. Know that you can make a strong argument even if you write in the third person. Third person writing allows you to sound more assertive, credible, and academic.

 Presenting Your Own Views: Disagreement or Correction

You may find that at times the only response you have to a text or to an author is complete disagreement.

X's claims about _____ are completely misguided.

X presents a long metaphor comparing _____ to _____;
in the end, the comparison is unconvincing because _____.

It can be tempting to disregard a source completely if you detect a piece
of information that strikes you as false or that you know to be untrue.

Although X reports that _____, recent studies indicate that is
not the case.

While X and Y insist that _____ is so, an examination of their
figures shows that they have made an important miscalculation.

SG8   Presenting and Countering Objections to Your Argument

Effective college writers know that their arguments are stronger when
they can anticipate objections that others might make.

Some will object to this proposal on the grounds that _____.

Not everyone will embrace _____; they may argue instead
that _____.

Countering, or responding to, opposing voices fairly and respectfully
strengthens your writing and your *ethos*, or credibility.

X and Y might contend that this interpretation is faulty; however,
_____.

Most _____ believe that there is too much risk in this
approach. But what they have failed to take into consideration is
_____.

Academic Writers Persuade by Putting It All Together

Readers of academic writing often want to know what's at stake in a particular debate or text. Aside from crafting individual sentences, you must,
of course, keep the bigger picture in mind as you attempt to persuade,
inform, evaluate, or review.

SG9   Presenting Stakeholders

When you write, you may be doing so as a member of a group affected
by the research conversation you have entered. For example, you may be

among the thousands of students in your state whose level of debt may change as a result of new laws about financing a college education. In this case, you are a *stakeholder* in the matter. In other words, you have an interest in the matter as a person who could be impacted by the outcome of a decision. On the other hand, you may be writing as an investigator of a topic that interests you but that you aren't directly connected with. You may be persuading your audience on behalf of a group of interested stakeholders—a group of which you yourself are not a member.

You can give your writing some teeth if you make it clear who is being affected by the discussion of the issue and the decisions that have been or will be made about the issue. The groups of stakeholders are highlighted in the following sentences.

> Viewers of Kurosawa's films may not agree with X that _____.

> The research will come as a surprise to parents of children with Type 1 diabetes.

> X's claims have the power to offend potentially every low-wage earner in the state.

> Marathoners might want to reconsider their training regimen if stories such as those told by X and Y are validated by the medical community.

SG10 Presenting the "So What"

For readers to be motivated to read your writing, they have to feel as if you're either addressing something that matters to them or addressing something that matters very much to you or that should matter to us all. Good academic writing often hooks readers with a sense of urgency—a serious response to a reader's "So what?"

> Having a frank discussion about _____ now will put us in a far better position to deal with _____ in the future. If we are unwilling or unable to do so, we risk _____.

> Such a breakthrough will affect _____ in three significant ways.

> It is easy to believe that the stakes aren't high enough to be alarming; in fact, _____ will be affected by _____.

> Widespread disapproval of and censorship of such fiction/films/art will mean _____ for us in the future. Culture should represent _____.

_____ could bring about unprecedented opportunities for _____ to participate in _____, something never seen before.

New experimentation in _____ could allow scientists to investigate _____ in ways they couldn't have imagined _____ years ago.

SG11 Presenting the Players and Positions in a Debate

Some disciplines ask writers to compose a review of the literature as a part of a larger project—or sometimes as a freestanding assignment. In a review of the literature, the writer sets forth a research question, summarizes the key sources that have addressed the question, puts the current research in the context of other voices in the research conversation, and identifies any gaps in the research.

Writing that presents a debate, its players, and their positions can often be lengthy. What follows, however, can give you the sense of the flow of ideas and turns in such a piece of writing.

_____ affects more than 30% of children in America, and signs point to a worsening situation in years to come because of A, B, and C. Solutions to the problem have eluded even the sharpest policy minds and brightest researchers. *(Student writer states the problem.)*

In an important 2003 study, W found that _____, which pointed to more problems than solutions. [. . .] Research by X and Y made strides in our understanding of _____ but still didn't offer specific strategies for children and families struggling to _____. [. . .] When Z rejected both the methods and the findings of X and Y, arguing that _____, policy makers and health-care experts were optimistic. [. . .] *(Student writer summarizes the views of others on the topic.)*

Too much discussion of _____, however, and too little discussion of _____, may lead us to solutions that are ultimately too expensive to sustain. *(Student writer presents her view in the context of current research.)*

Appendix: Verbs Matter

Using a variety of verbs in your sentences can add strength and clarity as you present others' views and your own views.

When you want to present a view fairly neutrally

acknowledges	observes
adds	points out
admits	reports
comments	suggests
contends	writes
notes	

X points out that the plan had unintended outcomes.

When you want to present a stronger view

argues	emphasizes
asserts	insists
declares	

Y argues in favor of a ban on _____; but Z insists the plan is misguided.

When you want to show agreement

agrees
confirms
endorses

An endorsement of X's position is smart for a number of reasons.

When you want to show contrast or disagreement

compares	refutes
denies	rejects
disputes	

The town must come together and reject X's claims that _____ is in the best interest of the citizens.

When you want to anticipate an objection

admits
acknowledges
concedes

Y admits that closer study of _____, with a much larger sample, is necessary for _____.

Acknowledgments (*continued from page iv*)

Tim Adams, "Nick Bostrom on Artificial Intelligence: 'We're Like Children Playing with a Bomb,'" *The Guardian*, June 12, 2016. Copyright © Guardian News & Media Ltd., 2016. Reprinted by permission.

Ross Alloway and Tracy Alloway, "The End of IQ (and the Dawn of Working Memory)," originally appeared in *The Huffington Post*, October 28, 2013. Copyright © 2013 by Tracy Alloway. Used with permission.

Irina Aristarkhova, "#MeToo in the Art World," *The Conversation*, https://theconversation.com, May 3, 2018. Reprinted by permission.

Emily Atkin, "The Sexism of 'Genius,'" *The New Republic*, March 15, 2018. Copyright © 2018 by New Republic. All rights reserved. Used under license.

Philip Ball, "'Wisdom of the Crowd': The Myths and Realities," *BBC Future*, July 7, 2014. Article Supplied by BBC Studios.

Frans de Waal, "Magic Wells" from *Are We Smart Enough to Know How Smart Animals Are?* by Frans de Waal. Copyright © 2016 by Frans de Waal. Used by permission of W. W. Norton & Company, Inc.

Adam Elkus, "Meet the Bots: Artificial Stupidity can be Just as Dangerous as Artificial Intelligence," *Slate*, April 13, 2015. Copyright © 2015 by The Slate Group. All rights reserved. Used under license.

Matthew Francis, "Cognitive Celebrity," *Aeon*, July 22, 2014. Reprinted by permission of Aeon Media Group Ltd.

Howard Gardner, Excerpt from "The Idea of Multiple Intelligences" from *Frames of Mind: The Theory of Multiple Intelligences*, Basic Books, 1983. Copyright © 1983 by Howard Gardner. Republished with permission of Basic Books; permission conveyed through Copyright Clearance Center, Inc.

From Malcolm Gladwell, "None of the Above," *The New Yorker*, December 17, 2007. Reprinted with permission from the author.

"When Smart Is Dumb" from *Emotional Intelligence: Why It Can Matter More Than IQ* by Daniel Goleman, copyright © 1995 by Daniel Goleman. Used by permission of Bantam Books, an imprint of Random House, a division of Random House LLC. All rights reserved.

Jane Goodall, "At Long Last I Belong" from *My Friends the Wild Chimpanzees* by Jane Goodall, copyright © 1967 by the National Geographic Society. Reprinted by permission.

Adam Grant, "The Dark Side of Emotional Intelligence," *The Atlantic*, January 2, 2014. Copyright © 2014 The Atlantic Media Co., as first published in *The Atlantic Magazine*. All rights reserved. Distributed by Tribune Content Agency, LLC.

From Diane F. Halpern, "Sex Differences in Intelligence," *American Psychologist*, Vol. 52, No. 10, October 1997. Copyright © 1997 American Psychological Association. Reproduced by permission.

David Z. Hambrick, "What Makes a Prodigy?" *Scientific American*, September 22, 2015. Reproduced with permission. Copyright © 2020 Scientific American, a division of Nature America, Inc. All rights reserved.

John Horgan, "Do Fish Suffer?" *Scientific American Blog Network*, November 21, 2017. Copyright © 2017 Scientific American, a division of Nature America, Inc. All rights reserved. Reprinted by permission.

Claudia Kalb, "What Makes a Genius?" *National Geographic*, May 12, 2017. Reprinted by permission.

Will Knight, "The Dark Secret at the Heart of AI," republished with permission of the Association of Alumni and Alumnae of the Massachusetts Institute of Technology from *MIT Technology Review*, April 11, 2017; permission conveyed through Copyright Clearance Center, Inc.

Ray Kurzweil, "What Is AI, Anyway?" from *The Age of Intelligent Machines*, pp. 13–21, copyright © 1990 Massachusetts Institute of Technology, by permission of The MIT Press.

Jennifer Lee, "The Truth about Asian Americans' Success," *CNN*, August 3, 2015. Copyright © 2015 by Turner Broadcasting Systems, Inc. All rights reserved. Used under license.

John D. Mayer, "We Need More Tests, Not Fewer," *The New York Times*, March 10, 2014. Copyright © 2014 by The New York Times Company. All rights reserved. Used under license.

Cade Metz, "Google's Artificial Brain Is Pumping Out Trippy—and Pricey—Art," *Wired*, February 29, 2016. © Conde Nast. Reprinted by permission.

Rachel Monroe, "The Cat Psychic." Copyright © 2016 by Rachel Monroe. Originally printed in *Hazlitt Magazine*, May 12, 2016. Reprinted by permission from the Author.

Daniel H. Pink, "What Kind of Genius Are You?" *Wired*, July 1, 2006. © Conde Nast. Reprinted by permission.

Alicia Puglionesi, "How Counting Horses and Reading Dogs Convinced Us Animals Could Think," *Atlas Obscura*, May 12, 2016. Copyright © 2016 by Atlas Obscura. Used with permission.

Sam Riches, "The Genius Problem," *Pacific Standard*, September 14, 2015. Copyright © 2015 The Social Justice Foundation. Reprinted by permission.

Mike Rose, "Blue-Collar Brilliance," *The American Scholar*, Vol. 78, No. 3, Summer 2009. Copyright © 2009 by the author. Reprinted by permission.

Lily Rothman, "A Cultural History of Mansplaining" © 2012 Lily Rothman, as first published on *TheAtlantic.com*. Reprinted by permission of the author.

William Saletan, "Stop Talking about Race and IQ," *Slate*, April 27, 2018. Copyright © 2018 by The Slate Group. All rights reserved. Used under license.

Allie Shaw, "Alexa, Siri, Sophia: Deconstructing AI's Subliminal Gender Bias," *Swaay Beta*, April 5, 2018. Reprinted by permission of SWAAY Media.

Dinitia Smith, "A Thinking Bird or Just Another Birdbrain?" *The New York Times*, October 9, 1999. Copyright © 1999 by The New York Times Company. All rights reserved. Used under license.

Philip Sopher, "What Animals Teach Us about Measuring Intelligence," *The Atlantic*, February 27, 2015. Copyright © 2015 The Atlantic Media Co., as first published in *The Atlantic Magazine*. All rights reserved. Distributed by Tribune Content Agency, LLC.

Mark Joseph Stern, "Are Gay People Smarter Than Straight People?" *Slate*, September 30, 2013. Copyright © 2013 by The Slate Group. All rights reserved. Used under license.

Robert J. Sternberg, "Commentary: What Is 'Successful' Intelligence?" *Education Week*, November 13, 1996. Reprinted by permission of the author.

From Alan Turing, "Computing Machinery and Intelligence," *Computing Machinery and Intelligence, Mind, New Series*, Vol. 59, No. 236 (October 1950). Published by Oxford University Press on behalf of the Mind Association. Reprinted by permission.

Index of Authors and Titles